普通高等学校规划教材

International Trade

乔亚洲　编著

人民交通出版社股份有限公司
China Communications Press Co.,Ltd.

内 容 提 要

本书是一本全英文教材,不同于以往的涵盖全部国际经济学内容的大部头原版教材,它更加适合我国国际贸易课程双语教学的课时安排,书中有针对性地对国际贸易知识进行系统论述。全书分为简介、贸易理论、贸易保护、外贸政策、贸易工具、经济一体化、世界贸易组织、跨国公司及我国的对外贸易九章。篇幅更为合理,实用性更强,具有较大的实践指导价值。

本书可作为高等院校本专科国际贸易课程双语教材使用,同时也可作为广大国际贸易工作者的参考书。

图书在版编目(CIP)数据

国际贸易 = International Trade:汉、英 / 乔亚洲编著. — 北京:人民交通出版社股份有限公司,2017.8

ISBN 978-7-114-14095-2

Ⅰ. ①国… Ⅱ. ①乔… Ⅲ. ①国际贸易—双语教学—高等学校—教材 Ⅳ. ①F74

中国版本图书馆CIP数据核(2017)第199674号

普通高等学校规划教材

书　　名:	International Trade
著 作 者:	乔亚洲
责任编辑:	富砚博　郭红蕊
出版发行:	人民交通出版社股份有限公司
地　　址:	(100011)北京市朝阳区安定门外外馆斜街3号
网　　址:	http://www.ccpress.com.cn
销售电话:	(010)59757973
总 经 销:	人民交通出版社股份有限公司发行部
经　　销:	各地新华书店
印　　刷:	北京鑫正大印刷有限公司
开　　本:	787×1092　1/16
印　　张:	11.25
字　　数:	260千
版　　次:	2017年8月　第1版
印　　次:	2017年8月　第1次印刷
书　　号:	ISBN 978-7-114-14095-2
印　　数:	0001-3000册
定　　价:	30.00元

(有印刷、装订质量问题的图书由本公司负责调换)

前　　言

随着我国融入全球经济一体化的进程加速,全球化经济呼唤既具有扎实专业知识又拥有娴熟外语语言技能的复合型人才,而这种需求是单纯的语言型外语专业或外语能力平平的单一专业教育所不能满足的,使用双语或全英文讲授专业课程已成为国内高校经管类专业的发展趋势。

由于我国长期缺乏讲第二语言(包括英语)的环境,开展双语教学面临着特殊困难,因此,选用合适的教材就成为双语教学成功的一个重要条件。目前,国内各类学科的双语教学大多使用原版教材,这类教材虽能保证语言的原汁原味,但具体到某门学科,一些国外原版教材的不足便凸显出来。以国际贸易课程为例,由于国外的国际贸易类教材很少,因此,一些只学国际贸易课程的学生也不得不购买涵盖全部国际经济学内容的大部头教材,师生用起来既不顺手,又造成了不小的浪费。

为顺应国内开展双语教学的需要,编者在查阅国内外大量文献的基础上,独立编著本书。在编写过程中,充分考虑到我国国际贸易双语教学的课时安排、内容设置以及学生的接受能力,篇幅更为合理,价格大大降低,非常适合本科双语教学使用,同时也可作为广大国际贸易工作者的参考书。

本书在编写过程中,四川大学研究生曹玲在资料查询和稿件校对方面付出了辛勤的劳动,在此致以诚挚的谢意!

由于编者学识和水平所限,本书难免存在疏漏和不足之处,敬请各位老师和读者交流指正。

乔亚洲
2017 年 5 月

Contents

Chapter 1 Introduction 1
  1.1 The Need for International Trade 1
  1.2 Division of Labor 3

Chapter 2 Theories of International Trade 5
  2.1 The Theory of Absolute and Comparative Advantage 5
  2.2 Factor Proportions Trade Theory 11
  2.3 The Product Cycle Theory 18
  2.4 New Trade Theory 23
  2.5 Intra-Industry Trade 25
  2.6 The Competitive Advantage of Nations 30

Chapter 3 Theory of Trade Protection 36
  3.1 Trade Theory of Mercantilism 36
  3.2 Government Intervention 41

Chapter 4 Foreign Trade Policy 47
  4.1 Trade Policy 47
  4.2 Pushing Exports 51

Chapter 5 Instruments of Trade Policy 56
  5.1 Tariff Barriers 56
  5.2 Non-Tariff Barriers 62
  5.3 Case Study 72

Chapter 6 Economic Integration 79
  6.1 Economic Integration: Overview 79
  6.2 Trade Creation and Trade Diversion 82
  6.3 Regional Economic Integration 83
  6.4 Trading Blocs 92

Chapter 7 GATT and WTO 108
  7.1 Brief History 108
  7.2 WTO 114

7.3　China and WTO ·· 120
Chapter 8　Foreign Direct Investment and Transnational Corporations ············ 123
　8.1　Case Study: Starbucks' Foreign Direct Investment ································ 123
　8.2　Introduction ··· 125
　8.3　Horizontal Foreign Direct Investment ··· 131
　8.4　Vertical Foreign Direct Investment ··· 137
　8.5　Entry Strategies ·· 140
Chapter 9　Chinese Foreign Trade ·· 155
　9.1　Historic Progress in Chinese Foreign Trade ··· 155
　9.2　Reform of and Improvements to Chinese Foreign Trade System ············ 158
　9.3　The Development of Chinese Foreign Trade Contributes to the World Economy ······ 160
　9.4　Promoting Basically Balanced Growth of Foreign Trade ······················· 162
　9.5　Constructing All-Round Economic and Trade Partnerships with Mutually
　　　 Beneficial Cooperation ·· 165
　9.6　Realizing Sustainable Development of Foreign Trade ··························· 167
References ·· 172

Chapter 1   Introduction

1.1   The Need for International Trade

A country may benefit from free trade even if it is less efficient than all other countries in every industry.

It makes sense that one firm would be more successful than another firm in a local market if it could produce its output more efficiently, at a lower cost than that of the second firm. If the two firms produce identical products, then the less efficient firm is likely to be driven out of business, generating losses. If we extend this example to an international market then it would also make sense that a more efficient foreign firm would absorb business from a less efficient domestic firm. Finally, suppose all domestic firms in all industries were less efficient than all firms in all industries in foreign countries, it would then seem logically impossible for any domestic firm to succeed in competition in international markets with foreign firms. International competition would seemingly have only negative effects upon the less efficient domestic firms and countries.

This seemingly logical conclusion is refuted by the Ricardian model of comparative advantage. Ricardo demonstrated the surprising result that less efficient firms in a country can indeed compete with foreign firms in international markets. In addition, by moving to free trade, the less efficient country can generate welfare improvements for everybody in the country. Free trade can even benefit a country that is less efficient in producing everything.

What's more, in a free market system, differences in prices and profit-seeking behaviors are all that is needed to induce countries to produce and export the "right" goods and trade to the national benefit.

There are a number of benefits that the citizens and firms of a country may enjoy as a result of being able to trade freely with the citizens and firms of another country.
- ➢ The benefits of specialization;
- ➢ The benefits of competition;
- ➢ The benefit of choice.

By specializing in the production of goods and services, the firms of a country will produce with a higher level of productive efficiency. The surplus produced can then be traded with the surplus of other countries. By specializing in the production of goods and services where there is an absolute or comparative advantage there is an overall gain in welfare. Increasing global competition will encourage allocative and productive efficiency.

The concepts of consumer and producer surplus can be used to assess the benefits of free trade. The difference between the amount that consumers would be prepared to pay for a goods or service rather than go without, and the price that they actually pay is called consumer surplus. It is used as a measure of satisfaction or welfare of consumers. The difference between the price that producers would be prepared to sell their produce at and the price that they actually sell it at is the producer surplus. There two together is a measure of the welfare of the product.

Just as shown in Figure 1.1.

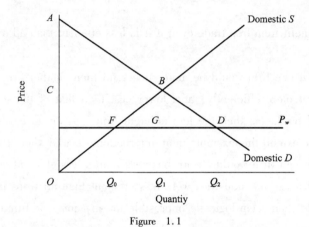

Figure 1.1

In a perfectly competitive market in a closed economy where the equilibrium market price and quantity are Q_0 and P_0, the consumer surplus is shown by the area ABC. The producer surplus is shown by the area CBO. The total level of welfare would be equal to the area ABO.

If the country now takes part in world trade, citizens of that country can buy goods and services at the world price of of P_w. This is below the domestic equilibrium market price of P_0. The horizontal world price line indicates that domestic producers have to accept the world price and cannot influence it due to their limited size. They are price takers. Domestic consumers can purchase all they need from other countries at the price P_w. In the model above domestic consumers will consumer Q_2 of which Q_0 will be purchased from domestic producers and $Q_2 - Q_0$ imported.

As a result of international trade consumer surplus has increased to $AD\ P_w$. Consumers have gained $CBF\ P_w$ of consumer surplus at the expense of domestic producers who have seen their producer surplus fall to P_wFO. Consumers have also achieved consumer surplus, FBG as they are now able to buy the goods from more efficient foreign producers. There is also an additional gain in welfare, BGD, which has resulted simply from consumers buying more goods because of the lower price. Overall society has experienced a welfare gain of BFD.

In addition, it should note that consumers have also gained as a result of additional choice. As many factors of production are not geographically mobile, world trade will be increased by the range of choice of goods and services that people can enjoy.

1.2 Division of Labor

1.2.1 Definition

Division of labor or specialization is the specialization of cooperative labor in specific, and circumscribed tasks and roles, intended to increase the productivity of labor. Historically, the growth of a more and more complex division of labor is closely associated with the growth of total output and trade, the rise of capitalism and of the complexity of industrialization processes. Later, the division of labor reached the level of a scientifically-based management practice with the time and motion studies associated with Taylorism.

1.2.2 Global Division of Labor

There exist as yet few comprehensive studies of the global division of labor (an intellectual challenge for researchers), although the ILO (International labor Organization, Figure 1.2) and national statistical offices can provide plenty of data on request for those games to try.

In one study, Deon Filmer estimated that 2474 million people participated in the global non-domestic labor force in the mid-1990s. Of these,

Figure 1.2

- around 15%, or 379 million people worked in industry;
- a third, or 800 million worked in services;
- over 40%, or 1074 million worked in agriculture.

The majority of workers in industry and services were wage & salary earners – 58 percent of the industrial workforce and 65 percent of the services workforce. But a big portion was self-employed or involved in family labor. Filmer suggested the total of employees worldwide in the 1990s was about 880 million, compared with around a billion working on own account on the land (mainly peasants), and some 480 million working on own account in industry and services.

1.2.3 Types of Specialization

Geographical specialization: Land use is naturally suited to specific situation.

Labor specialization: achieved when the population process is broken into tiny tasks. The idea is referred to as the division of labor.

1.2.4 Advantages

The productivity gains of the division of labor are important within any type of production process, ranging from pin manufacture to legal practice and medical care. Productivity gains result from a number of mechanisms, as follows:

(1) Freeing workers to focus on tasks that they are best at;

(2) Learning Curve efficiencies.

①More repetitions lead into learning faster ways to perform the task, causing:

➤ more efficient in terms of time, which is equal;

➤ increases productivity because training time is reduced and the worker is productive on a short amount of time;

➤ concentration on one repetitive task makes workers more skilled at performing that task.

②Might also cause Steepening of the Learning Curve.

➤ reduces the time needed for training because the task is simplified;

➤ increase in meta-capabilities like ability to learn further new tasks.

(3) Little time is spent on moving between tasks, so overall wasted time is reduced.

(4) The overall quality of the product will increasingly bring welfare gains to the consumer.

(5) It becomes possible to influence how production takes place.

1.2.5 Disadvantages

(1) Disconnection from effects of actions – the worker may not feel responsible for the result of the process in which he/she contributes to.

(2) Lack of motivation.

Productivity of labor may decrease while absenteeism may rise.

①repetitive motion disorder: can be a factor in many manual jobs;

②growing dependency: a break in production may cause problems to the entire process;

③loss of flexibility: workers may have limited knowledge while not many jobs opportunities are available;

④higher start-up costs: high initial costs necessary to buy the specialist machinery lead to a higher break-even point.

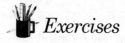
Exercises

1. Define the key term: division of labor.
2. What are the types of specialization?
3. Talk about the advantages of division of labor.

Chapter 2 Theories of International Trade

2.1 The Theory of Absolute and Comparative Advantage

2.1.1 David Ricardo

David Ricardo (1772-1823, Figure 2.1) was a British economist who developed two economic theories that are still valued today – distribution theory and the theory of comparative advantage. Ricardo's theory of comparative advantage is particularly important because it was the first to concretely articulate the value of free trade.

Ricardo was born on April 18, 1772. He is the third one of 17 children. Both his father, Abraham Israel Ricardo and his mother, Abigail Delvalle, were practicing Sephardic Jews. Abraham Ricardo was a successful merchant banker, and the family was very wealthy. During David's childhood the family lived in Amsterdam but moved to London when he was a teen. Ricardo received little formal education, and going to work for his father at age 14.

Figure 2.1

At age 21, Ricardo defied his parents' wish to marrying a Quaker, Priscilla Ann Wilkinson, and was disinherited and cut off from his family. He went to work on his own as a stockbroker, and was so fabulously succeeded that he was able to retire at age 42 and concentrate solely on his economic and political writings. At his death, his estate was worth approximately £ 725,000, and produced a yearly income of £ 28,000 (about 1.15 million in modern U.S. dollars).

As one of the foremost of the classical economists, Ricardo was friends with several leading economic thinkers of his day, including Thomas Malthus and Jean-Baptiste Say. Ricardo particularly credited his conversations with Malthus for spurring him to think about political economy in new ways. Ricardo wrote these conversations: "My discussions with Malthus have been innumerable, and in my eagerness to convince him that he was wrong, on some points on which we differed, I was led into a deeper consideration of many parts of the subject than I had before given them, and though I have failed to convince him, and may not have satisfied others, I have convinced myself."

Like Malthus, Ricardo took an essentially pessimistic view of the future of human society and agreed with many of his views on the inevitability of human population explosion. Working with Malthus he developed Distribution Theory, which was the first economic theory to make use of the idea of diminishing returns. Distribution theory states that as population grows, more land will have to be cultivated and the return from this land will not be constant because the amount of capital available will not grow at the same rate – newly cultivated land will suffer from diminishing returns and eventually returns will not be enough to attract any further capital. At this point, argued Ricardo, the maximum level of "economic rent" will have been earned – capital will no longer be invested in opening new lands for cultivation, and will instead be shifted to other activities.

Distribution is still valued as a theory today, but even more revered is a theory Ricardo put forward about International Trade that has come to be called "the theory of comparative advantage". Ricardo recognized that if two countries have different opportunity costs for different goods, they will both come out ahead if they specialize in manufacturing and trading those goods in which they have a lower opportunity cost (or "comparative advantage"), even if one country has an absolute advantage in producing all the goods. This theory is quite powerful and has become the strongest, most convincing argument in favor of free trade. For this theory alone, Ricardo is virtually worshipped by many modern economists.

Ricardo also published treatises on the British monetary system, rent and wages, and on an idea for a national bank. Ricardo became a Member of Parliament in 1819 and served until his sudden death on September 11, 1823, from complications resulting from an untreated ear infection. He was survived by his wife and seven children.

2.1.2 Absolute and Comparative Advantage

2.1.2.1 Adam Smith's Theory of Absolute Advantage

In the late 18th and early 19th centuries, first Adam Smith and then David Ricardo explored the basis for international trade as part of their efforts to make a case for free trade. Their writings responded to the doctrine of mercantilism that prevailed at the time (see accompanying box). Their classic theories swayed policymakers for the whole century, even though today we view them as only special cases of a more basic, and more powerful, theory of trade.

In his *Wealth of Nations*, Adam Smith promoted free trade by comparing nations to households. Every household finds it worthwhile to produce only some of the products it consumes, and to buy other products using the proceeds from what the household can sell to others. The same should apply to nations.

It is the maxim of every prudent master of a family, never to attempt to make at home what it will cost...more to make than to buy. The tailor does not attempt to make his own shoes, but buys them from the shoemaker.

What is prudent in the conduct of every private family can scarce be folly in that of a great kingdom. If a foreign country can supply us with a commodity cheaper than what we ourselves can make it, better buy it from them with some part of the product of our own industry, employed in a

Chapter 2 Theories of International Trade

way in which we have some advantages.

An example can show Smith's reasoning. The two "countries" in the example are the United States and the rest of the world. The two products are wheat and cloth (perhaps broadly representing agricultural products and manufactured products). Each product is produced using one resource called labor. (Smith focused on labor because he thought that all "value" was determined by and measured in hours of labor. In this respect, he was imitated by David Ricardo and Karl Marx, who also believed that labor was the basis for all value. We don't have to take this literally – we can consider "labor" to be a bundle of resources which are used to produce products.)

Suppose that the United States is better than the rest of the world at producing wheat, and the rest of the world is better than the United States at producing cloth, it is probably not a surprise that international trade can create benefits, because the United States can focus on producing what it does best (wheat) and export it and the rest of the world can focus on producing what it does best (cloth) and export it. Let's look at this more closely.

What do we mean by "better at producing?" We can indicate each country's ability to produce each product in one of two equivalent ways. First, we measure labor productivity – the number of u- nits of output that a worker can produce in one hour. Second, we can look at the number of hours that it takes a worker to produce one unit of output – this is just the reciprocal of labor productivity. Here are some numbers for our example (see Table 2.1):

Table 2.1

	in the United States	in the rest of the world
Productivity:		
Yard of cloth per labor hour	0.25	<1.0
Bushels of wheat per labor hour	0.5	>0.4
Labor hours to make:		
1 yard of cloth	4.0	>1.0
1 bushel of wheat	2.0	<2.5

In this numerical example, the United States has an absolute advantage in producing wheat, because the U.S. labor productivity in wheat is higher than the rest of the world's labor productivity in wheat. Similarly, the rest of the world has an absolute advantage in producing cloth.

If there is no trade, then each country will have to produce both products to satisfy its demand for the products. If the countries then open to free trade, each can shift its labor resources toward producing the goods in which it has the absolute advantage. In the United States, shifting 1 hour of labor results in a decrease of 0.25 yards of cloth and in an increase of 0.5 bushels of wheat. In the rest of the world, shifting 1 hour of labor results in a decrease of 0.4 bushels of wheat and an in- crease of 1 yard of cloth. Total world production increased. For each product, production using la- bor that has high productivity replaces production using labor that has low productivity.

International trade makes these shifts in production possible even if consumers in each country want to buy something different from what is produced in the country. For instance, in the United States the apparent shortage of (or apparent excess demand for) clothing (as clothing production decreases) is met by imports of clothing from the rest of the world. The United States pays for these imports of clothing by exporting some of the extra wheat product.

Thus, Adam Smith showed the benefits of free trade by showing that global production efficiency is enhanced because trade allows each country to exploit its absolute advantages in producing some product(s). At least one country is better off with trade, and this country's gain is not at the expense of the other country. In many cases both countries will gain from trade by splitting the benefits of the enhanced global production.

Smith's reasoning was fundamentally correct, and it helped to persuade some governments to dismantle inefficient barriers to international trade over the 100 years after he wrote *Wealth of Nation*. Yet his argument failed to put to rest a fear that others had already expressed before he wrote that is what if our country has no absolute advantage? What if the foreigners are better at producing everything than we are? Will they want to trade? If they do, should we want to? That fear existed in the minds of many of Smith's English contemporaries, who worried that the Dutch were more productive than they at making anything. It persists into the 21st century too. In the wake of World War II, many nations thought they could not possibly compete with the highly productive Americans at anything and wondered how they could gain from free trade. Today, some Americans have the same fear in reverse: Aren't foreigners getting better at making everything that enters international trade, and won't the United States be hurt by free trade? We turn next to the theory that first answered these fears and established a fundamental principle of international trade.

2.1.2.2 Ricardo's Theory of Comparative Advantage

David Ricardo's main contribution to our understanding of international trade ways shows that there is a basis for beneficial trade whether countries have any absolute advantage or not. His contribution is based on a careful examination of opportunity cost. The opportunity cost of producing more of a product that is given up. The opportunity cost exists because production resources must be shifted from the other product to this product. (We already used this idea in the discussion of absolute advantage, when we shifted labor from producing one product to producing the other product.)

Ricardo's writings in the early 19th century demonstrated the principle of comparative advantage: A country will export the goods and services that it can produce at a low opportunity cost and import the goods and services that it would otherwise produce at a high opportunity cost.

The key word here is *comparative*, means "relative" and "not necessarily absolute". Even if one country is absolutely more productive at producing everything and the other country is absolutely less productive, they both can gain by trading with each other as long as their relative (dis)advantages in making different goods are different. Each of these countries can benefit from trade by exporting products in which it has the greatest relative advantage (or least relative disadvantage), and importing products in which it has the least relative advantage (or the greatest relative disadvantage).

Chapter 2 Theories of International Trade

Ricardo's approach is actually a double comparison between countries and between products.

Ricardo drove home the point with a simple numerical example of gains from trading two products (cloth and wine) between two countries (England and Portugal). Here is a similar illustration, using wheat and cloth in the United States and the rest of the world (See Table 2.2):

Table 2.2

	in the United States	in the rest of the world
Productivity:		
Yard of cloth per labor hour	0.25	<1.0
Bushels of wheat per labor hour	0.5	<0.67
Labor hours to make:		
1 yard of cloth	4.0	>1.0
1 bushel of wheat	2.0	>1.5

Here, one country has inferior productivity in both goods. The United States has absolute disadvantages in both goods – lower productivity or larger numbers of hours to produce one unit of each goods. What products (if any) will the United States export or import? Can trade bring net national gains to both countries?

As in the absolute-advantage case, we can start from imagining the two countries separately with no trade between them. Each country will have to produce both products to meet local demands for the two products. What will determine the product prices by conditions within each country? To keep our focus on real values and activities, we are going to try to ignore money as long as we can. Rather than looking at money prices (dollars per bushel or dollars per yard), we will use the relative price – the ratio of one product price to another product price. It's as if we are in a world without money, a world of barter between real products like wheat and cloth.

Ricardo, like Smith, believed that, in competitive markets, product prices reflect the costs of the labor needed to produce the products. With no trade, 4 hours of labor in the United States could produce either 2 bushels of wheat or 1 yard of cloth. The price of 1 yard of cloth is more than 2 bushels of wheat in the United States. (Two bushels of wheat are also the opportunity cost of producing cloth in the United States – product prices reflect costs.) In the rest of the world, 1 hour of labor could produce 1 yard of cloth or 2/3 bushels of wheat. The price (and the opportunity cost) of a yard of cloth is 0.67 bushels of wheat in the rest of the world. Thus, within the two isolated economies, national prices would follow the relative labor costs of cloth and wheat (See Table 2.3):

Table 2.3

	In the United States	In the rest of the world
With no international trade:		
Price of cloth	2.0 bushels/yard	0.67 bushel/yard
Price of wheat	0.5 yard/bushel	1.5 yards/bushel

There is really only one ratio in each country because the price of wheat is just the reciprocal of the price of cloth.

Now let trade be possible between the United States and the rest of the world. Somebody will notices the difference between the national prices for each goods and will try to profit from that difference. The principle is simple and universal: As long as prices differ in two places (by more than any cost of transporting between the places), there is a way to profit through arbitrage – buying at the low price in one place and selling at the high price in the other place.

Perhaps the first alert person will think of sending cloth to the United States in exchange for U.S. wheat. Considering the arbitrage profit that the person could make, she acquires cloth in the rest of the world, giving up 0.67 bushels of wheat for each yard, then ships this cloth to the United States and sells it there for 2.0 bushels per yard. To keep things simple, we will usually assume that the cost of transporting products between the countries is zero. Therefore, by buying low (at 0.67) and selling high (at 2.0), she can make an arbitrage profit of 1.33 bushels of wheat for each yard of cloth that she exports from the rest of the world (and imports into the United States). Somebody else could profit by acquiring wheat in the United States at the low price of 0.5 yards per bushel, shipping the wheat to the rest of the world, and selling it for the higher price of 1.5 yards per bushel.

The opening of profitable international trade will start pushing the two separate national price ratios toward a new worldwide equilibrium. As people remove cloth from the rest of the world by exporting it, cloth becomes more expensive relative to wheat in the rest of the world. Meanwhile, cloth becomes cheaper in the United States, thanks to the additional supply of cloth imported from the rest of the world. So, cloth tends to be more expensive where it was cheap at first and cheaper where it was more expensive (A similar process occurs for wheat). The tendencies continue until the two national relative prices become one world equilibrium relative price. Normal trade on an ongoing basis will be conducted at this equilibrium relative price.

What will the equilibrium international price be? We cannot say that without knowing how strongly the two countries demand each of the two products. We do know something – the equilibrium international price ratio must fall within the range of the two price ratios that prevailed in each country before trade began:

$$2.0 \geqslant \text{International price of cloth} \geqslant 0.67 \text{ (bushel/yard)}$$

Or, equivalently,

$$0.5 \leqslant \text{International price of wheat} \leqslant 1.5 \text{ (yard/bushel)}$$

Why? Consider what would happen if this was not true, for instance, an international price of only 0.4 bushel per yard. At this low price of cloth, the rest of the world would want to import cloth and export wheat because the price of cloth on the international market is now below the cost of producing cloth at home (0.67 bushel/yard). No deal could be made, though. At this low cloth price, the United States would also want to import cloth and export wheat. No equilibrium is possible, and the cloth price would be pushed up as a result of the excess demand for cloth. (Similar reasoning applies to show the lack of equilibrium if the cloth price is above 2 bushels/yard.) The only way for the two sides to agree on trading is to have the cloth price somewhere in the range 0.67 to 2.0 bushels/yard.

Supposing that the strengths of demand for the products, which we will examine more closely later in this chapter, lead to an equilibrium international cloth price that has the convenient value of 1 bushel/yard, both countries gain from international trade. The United States gains:
➢ It produces a bushel of wheat by giving up only 0.5 yard of cloth.
➢ It can export this bushel and receive 1 yard of cloth.

The rest of the world gains:
➢ It produces a yard of cloth by giving up only 0.67 bushel of wheat.
➢ It can export this yard and receive 1 bushel of wheat.

How do absolute advantage and comparative advantage relate to each other? Smith's example of each country having an absolute advantage in one product is also a case of comparative advantage. Our detailed analysis of comparative advantage could be applied to the numerical example of absolute advantage in the previous section. But comparative advantage is more general and powerful. A country will have a comparative advantage even if it has no absolute advantage. The basis for trade and the gains from trade arose from differences between the countries in opportunity costs of the goods. In our numerical example of comparative advantage, the opportunity cost of a bushel of wheat within the United States (0.5 yards/bushel) is lower than this opportunity cost in the rest of the world (1.5 yard/bushel). The United States will export wheat, even though it has an absolute disadvantage in producing both wheat and cloth.

2.2 Factor Proportions Trade Theory

2.2.1 The Heckscher-Ohlin (Factor Proportions) Model Overview

The factor proportions model was originally developed by two Swedish economists, Eli Heckscher and his student Bertil Ohlin in the 1920s. Many elaborations of the model were provided by Paul Samuelson after the 1930s, and thus sometimes the model is referred to as the Heckscher-Ohlin-Samuelson (or HOS) Model. In the 1950s and 60s some noteworthy extensions to the model were made by Jaroslav Vanek and so occasionally the model is called the Heckscher-Ohlin-Vanek model. Here we will simply call all versions of the model either the "Heckscher-Ohlin (or H-O) Model" or simply the more generic "Factor Proportions Model".

The H-O model incorporates a number of realistic characteristics of production that are left out of the simple Ricardian model. Recalling that in the simple Ricardian model only one factor of production, labor, is needed to produce goods and services, the productivity of labor is assumed to vary across countries, which implies a difference in technology between nations. It was the difference in technology that motivated advantageous international trade in the model.

The standard H-O model begins by expanding the number of factors of production from one to two. The model assumes that labor and capital are used in the production of two final goods. Here, capital refers to the physical machines and equipment that are used in production. Thus, machine tools, conveyers, trucks, forklifts, computers, office buildings, office supplies and much more are considered as capital.

All productive capital must be owned by someone. In a capitalist economy, most of the physical capital is owned by individuals and businesses. In a socialist economy productive capital would be owned by the government. In most of economies today, the government owns some of the productive capitals but private citizens and businesses own most of the capital. Any person who owns common stock issued by a business has an ownership share in that company and is entitled to dividends or income based on the profitability of the company. As such, that person is a capitalist, i.e., an owner of capital.

The H-O model assumes private ownership of capital. Use of capital in production will generate income for the owner. We will refer to that income as capital "rents". Thus, whereas the worker earns "wages" for his or her efforts in production, the capital owner earns rents.

The assumption of two productive factors, capital and labor, allows for the introduction of another realistic feature in production; that of differing factor proportions both across and within industries. When one considers a range of industries in a country, it is easy to convince oneself that the proportion of capital to labor used varies considerably. For example, steel production generally involves large amounts of expensive machines and equipment spread over perhaps hundreds of acres of land, but also uses relatively few workers. In the tomato industry, in contrast, harvesting requires hundreds of migrant workers to hand-pick and collects each fruit from the vine. The amount of machinery used in this process is relatively small.

In the H-O model, we define the ratio of the quantity of capital to the quantity of labor used in a production process as the capital-labor ratio. We imagine, and therefore assume, that different industries producing different goods and have different capital-labor ratios. It is this ratio (or proportion) of one factor to another that gives the model its generic name: the Factor Proportions Model.

In a model in which each country produces two goods, an assumption must be made as to which industry has the larger capital-labor ratio. Thus, if the two goods that a country can produce are steel and clothing, and if steel production uses more capital per unit of labor than is used in clothing production, then we would say the steel production is capital-intensive relative to clothing production. Also, if steel production is capital intensive, then it implies that clothing production must be labor-intensive relative to steel.

Another realistic characteristic of the world is that countries have different quantities, or endowments, of capital and labor available for use in the production process. Thus, some countries like the U. S. are well endowed with physical capital relative to their labor force. In contrast, many less developed countries have very little physical capital but are well endowed with large labor forces. We use the ratio of the aggregate endowment of capital to the aggregate endowment of labor to define relative factor abundance between countries. Thus if, for example, the U. S. has a larger ratio of aggregate capital per unit of labor than France's ratio, we would say that the U. S. is capital-abundant relative to France. By implication, France would have a larger ratio of aggregate labor per unit of capital and thus France would be labor-abundant relative to the U. S. .

The H-O Model assumes that the only difference between countries is these variations in the relative endowments of factors of production. It is ultimately shown that trade will occur, trade will be nationally advantageous, and trade will have characterized effects upon prices, wages and rents, when the nations differ in their relative factors endowments and when different industries use factors in different proportions.

It is worth emphasizing that a fundamental distinction between the H-O model and the Ricardian Model. Whereas the Ricardian model assumes that production technologies differ between countries, the H-O Model assumes that production technologies are the same. The reason for the identical technology assumption in the H-O Model is perhaps not so much because it is believed that technologies are really the same; although a case can be made for that, instead the assumption is useful that it enables us to see precisely how differences in resource endowments is sufficient to cause trade and it shows what impacts will arise entirely due to these differences.

2.2.2 The Main Results of the H-O Model

There are four main theorems in the H-O Model: the Heckscher-Ohlin theorem, the Stolper-Samuelson Theorem, the Rybczynski theorem and the factor-price equalization theorem. The Stolper-Samuelson and Rybczynski theorems describe relationships between variables in the model while the H-O and factor-price equalization theorems present some of the key results of the model. Applications of these theorems also allow us to derive some other important implications of the model. Let us begin with the H-O theorem.

2.2.2.1 The Heckscher-Ohlin Theorem

The H-O theorem predicts the pattern of trade between countries based on the characteristics of the countries. The H-O theorem says that a capital-abundant country will export the capital-intensive goods while the labor-abundant country will export the labor-intensive goods.

Here's the reason.

A capital-abundant country is one that is well endowed with capital relative to the other country. This gives the country a propensity for producing the goods which uses relatively more capital in the production process, i. e., the capital-intensive goods. As a result, if these two countries were not trading initially, i. e., they were in autarky, the price of the capital-intensive goods in the capital-abundant country would be bid down (due to its extra supply) relative to the price of the goods in the other country. Similarly, in the labor-abundant country the price of the labor-intensive goods would be bid down relative to the price of that goods in the capital-abundant country.

Once trade is allowed, profit-seeking firms will move their products to the markets that temporarily have the higher price. Thus, the capital-abundant country will export the capital-intensive goods since the price will be temporarily higher in the other country. Likewise the labor-abundant country will export the labor-intensive goods. Trades flows will rise until the price of both goods are equalized in the two markets.

The H-O theorem demonstrates that differences in resource endowments as defined by national abundances are one reason that international trade may occur.

2.2.2.2 The Stolper-Samuelson Theorem

The Stolper-Samuelson theorem describes the relationship between changes in output, or goods, prices and changes in factor prices such as wages and rents within the context of the H-O model. The theorem was originally developed to illuminate the issue of how tariffs would affect the income of workers and capitalists (i.e., the distribution of income) within a country, however, the theorem is just as useful when applied to trade liberalization.

The theorem states that if the price of the capital-intensive goods rises (for whatever reason) then the price of capital, the factor used intensively in that industry will rise, while the wage rate paid to labor will fall. Thus, if the price of steel was to rise, and if steel was capital-intensive, then the rental rate on capital would rise while the wage rate would fall. Similarly, if the price of the labor-intensive goods was to rise then the wage rate would rise while the rental rate would fall.

The theorem was later generalized by Ronald Jones who constructed a magnification effect for prices in the context of the H-O Model. The magnification effect allows for analysis of any change in the prices of both goods and provides information about the magnitude of the effects on the wages and rents. Most importantly, the magnification effect allows one to analyze the effects of price changes on real wages and real rents earned by workers and capital owners. This is instructive since real returns indicate the purchasing power of wages and rents after accounting for the price changes and thus are a better measure of well-being than simply the wage rate or rental rate alone.

Since prices change in a country when trade liberalization occurs, the magnification effect can be applied to yield an interesting and important result. A movement to free trade will cause the real return of a country's relatively abundant factor to rise, while the real return of the country's relatively scarce factor will fall. Thus, if the U.S. and France are two countries that move to free trade, and if the U.S. is capital-abundant (while France is labor-abundant) then capital owners in the U.S. will experience an increase in the purchasing power of their rental income (i.e., they will gain) while workers will experience a decline in the purchasing power of their wage income (i.e., they will lose). Similarly, workers will gain in France, but capital owners will lose.

What's more, the abundant factor of the country benefits regardless in which industry it is employed. Thus, capital owners in the U.S. would benefit from trade even if their capital is used in the declining import-competing sector. Similarly, workers would lose in the U. S. even if they are employed in the expanding export sector.

The reasons for this result are somewhat complicated but the gist can be given fairly easily. When a country moves to free trade, the price of its exported goods will rise while the price of its imported goods will fall. The higher prices in the export industry will inspire profit-seeking firms to expand production. At the same time, the import-competing industry, suffering from falling prices, will want to reduce production to cut its losses. Thus, capital and labor will be laid off in the import-competing sector but will be in demand in the expanding export sector. However, a problem arises in that the export sector is intensive on the country's abundant factor, let's say capital. This means that the export industry wants relatively more capital per worker than the ratio of factors that the import-competing industry is laying off. In the transition there will be an excess demand for capital, which will bid up its price, and an excess supply of labor, which will bid down its price. Hence, the capital owners in both industries experience an increase in their rents while the workers in both industries experience a decline in their wages.

2.2.2.3 The Factor-Price Equalization Theorem

The factor-price equalization theorem says that when the prices of the output goods are equalized between countries, as when countries move to free trade, then the prices of the factors (capital and labor) will also be equalized between countries. This implies that free trade will equalize the wages of workers and the rents earned on capital throughout the world.

The theorem derives from the assumptions of the model, the most critical of which is the assumption that the two countries share the same production technology and that markets are perfectly competitive. In a perfectly competitive market, factors are paid on the basis of the value of their marginal productivity, which in turn depends upon the output prices of the goods. Thus, when prices differ between countries, are their marginal productivity and hence are their wages and rents. However, once goods prices are equalized, as they are in free trade, the value of marginal products is also equalized between countries and hence, the countries must also share the same wage rates and rental rates.

Factor-price equalization formed the basis for some arguments often heard in the debates leading up to the approval of the North American Free Trade Agreement (NAFTA) between the U. S., Canada and Mexico. Opponents of NAFTA feared that free trade with Mexico would lower U. S. wages to the level of Mexico. Factor-price equalization is consistent with this fear, although a more likely outcome would be a reduction in U. S. wages coupled with an increase in Mexican wages.

Furthermore, we should note that the factor-price equalization is unlikely to apply perfectly in the real world. The H-O Model assumes that technology is the same between countries in order to focus on the effects of different factor endowments. If production technologies differ across countries, as we assumed in the Ricardian model, then factor prices would not equalize once goods prices equalize. As such a better interpretation of the factor-price equalization theorem applied to real world settings is that free trade should cause a tendency for factor prices to move together, if some of the trade between countries is based on differences in factor endowments.

2.2.2.4 The Rybczynski Theorem

The Rybczynski theorem demonstrates the relationship between changes in national factor endowments and changes in the outputs of the final goods within the context of the H-O Model. Briefly stated, it says that an increase in a country's endowment of a factor will cause an increase in output of the goods which uses that factor intensively, and a decrease in the output of the other goods. In other words, if the U.S. experiences an increase in capital equipment, then that would cause an increase in output of the capital-intensive goods, steel and a decrease in the output of the labor-intensive goods, clothing. The theorem is useful in addressing issues such as investment, population growth and hence labor force growth, immigration and emigration, all within the context of the H-O Model.

The theorem was also generalized by Ronald Jones who constructed a magnification effect for quantities in the context of the H-O Model. The magnification effect allows for analysis of any change in both endowments and provides information about the magnitude of the effects on the outputs of the two goods.

2.2.2.5 Aggregate Economic Efficiency

The H-O Model demonstrates that when countries move to free trade, they will experience an increase in aggregate efficiency. The change in prices will cause a shift in production of both goods in both countries. Each country will produce more of its export goods and less of its import goods. Unlike the Ricardian model, however, neither country will necessarily specialize in production of its export goods. Nevertheless, the production shifts will improve productive efficiency in each country. Also, due to the changes in prices, consumers, the aggregate will experience an improvement in consumption efficiency. In other words, national welfare will rise for both countries when they move to free trade.

However, this does not imply that everyone benefits. As was discussed above, the model clearly shows that some factor owners will experience an increase in their real incomes while others will experience a decrease in their factor incomes. Trade will generate winners and losers. The increase in national welfare essentially means that the sum of the gains to the winners will exceed the sum of the losses to the losers. For this reason, economists often apply the compensation principle.

The compensation principle states that as long as the total benefits exceed the total losses in the movement to free trade, then it must be possible to redistribute income from the winners to the losers such that everyone has at least as much as they had before trade liberalization occurred.

The "standard" H-O Model refers to the case of two countries, two goods and two factors of production. The H-O Model has been extended to many countries, many goods and many factors cases, but most of the exposition in this text, by economists in general, is in reference to the standard case.

2.2.3 The Leontief Paradox(Figure 2.2)

The Heckscher-Ohlin theory has been one of the most influential theoretical ideas in international economics. Most economists prefer the Heckscber-Ohlin theory to Ricardo's theory because it makes fewer simplifying assumptions. Because of its influence, the theory has been subjected to many empirical tests. Beginning with a famous study published in 1953 by Wassily Leontief (winner of the Nobel Prize in economics in 1973), many of these tests have raised questions about the validity of the Heckscher-Ohlin theory. Using the Heckscher-Ohlin theory, Leontief postulated that since the United States was relatively abundant in capital compared to other nations, the United States would be an exporter of capital-intensive goods and an importer of labor-intensive goods. To his surprise, he found that U.S. exports were less capital intensive than U.S. imports. Since this result was at variance with the predictions of the theory, it has become known as the Leontief paradox.

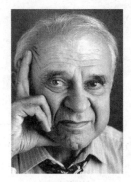

Figure 2.2

No one is quite sure why we observe the Leontief paradox. One possible explanation is that the United States has a special advantage in producing new products or goods made with innovative technologies. Such products may be less capital intensive than products whose technology has had time to mature and become suitable for mass production. Thus, the United States may be exporting goods that heavily using skilled labor and innovative entrepreneurship, such as computer software, while importing heavy manufacturing products that use large amounts of capitals. Some more recent empirical studies tend to confirm this. Tests of the Heckscher-Ohlin theory using data for a large number of countries tend to confirm the existence of the Leontief paradox.

This leaves economists with a difficult dilemma. They prefer the Heckscher-Ohlin theory on theoretical grounds, but it is a relatively poor predictor of real-world international trade patterns. On the other hand, the theory they regard as being too limited, Ricardo's theory of comparative advantage, actually predicts trade patterns with greater accuracy. The best solution to this dilemma may be to return to the Ricardo's idea that trade patterns are largely driven by international differences in productivity.

Thus, one might argue that the United States exports commercial aircraft and imports automobiles not because its factor endowments are especially suited to aircraft manufacture and not suited to automobile manufacture, but because the United States is more efficient at producing aircraft than automobiles. A key assumption in the Heckscher-Ohlin theory is that technologies are the same across countries. This may not be the case. Differences in technology may lead to differences in productivity, which in turn, drives international trade patterns. Thus, Japan's success in exporting automobiles in the 1970s and 1980s was based not just on the relative abundance of capital, but also on its development of innovative manufacturing technology that enabled it to achieve higher productivity levels in automobile production than other countries that also had abundant capital. The newest empirical work strongly suggests that this theoretical explanation may be correct. The new research shows that once differences in technology across countries are controlled for, countries do indeed export those goods that make intensive use of factors that are locally abundant, while importing goods that make intensive use of factors that are locally scarce. In other words, once the impact of differences of technology on productivity is controlled for, the Heckscher-Ohlin seems to gain predictive power.

2.3 The Product Cycle Theory

The product cycle theory (PCT) of trade builds on the imitation lag hypothesis in its treatment of delay in the diffusion of technology. However, the PCT also relaxes several other assumptions of traditional trade theory and is more complete in its treatment of trade patterns. This theory was developed in 1966 by Raymond Vernon.

The PCT is concerned with the life cycle of a typical "new product" and its impact on international trade. Vernon developed the theory in response to the failure of the United States – the main country to do so – to conform empirically to the Heckscher-Ohlin model. Vernon emphasizes manufactured goods, and the theory begins with the development of a new product in the United States. The new product will have two principal characteristics: (a) it will cater to high-income demands because the United States is a high-income country; and (b) it promises, in its production process, to be labor-saving and capital-using in nature (It is also possible that the product itself – for example, a consumer durable such as a microwave oven – will be labor-saving for the consumer). The reason for including the potential labor-saving nature of the production process is that the United States is widely regarded as a labor-scarce country. Thus, technological change will emphasize production processes with the potential to conserve this scarce factor of production.

The PCT divides the life cycle of this new product into three stages. In the first stage, the new product stage, the product is produced and consumed only in the United States. Firms produce in the United States because that is where demand is located, and these firms wish to stay close to the market to detect consumer response to the product. The characteristics of the product and the production process are in a state of change during this stage as firms seek to familiarize themselves with the product and the market. No international trade takes place.

The second stage of the life cycle is called the maturing product stage. In this stage, some general standards for the product and its characteristics begin to emerge, and mass production techniques start to be adopted. With more standardization in the production process, economies of scale start to be realized. This feature contrasts with Heckscher-Ohlin and Ricardo, whose theories assumed constant returns to scale. In addition, foreign demand for the product grows, but it is associated particularly with other *developed* countries, since the product is catering to high-income demands. This rise in foreign demand (assisted by economies of scale) leads to a trade pattern whereby the United States exports the product to other high-income countries.

Other developments also occur in the maturing product stage. Once U. S. firms are selling to other high-income countries, they may begin to assess the possibilities of producing abroad in addition to producing in the United States. If the cost picture is favorable (means that production abroad costs less than production at home plus transportation costs), then U. S. firms will tend to invest in production facilities in the other developed countries. If this is done, export displacement of U. S. produced output occurs. With a plant in France, for example, not only France but other European countries can be supplied from the French facility rather than from the U. S. plant. Thus, an initial export surge by the United States is followed by a fall in U. S. exports and a likely fall in U. S. production of the goods. This relocation-of-production aspect of the PCT is a useful step, because it recognizes – in contract to H-O and Ricardo – that capital and management are not immobile internationally. This feature is also consistent with the very large amount of direct investment by U. S. firms in Western Europe during the 1960s and 1970s and, in a more recent context, by Japanese firms in rapidly growing countries in Asia (such as China, and South Korea etc.).

Vernon also suggested that, in this maturing product stage, the product might now begin to flow from Western Europe to the United States, because with capital more mobile internationally than labor, the price of capital across countries was unlikely to diverge as much as the price of labor. With relative commodity prices thus heavily influenced by labor costs, and with labor costs lower in Europe than in the United States, Europe might be able to undersell the United States in this product (Remember that Vernon was written in 1966; it is less true today than those of the United States that Europe's labor costs are lower). Relative factor endowments and factor prices, which played such a large role in Heckscher-Ohlin, have not been completely ignored in the PCT.

The final stage is the standardized product stage. By this time in the product's life cycle, the characteristics of the product itself and of the production process are well known; the product is familiar to consumers and the production process to producers. Vernon hypothesized that production may shift to the developing countries. Labor costs again play an important role, and the developed countries are busy introducing other products. Thus, the trade pattern is that the United States and other developed countries may import the product from the developing countries. Figure 2.3 summarizes the production, consumption, and trade pattern for China and the United States.

In summary, the PCT postulates a dynamic comparative advantage because the country source of exports shifts throughout the life cycle of the product. Early on, the innovating country exports the goods, but then it is displaced by other developed countries – which in turn are ultimately displaced by the developing countries. A casual glance at product history yields this kind of pattern in a general way. For example, electronic products such as television receivers were for many years a prominent export of the United States, but Europe and especially Japan emerged as competitors, causing the U. S. share of the market to diminish dramatically. Recently, Japan has been threatened by South Korea and other Asian producers. The textile and apparel industry is another example where developing countries (especially China, South Korea and Singapore. ect.) have become major suppliers in the world market, displacing in particular the United States and Japan. Automobile production and export location also shifted relatively from the United States and Europe to Japan and later still to countries such as South Korea and Malaysia. This dynamic comparative advantage, together with factor mobility and economies of scale, makes the product cycle theory an appealing alternative to the Heckscher-Ohlin model.

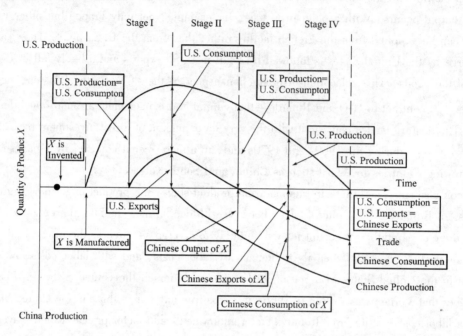

Figure 2.3

There is no single all-encompassing test (such as the Leontief test of Heckscher-Ohlin) to verify empirically the product cycle theory. Instead, researchers have examined particular features of the PCT to see if they are consistent with real-world experience. For example, new product development is critical to the PCT, and it is often the result of research and development (R&D) expenditures. Therefore, economists hypothesize that, in the U.S. manufacturing sector, there should be a positive correlation between R&D expenditures and successful export performance by industry. A number of tests indicated this result, including those by Donald Keesing (1967) and William Gruber, Dileep Mehta and Vernon (1967). Kravis and Lipsey (1992) found that high R&D intensity was positively associated with large shares of exports by U.S. multinational companies (MNCs). Further more, over the last 25 years, greater shares of U.S. MNC exports have come from overseas production, which is consistent with the direct-investment and export-displacement features of the PCT. In addition, in 1969, Louis Wells examined the income elasticity of demand of the fastest growing U.S. exports and found that trade in "high-income" products indeed grew more rapidly than other products – again, an occurrence is consistent with the PCT.

Among the many other empirical works is Gary Hufbauer's (1966) study on trade in synthetic materials. Hufbauer found that the United States and other developed countries tended to export new products while developing countries tended to export older products. Gruber, Meht and Vernon (1967) also discovered that research-intensive U. S. industries had a high propensity on aborad investment. This is consistent with the maturing product stage of the theory. In 1972, John Morrall found that U. S. industries that were successful exporters also tended to have relatively high expenditures on non-payroll costs such as advertising, sales promotion, and so forth. This finding is consistent with the product cycle theory since production of new products involves such spending. Many other studies of PCT features have shown consistency between real-world experience and aspects of the theory.

Raymond Vernon (1979) later suggested that the PCT might need to be modified. The main alteration concerns the location of the production of the goods when the goods is first introduced. Multinational firms today have subsidiaries and branches worldwide, and knowledge of conditions outside the United States is more complete than it was at the time of Vernon's original writing in 1966. Thus, the new product may be produced first not in the United States but outside the country. In addition, per capita income differences between the United States and other developed countries are now not as great as in 1966, so catering to high-income demands no longer implies catering to U. S. demands alone. Even with this modification, the salient features of scale economies, direct investment overseas, and dynamic comparative advantage still distinguish the product cycle theory from the Heckscher-Ohlin model.

One hesitates, however, to distinguish the product cycle theory so clearly from the Heckscher-Ohlin model. Elias Dinopoulos, James Oehmke, and Paul Segerstrom (1993) constructed a theoretical model that has PCT-type trade emerging as a *result* of differing factor endowments across countries. The model utilizes three production sectors in each country: an innovating high-technology sector and "outside-goods" sector that are engaged in no product innovation, and a sector that supplies R&D services to the high-technology sector. Like H-O, there are only two factors (capital and labor) identical production functions across countries, and constant returns to scale. Assuming that the R&D sector is the most capital-intensive sector, a capital-abundant country produces a great deal of R&D. This enables a firm in the high-technology sector in that country to obtain a temporary monopoly in a new product – with patent protection – and then to export the product. After the patent expires, production occurs abroad with some export from that location. While a complete explanation is beyond the scope of this book, Dinopoulos, Oemke and Segerstrom's model generates PCT-type trade as well as intra-industry trade (a concept discussed later) and a role for MNCs. Thus, Heckscher-Ohlin and the product cycle theory may well be complementary, not competing theories.

In similar fashion, James Markusen, James Melvin, William Kaempfer, and Keith Maskus (1995, p. 209) introduced the idea of a life cycle for new technologies containing elements of both the Dinopoulos, Oehmke and Segerstrom model and the product cycle model. Noting the growing importance of technology in the trade of industrialized countries, Markusen et al. Suggest that, just as there is a product cycle for consumer goods, there increasingly appears to be a cycle for techniques of production and machinery, as techniques and machines developed in industrialized countries eventually find their way into labor-abundant developing countries.

This technology cycle is driven by the capital-abundant, high-wage countries where there is a cost incentive and a sufficient market demand to warrant new labor-saving technologies and new product development. The capital-abundant countries thus produce a flow of new products and innovations, with firms often protected by a temporary monopoly via patents to produce for the home market. Since the new labor-saving technologies are not consistent with the relative factor abundances in the labor-abundant developing countries, those countries initially have little economic incentive to acquire the innovations. Consequently, capital-abundant countries export the new products utilizing the new technology. Eventually, however, as incomes start to rise in developing countries and even new technologies are produced in the developed countries, the machines embodying the original "new" technologies are exported by capital-abundant countries and the final products start being produced in the labor-abundant countries. Later, as in the product cycle theory, the machines themselves may be produced in the developing countries and exported from them.

Raymond Vernon has argued that, for many manufactured goods, comparative advantage may shift over time from one country to another. This is because these goods go through a product life cycle. This life cycle involves a stage during which goods are invented and tested in the market place. During this period of time, the production of the goods also undergoes considerable experimentation.

Later, when the product is successful and becomes firmly established in the marketplace, a standardization process occurs. During this period, competing products from different manufacturers take on an increasingly common appearance, and the manufacturing processes used to make the goods also become more and more identical. At this point, the product has matured. It may be sold for many years in this stage, or it may be displaced over time by new inventions.

How does the product life cycle relate to comparative advantage? The answer is simple. Early in a product's life, the country that invents the product has comparative advantage. As the country exports the goods to the rest of the world, and as the product becomes increasingly more standardized, it is possible for competing firms in other countries to begin and gain market share, if these firms have a cost advantage in large-scale manufacturing. In such instances, comparative advantages shifts from the inventing country to countries where manufacturing costs are lower.

Noting how this model can be used to reconcile the Leontief paradox, let us assume that the United States is an innovating country that produces many new products. The United States will have comparative advantage in recently invented manufactured goods. Because these goods have yet to become standardized, their production is apt to be quiet labor intensive. Investment in fixed capital is likely to be postponed until that it becomes certain what features are most popular with the public and how best to automate the production of the goods. Thus, U.S. exports will tend to be labor intensive. Because standardization involves the adoption of more capital-intensive production techniques, if later the United States loses comparative advantage in a goods and begins to import it, this goods will tend to be capital intensive.

The product life cycle model is a model that has limited applicability. It represents an attempt to explain trade in manufactured products that require some degree of technical sophistication in their invention, design and development. In some cases, the theory seems to fit the facts. For instance, color television was invented in the United States, and in the early days of the product, the United States produced and exported this goods. Then, over time, the production of color televisions has shifted almost entirely to countries such as Japan, Korea and elsewhere.

For other sophisticated products, such as computers and aircraft, the model seems to do less well. The United States, which took the lead in the development of these goods, still retains substantial comparative advantage despite the fact that each is now a relatively mature product. These examples point to the fundamental weakness of the product life cycle model — its inability to generalize its predictions about the timing of changes in the location of comparative advantage.

2.4 New Trade Theory

New Trade Theory (NTT) is the economic critique of international free trade from the perspective of increasing returns to scale and the network effect. Some economists have asked whether it might be effective for a nation to shelter infant industries until they had grown to a sufficient size large enough to compete internationally.

New Trade theorists challenge the assumption of diminishing returns to scale, and some argue that using protectionist measures to build up a huge industrial base in certain industries will then allow those sectors to dominate the world market (via a Network effect).

They wondered whether free trade would have prevented the development of the Japanese auto industries in the 1950s, when quotas and regulations prevented import competition. Japanese companies were encouraged to import foreign production technology but were required to produce 90 percent of parts domestically within five years. It is said that the short-term hardship of Japanese consumers (who were unable to buy the superior vehicles produced by the world market) was more than compensated for by the long-term benefits to producers, who gained time to out-compete their international rivals.

Less quantitative form of this "infant industry" argument against totally free trade has been advanced by trade theorists since at least 1848.

2.4.1 The Impact of Theory

Although there was nothing particularly "new" about the idea of protecting "infant industries" (an idea offered in theory since the 18th century, and in trade policy since the 1880s). What was new in "New Trade Theory" was the rigour of the mathematical economics used to model the increasing returns to scale, and especially the use of the network effect to argue that the formation of important industries was path dependent in a way which industrial planning and judicious tariffs might control.

The model they developed was highly technical, and predicted the possibilities of national specialization-by-industry observed in the industrial world (movies in Hollywood, watches in Switzerland, etc). The story of path-dependent industrial concentrations sometimes leads to the monopolistic competition.

2.4.2 Econometric Testing

The econometric evidence for NTT was mixed, and again, highly technical. Due to the timescales required and the particular nature of production in each "monopolizable" sector, statistical judgements have been hard to make. In many ways, there is too limited a dataset to produce a reliable test of the hypothesis which doesn't require arbitrary judgements from the researchers.

Japan is cited as a evidence of the benefits of "intelligent" protectionism, but critics of NTT have argued that the empirical support post-war Japan offers for beneficial protectionism is unusual, and that the NTT argument is based on a selective sample of historical cases. Although many examples (like Japanese cars) can be cited where a "protected" industry subsequently grew to world status, regressions on the outcomes of such "industrial policies" (including the failures) have been less conclusive.

2.4.3 History of the Theory's Development

The theory was initially associated with Paul Krugman in the late 1970s; Krugman claims that he heard about monopolistic competition from Robert Solow. Looking back in 1996, Krugman wrote that international economics a generation earlier had completely ignored returns to scale. "The idea that trade might reflect an overlay of increasing-returns specialization on comparative advantage was not there at all: instead, the ruling idea was that increasing returns would simply alter the pattern of comparative advantage." In 1976, however, MIT-trained economist Victor Norman had worked out the central elements of what came to be known as the Helpman-Krugman theory. He wrote it up and showed it to Avinash Dixit. However, they both agreed the results were not very significant. Indeed Norman never had the paper typed up, much less been published. Norman's formal stake in the race comes from the final chapters of the famous Dixit-Norman book.

James Brander, a PhD at Stanford at the time, was undertaking similarly innovative work using models from industrial organisation theory – cross-hauling – to explain two – way trade in similar products.

2.4.4 "New" New Trade Theory

M. J. Melitz and Pol Antras stated a new trend in the study of international trade. While new trade theory put emphasis on the growing trend of intermediate goods, this new trend emphasizes firm level differences in the same industry of the same country and this new trend is frequently called "new" new trade theory (NNTT). NNTT stresses the importance of firms rather than sectors in understanding the challenges and the opportunities countries face in the age of globalization.

As international trade is increasingly liberalized, industries of comparative advantage are expected to expand, while those of comparative disadvantage are expected to shrink, leading to an uneven spatial distribution of the corresponding economic activities. Within the very same industry, some firms are not able to cope with international competition while others thrive. The resulting intra-industry reallocations of market shares and productive resources are much more pronounced than inter-industry reallocations driven by comparative advantage.

2.4.5 Theoretical Foundations

New trade theory and "new" new trade theory (NNTT) need their own trade theory. New trade theories are often based on assumptions such as monopolistic competition and increasing returns to scale. One of the typical explanations, given by P. Krugman, depends on the assumption that all firms are symmetrical, meaning that they all have the same production coefficients. This is too strict as an assumption and deprived general applicability of Krugaman's explanation. Shiozawa, based on much more general model, succeeded in giving a new explanation on why the traded volume increases for intermediates goods when the transport cost decreases.

"New" new trade theory (NNTT) also needs new theoretical foundation. Melitz and his followers concentrate on empirical aspects and pay little interest on theoretical aspects of NNTT. Shiozawa's new construction, or Ricardo-Sraffa trade theory, enables Ricardian trade theory to include choice of techniques. Thus the theory can treat a situation where there are many firms with different production processes. Based on this new theory, Fujimoto and Shiozawa analyze how different production sites, either of competing firms or of the same firms locating in the different countries, compete.

2.5 Intra-Industry Trade

2.5.1 Alternative Theories of Trade

When the facts change, theories often need to be charged with them. Here we explore facts about world trade and the leading theories that try to explain the aspects that are not consistent with the standard theory.

One key fact is the importance of two-way trade by a country in very similar products – both exporting and importing products in the same industry. Another key fact is the dominance of a few large firms in some world industries. These facts point us toward considering theories based on types of market structure different from the perfectly competitive markets of standard trade theory. We will examine three major alternatives:

➢ Monopolistic competition (with its emphasis on product differentiation);

➤ Global oligopoly;

➤ Industries that concentrate in a few places because of scale economies that arise from interactions among the firms located within each area.

2.5.2 Trade Facts in Search of Better Theory

According to the trade theory based on comparative advantage, nations should trade with each other to exploit their production-side differences. We would expect that industrialized countries (like the United States, Japan and Germany) would trade with the developing countries. This part of the trade pattern is generally well explained by comparative-advantage theory.

According to comparative-advantage theory, nations that are similar in their production-side capabilities (and in their general demand patterns) should trade little with each other. Industrialize countries are similar in many aspects of their factor endowments (physical capital, skilled labor and unskilled labor) and also in their technologies and technological capabilities. Comparative-advantage theory predicts that these countries should trade rather little with each other, except for some trade based in primary products (for instance, food products and minerals) resulting from differences in endowments of arable land and natural resources.

In fact, industrialized countries trade extensively with each other. Trade between industrialize countries is about half of all world trade volume. Over 70 percent of the exports of industrialize countries go to other industrialize countries, and about four-fifths of these exports are nonfood manufactured products. These facts appear to be inconsistent with comparative advantage theory.

2.5.3 The Rise of Intra-Industry Trade

Perhaps there is still some comparative advantage basis for production specialization across industries among the industrialized countries. That is, perhaps each industrialize country specializes in and exports products in a particular range of industries, exploiting some subtle production side comparative advantage. A close look at the data suggests that this is not true. Much trade in manufactured goods between industrialize countries is intra-industry trade-two-way trade in which the country both exports and imports the same or very similar products (products in the same industry). Economists coined this term in the 1970s to describe such trade as Hondas for Volkswagens, French wine for Italian wine, or Boeing airplanes for Airbus airplanes.

To describe the phenomenon more carefully, specialists divide a country's trade in an industry's products into the part that is net trade (or industrialize trade) and the part that is intra-industry trade. Net trade is the value of the difference between exports and imports for the product. Net trade is positive (net exports) if the country's exports of the product are larger; it is negative (net imports) if imports of the product are larger. We use theories of comparative advantage to try to explain a country's net trade in different products.

The importance of intra-industry trade in a country's overall trade (in total or for a broad class of industries such as manufacturing) can be calculated as an index using information on the exports

(X) and imports (M) of each constituent industry:

$$\text{Intra-industry trade (IIT) share} = 1 - \left(\frac{\text{Sum of} |X - M|}{\text{Sum of } X + M}\right)$$

Intra-Industry Trade (IIT) as a percentage of trade in nonfood manufactured goods with other industrialized countries.

The absolute values of ($X - M$) are the magnitudes of net trade for each constituent industry. The IIT share is a number between 0 and 1 (or 100 percent). If all trade is between industries, then for each industry either exports (X) or imports (M) is 0. In this extreme case, all trade is inter-industry, and the IIT share is 0. At the other extreme, if all trade involves matched exports and imports ($X = M$) for each industry, the IIT share is 1 (or 100 percent). If some trade is net trade and some trade is intra-industry trade, the IIT share will have a value between 0 and 1, with its size indicating the importance of the part that is intra-industry trade.

Table 2.4 reports information on the importance of intra-industry trade in the trade of nonfood manufactured products among industrialized countries. The estimates are based on dividing this sector into almost 1000 different industries so that they presumably are not biased by a failure of disaggregation the sector's products into meaningful and narrowly defined industries. For five of the six countries shown, by 1987 IIT was more than half of the country's overall trade in these products with other industrialized countries. Japan is an exception (Some have blamed Japanese government policies for making Japan different in its dearth of intra-industry trade, but this has not been proved or disproved decisively). In addition, the importance of intra-industry trade has tended to rise over time. This is true of all the countries shown in Table 2.4 except Japan.

Table 2.4

Country	1970	1987
the United States	45.3	51.0
Canada	44.8	55.7
Japan	23.6	22.2
West Germany	58.9	65.5
France	65.5	72.3
the United Kingdom	57.8	63.8

We also know from other studies that IIT is more prevalent where trade barriers and transport costs are low, such as within free-trade areas like the European Union. In Table 2.4, the IIT shares are particularly high for the three European countries. Furthermore, IIT is more characteristic of the (high-income) industrialized countries, and IIT shares tend to be lower for the (low-income) developing countries.

In the analysis of intra-industry trade, a well-defined industry would consist of products viewed as close substitutes by consumers and produced using very similar factor intensities. The latter is needed to conform to the definition of an industry stressed in the factor-proportions theory. Although we cannot prove that each of these nearly 1 000 industries meets this definition, it seems unlikely that the industries are too aggregated. If the industry definition is too aggregated, estimates of the IIT share tend to be biased upward because some inter-industry trade (measured at the correct level of individual industries) can appear to be intra-industry trade when several industries are incorrectly added up into a single too-broad "industry".

Intra-industry trade seems to can for a different kind of analysis from the standard trade models. While there are several reasons that we might observe or measure intra-industry trade, the major explanation focuses on the role of product differentiation — consumers view the products of an industry as close but not perfect substitutes for each other. If IIT is based on two-way trade in varieties of the same basic product, then growth in IIT over time and higher IIT for higher-income countries can be understood partly from the demand side. Income growth shifts demand toward luxuries, and product variety is a luxury. The higher incomes of consumers, the more consumers can seek variety in the products that they buy. Thus, affluent people to vary their choices of wines, beers, automobiles, music, clothing, travel experiences and so on. Some varieties will be imported, while the varieties produced in the country, can be exported to affluent consumers in other countries.

Yet, demand effects cannot be the whole story. Why are products produced in only a limited number of varieties, rather than in the nearly infinite number of varieties that would be appropriate to match precisely the tastes of each individual consumer in the world? That is, why are differentiated products generally not produced to be fully customized to the specific demand of each individual? Something on the supply side limits the actual number of varieties offered on the market. Full customization (with each variety produced at a small individual scale) would be too costly. Scale economies in some aspect of production (or distribution) encourage larger production for each variety. Thus, scale economies limit the number of different varieties offered into the market.

2.5.4 Global Industries Dominated by a Few Large Firms

One major set of facts about actual trade that may require theory beyond comparative advantage is the substantial trade among industrialized countries, much of which involves exchanges of very similar products (intra-industry trade). The second major set of facts about actual trade that challenges the standard theory involves a departure from the assumption of highly competitive international markets.

Some important industries in the world are dominated by a few large firms. Productions of commercial aircraft are dominated by two firms: Boeing and Airbus. Production of microprocessors is dominated by Intel and Motorola. In such industries as steel, five firms account for half or more of world sales.

Using our standard model to analyse these industries may not be appropriate. The assumption of perfect competition may not be suitable; rather, these industries are global oligopolies. In the latter part of this chapter we will discuss some aspects of international competition in this type of industry. One key departure from the standard theory is the importance of scale economies in the production activities of the firm. Exploiting substantial scale economies is an explanation of why a few firms come to dominate some industries.

2.5.5 Economies of Scale

Our standard theory of international trade assumed constant returns to scale. With constant returns to scale, average cost (or unit cost) does not change when the quantity of output changes, assuming both long-run adjustments of all factor inputs and constant factor input prices (The latter assumption is important). In the H-O approach, each industry actually experiences rising unit costs as it expands. This occurs because industry expansion actually drives up the price of the factor used intensively by the industry.

The major alternative theories of international trade use the existence of economies of scale as a major departure. The discussion of the basis for intra-industry trade and the discussion of global oligopolies both suggested a key role for scale economies. Economies of scale, or increasing returns to scale, exist if increasing expenditures on all inputs (with imput prices constant) increases the output quantity by a larger percentage. Therefore the average cost of producing each unit of output declines, as output increases. For instance, economies of scale exist if doubling all input amounts (labor, capital, and so forth) more than doubles output. Economies of scale are often not easy to measure precisely, but they appear to be of some importance in many industries.

In discussing scale economies, several distinctions are important. First, scale economies can be internal to each firm, or they can be external to the individual firm. Scale economies are internal if the expansion of the size of the firm itself is the basis for the decline its average cost. Larger firms may be able to reduce average cost through greater use of specialization by their works with more specialized machines, or the spreading of up-front fixed costs, such as research and development or production setup costs, over more units of output.

Scale economies external to the individual firm relate to the size of the entire industry within a specific geographic area. The average cost of the typical firm declines as the output of the industry within this area is larger. External scale economies can arise if concentrating the industry geographically gives rise to better input markets. For instance, the concentration of an industry's firm in a specific geographic area may attract greater local supplies of specialized services for the industry or larger pools of specialized kinds of labor required by the industry. External economies can also result as new knowledge about product and production technology diffuse quickly among firms in the area, through direct contacts among the firms or as skilled labor transfers from firm to firm. External scale economies appear to explain the clustering of some industries – high – technology semiconductor, computer and related producers in Silicon Valley; banking and finance in New York City; filmmaking in Hollywood (and in Bombay, India, known as Hollywood); stylish clothing, shoes and accessories in Italy; and watches in Switzerland. We will discuss the relationship of external scale economies to international trade in the last section of this chapter.

A second major distinction is the size or extent of scale economies, especially for economies that are internal to the firm. How much does average cost decline as output expands? How large should a firm be to exploit all (or most) economies of scale? The answers of these questions matter a lot for the type of structure that arises on the seller side of the market.

If scale economies are modest or moderate, then there is room in the industry for a large number of firms. If, in addition, products are differentiated, then we have a mild form of imperfect competition called monopolistic competition, a type of market structure in which a large number of firms compete vigorously with each other in producing and selling varieties of the basic product. Because each firm's product is somewhat different, each firm has some control over the price that it charges with its product. This contrasts with the perfectly competitive market structure used in standard trade theory. With perfect competition, each of the industry's small firms takes the market price as given and believes that it has no direct control or influence on this market price.

If scale economies are substantial over a large range of output, then it is likely that a few firms will grow to be large in order to reap the scale economies. If a few large firms dominate the global industry, perhaps because of substantial scale economies, then we have an oligopoly. The large firms in an oligopoly know that they can control or influence prices. A key issue in an oligopoly is how actively these large firms compete with each other. If they do not compete too aggressively, then it is possible for the firms to earn economic (or pure) profit, profit greater than the normal return of invested capital. In the extreme, the industry could be a global monopoly, in which one firm dominates the world industry.

2.6 The Competitive Advantage of Nations

2.6.1 Overview

(1) Porter is a famous Harvard business professor. He conducted a comprehensive study of 10 nations to learn what leads to success. Recently his company was commissioned to study Canada in a report called "Canada at the Crossroads".

(2) Porter believes standard classical theories on comparative advantage are inadequate (or even wrong).

(3) According to Porter, a nation attains a competitive advantage if its firms are competitive. Firms become competitive through innovation. Innovation includes technical improvements to the product or to the production process.

2.6.2 The Diamond-Four Determinants of National Competitive Advantage

Four attributes of a nation comprise Porter's "Diamond" of national advantage. They are:

(1) factor conditions (i.e. the nation's position in factors of production, such as skilled labor and infrastructure);

(2) demand conditions (i.e. sophisticated customers in domestic market);

(3) related and supporting industries and firm strategy, structure and rivalry (i. e. conditions for organization of companies and the nature of domestic rivalry).

2.6.2.1 Factor Conditions

(1) Factor conditions refer to inputs used as factors of production – such as labor, land, natural resources, capital and infrastructure. This sounds similar to standard economic theory, but Porter argues that the "key" factors of production (or specialized factors) are *created*, not inherited. Specialized factors of production are skilled labor, capital and infrastructure.

(2) "Non-key" factors or general use factors, such as unskilled labor and raw materials, can be obtained by any company and, hence, do not generate sustained competitive advantage. However, specialized factors involve heavy, and sustained investment. They are more difficult to duplicate. This leads to a competitive advantage if other firms cannot easily duplicate these factors, they are valuable.

(3) Porter argues that a lack of resources often actually helps countries to become competitive (call it selected factor disadvantage). Abundance generates waste, and scarcity generates an innovative mindset. Such countries are forced to innovate to overcome their problem of scarce resources. How true is this?

①Switzerland is the first country to experience labor shortages. They abandoned labor-intensive watches and concentrated on innovative/high-end watches.

②Japan has high-price land and so its factory space is at a premium. This leads to just-in-time inventory techniques (Japanese firms can't have a lot of stocks to take up space, so to cope with the potential of not have goods around when they need it, they innovated traditional inventory techniques).

③Sweden has a short building season and high construction costs. These two things combined created a need for pre-fabricated houses.

2.6.2.2 Demand Conditions

(1) Porter argues that a sophisticated domestic market is an important element to produce competitiveness. Firms that face a sophisticated domestic market are likely to sell superior products because the market demands high quality and a close proximity to such consumers, and enables the firm to better understand the needs and desires of the customers (this same argument can be used to explain the first stage of the IPLC theory when a product is just initially being developed and after it has been perfected, it doesn't have to be so close to the discriminating consumers).

(2) If the nation's discriminating values spread to other countries, then the local firms will be competitive in the global market.

(3) One example is the French wine industry. The French has sophisticated wine consumers. These consumers force and help French wineries to produce high quality wines. Can you think of other examples, or counter-examples?

2.6.2.3 Related and Supporting Industries

(1) Porter also argues that a set of strong related and supporting industries is important to the competitiveness of firms. This includes suppliers and related industries. This usually occurs at a regional level as opposed to a national level. Examples include Silicon Valley in the U.S., Detroit (for the auto industry) and Italy (leather-shoes or other leather goods industry).

(2) The phenomenon of competitors (and upstream and/or downstream industries) are located in the same area is known as clustering or agglomeration. What are the advantages and disadvantages of locating within a cluster? Some advantages to locating close to your rivals may be:

①potential technology knowledge spillovers;

②an association of a region on the part of consumers with a product and high quality and therefore some market power;

③or an association of a region on the part of applicable labor force.

(3) Some disadvantages to locating close to your rivals are: potential poaching of your employees by rival companies, and obvious increase in competition possibly decreasing mark-ups.

2.6.2.4 Firm Strategy, Structure and Rivalry

1. Strategy

(1) Capital Markets.

Domestic capital markets affect the strategy of firms. Some countries' capital markets have a long-run outlook, while others have a short-run outlook. Industries varied in how long the long-run is. Countries with a short-run outlook (like the U.S.) will tend to be more competitive in industries where investment is short-term (like the computer industry). Countries with a long run outlook (like Switzerland) will tend to be more competitive in industries where investment is long term (like the pharmaceutical industry).

What about Canada?

(2) Individuals' Career Choices.

Individuals base their career decisions on opportunities and prestige. A country will be competitive in an industry whose key personnel hold positions that are considered prestigious.

Does this appear to hold in the U.S. and Canada? What are the most prestigious occupations? What about Asia? What about developing countries?

2. Structure

Porter argues that the best management styles vary among industries. Some countries may be oriented toward a particular style of management. Those countries will tend to be more competitive in industries for which that style of management is suited.

For example, Germany tends to have hierarchical management structures composed of managers with strong technical backgrounds and Italy has smaller, family-run firms.

3. Rivalry

Porter argues that intense competition spurs innovation. Competition is particularly fierce in Japan, where many companies compete vigorously in most industries.

International competition is not as intense and motivating. With international competition, there are enough differences between companies and their environments to provide handy excuses to managers who were outperformed by their competitors.

2.6.3 The Diamond as a System

The points on the diamond constitute a system and are self-reinforcing.

Domestic rivalry for final goods stimulates the emergence of an industry that provides specialized intermediate goods. Keen domestic competition leads to more sophisticated consumers who come to expect upgrading and innovation. The diamond promotes clustering.

Porter provides a somewhat detailed example to illustrate the system. The example is the ceramic tile industry in Italy.

Porter emphasizes the role of chance in the model. Random events can either benefit or harm a firm's competitive position. These can be anything like major technological breakthroughs or inventions, acts of war and destruction or dramatic shifts in exchange rates.

One might wonder how agglomeration becomes self-reinforcing…

(1) When there is a large industry presence in an area, it will increase the supply of specific factors (i.e. workers with industry-specific training) since they will tend to get higher returns and less risk of losing employment.

(2) At the same time, upstream firms (i.e. those who supply intermediate inputs) will invest in the area. They will also wish to save on transport costs, tariffs and inter-firm communication costs and inventories, etc.

(3) At the same time, downstream firms (i.e. those using our industry's product as an input) will also invest in the area. This causes additional savings of the type listed before.

(4) Finally, attracted by the good set of specific factors, upstream and downstream firms and producers in related industries (i.e. those who use similar inputs or whose goods are purchased by the same set of customers) will also invest. This will trigger subsequent rounds of investment.

2.6.4 Implications for Governments

The government plays an important role in Porter's Diamond model. Like everybody else, Porter argues that there are some things that governments do that they shouldn't, and other things that they do not do but should. He says, "Government's proper role is as a catalyst and challenger; it is to encourage– or even push – companies to raise their aspirations and move to higher levels of competitive performance …"

Governments can influence all four of Porter's determinants through a variety of actions such as:

(1) subsidies to firms, either directly (money) or indirectly (through infrastructure);

(2) tax codes applicable to corporation, business or property ownership;

(3) educational policies that affect the skill level of workers;

(4) they should focus on specialized factor creation; (How can they do this?)

(5) they should enforce tough standards. (This prescription may seem counterintuitive. What is his rationale? Maybe to establish high technical and product standards including environmental regulations.)

The problem, of course, is through these actions, it becomes clear which industries they are choosing to help innovate. What methods do they use? What happens if they pick the wrong industries?

2.6.5 Criticisms

Although Porter theory is renowned, it has a number of critics.

(1) Porter developed this paper based on case studies and these tend to only apply to developed economies.

(2) Porter argues that only outward-FDI is valuable in creating competitive advantage, and inbound-FDI does not increase domestic competition significantly because the domestic firms lack the capability to defend their own markets and facing a process of market-share erosion and decline, however, there seems to be little empirical evidence to support that claim.

(3) The Porter model does not adequately address the role of MNCs. There seems to be ample evidence that the diamond is influenced by factors outside the country.

Are Porter's arguments persuasive? What arguments do you agree with and what arguments do you find unconvincing?

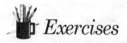
Exercises

1. Define the key terms listed below.

Distribution Theory;

Absolute Advantage;

Opportunity Cost;

Comparative Advantage;

The Leontief Paradox;

New Trade Theory.

2. "According to Ricardo's analysis, a country exports any goods whose production requires fewer labor hours per unit than the labor hours per unit needed to produce the goods in the foreign country. That is, the country exports any goods in which its labor productivity is higher than the labor productivity for the goods in the foreign country." Do you agree or disagree? Why?

Vinland has 30 million hours of labor in total per year. Moontied Republic has 20 million hours of labor per year.

①Which country has an absolute advantage in wine or in cheese?

②Which county has a comparative advantage in wine? In cheese?

③When trade is opened, which country exports wine? Which country exports cheese?

④Does each country gain from trade? Explain, referring to your graphs as is appropriate.

	Labor hours per bottle of wine	Labor hours per kilogram of cheese
Vinland	15	10
Moontied Republic	10	4

3. "According to the Heckscher-Ohlin theory, countries should engage in a lot of intra-industry trade." Do you agree or disagree? Why?

4. How many stages does the Product Cycle Theory contain? And explain the stages.

5. What are the Diamond-Four Determinants of National Competitive Advantages?

6. "For my country, imports are the good thing about international trade, whereas exports are more like the necessary evil." Do you agree or disagree? Why?

Chapter 3   Theory of Trade Protection

3.1   Trade Theory of Mercantilism

3.1.1   The Social Economic Background of the Emergence of Mercantilism

Mercantilism is an economic ideology and policy system representing benefits of the newly thrived commercial capitalism in the years from 15th century till 17th century during which the major European powers had finished their primitive accumulation of capital.

At the end of 15th century, the feudalist economy dominated the social economic life in Europe with its most important characteristic of self-sufficiency. Most of the population of Europe, that was about 60 million, was living in rural areas. The urban people accounted less than 20 percent of the total population. When we consider the economic structure at that time, we could find that agriculture was taking the dominant position in the economy. Only in some commercial cities, such as London, Paris, Rome, Milan, Lisbon, Amsterdam, Naples and Antwerp sporadically scattered some handicraft workshops manufacturing small amount of furniture, cooking utensils, clothing, pottery and metal handicraft. A specific production organization made merchants a dominant class in the society. They contracted different production stages of those daily necessities among the relevant workshops or craftsmen. By doing so, merchants supplied workshops or craftsmen with raw materials they each manufactured a particular part of the goods and then handed out what they manufactured to the merchants. At last, the merchants assigned particular producers to assemble the parts into finished goods to market. In this production organization all the workshops or craftsmen strongly depended upon the merchants to have their production and living.

Of course there was a few of long distance trade before the maritime discovery, for instance, trade across and around the Mediterranean and even land trade between European countries and India and China via the middle and west Asia. On the whole, however, commercial activities in Europe at that time were somewhat regional economic activity that mainly concentrated in cities and the areas around cities.

Rapacious greed for the tremendous benefits of trade from the East encouraged Europeans to increase trade with the Far Eastern Areas. Simultaneously, however, the Turk and the Arabian seriously menaced the safety of the trade routes and free circulation of the traded goods. The Turks occupied Constantinople (now Istanbul) the most important commercial center. Trade along the east coast of the Mediterranean was hindered. The Arabians exclusively controlled the routes from Europe to India via Egypt and the Red Sea. Consequently, European merchants were forced to find out a new route to the East. In addition, the eager desire to acquire more gold and silver from abroad and thus to explore a new source of revenue for the sovereignty was other impetuses to have the overseas explorations. Of course development of shipbuilding technology, marine sailing technology, advances of geography and astronomy, and some other scientific and technological progresses achieved by the Europeans then had actually offered the necessary material and technical conditions for the maritime discoveries.

In 1487, a brave sea captain named Bartholomew Diaz led an expedition that reached the southern tip of Africa. He found that the great continent narrows down to a point, or cape. This he named the Cape of Good Hope. He also discovered a vast new body of water, the Indian Ocean. His expedition had made the longest sea voyage in history, a distance of 3500 miles. At this point he was forced to return. He hoped someday to round this cape and continue on to Asia, but he never did.

The Portuguese explorer Vasco da Gama was to make the first all-water voyage to India in 1498. It was a great day for Portugal when da Gama returned with a cargo of species and jewels worth sixty times the cost of the voyage. Upon his return to Lisbon, he learned of another sailor who had gained fame. This man had reached land, which was thought to be part of Asia, by sailing west across the Atlantic. His name was Christopher Columbus(Figure 3.1).

Figure 3.1

An Italian sailor, Christopher Columbus, sponsored by Spanish Queen Isabella started his historical voyage early on the morning of August 3, 1492. His little fleet of three tiny ships and a crew of eighty-eight sailors left the port of Palos in southern Spain for the imaginary India since people believed that keep on sailing west they would finally reach India because the Earth is a round ball. After more than two months on October 11th, Columbus landed in the new world. We know today that Columbus had reached a tiny island in the Bahamas Islands, that he had reached America. But Columbus thought that he had reached an island off the coast of Asia. He named the island San Salvador, it was probably the island now known as Watling Island. The little fleet went on to explore other islands. Columbus discovered Cuba, Hispaniola (on which Haiti and Dominica are now situated), and other islands of the West Indies. Columbus was so sure that he had reached India that he called the friendly natives he met on these islands Indians. Columbus made three more voyages to the "Indies" that he had discovered. On the second trip, he had 17 ships and 1200 men. This time he discovered Puerto Rico and the Leeward Island. On his third voyage he reached the mainland of South America. His fourth voyage in 1502 carried him to the shores of the Central America. Each of his voyages made him more and more puzzled. According to his map, the lands he saw were part of India or China. Yet he found no gold, no palaces, no jewels and no silks. Instead he saw endless woods and half-naked savages.

Another great Portuguese navigator who should be mentioned is Ferdinand De Magellan. Because of his courage and skill in sailing around the world, Europeans finally found out the true size and shape of the earth on which they lived. Magellan believed that if he kept sailing southwest he could find a way around the new lands to Asia. Portugal at that time was beginning to enjoy the profits from her trade route around Africa to the East so she had no interest in Magellan's idea. Spanish king gave him five ships with full crews. On September 20th, 1519, Magellan's fleet set sail. Three years later, in 1522, one ship, the flagship Victoria, returned to Spain. Eighteen pale and exhausted men stood on the decks, this was all that remained of the almost three hundred who started out. Among them was not Magellan. He was killed in a battle with the natives when the fleet explored one of Philippine islands. The voyage that Magellan had planned but did not himself finish had many important results:

①It proved that the world is round;

②It proved that it is possible to reach the East by sailing west;

③It proved that America is not part of Asia, but a vast separated land;

④It opened men's eyes to the true size of the earth.

The discovery of the new continent and opening of the new sea route greatly encouraged development of overseas commerce. The successive thriving European powers, such as Spain, Portugal, Netherlands, Britain and France started their bloody colonialist exploitation and domination in Asia, Africa and America. Those colonial powers even engaged in the notorious trade of slaves in order to grab the wealth from abroad. A tremendous amount of wealth in terms of gold, silver, diamond, jewels and a lot of luxury goods, such as perfume, indigo, silk, coffee, pepper, clove and so on, in-flowed into Europe in a steady stream. International trade in the early years had completely broken geographical limitation. Sailing boats along the coast of the Mediterranean and traveling merchants, like Marco Polo, herding camels across the desert had been replaced by a number of large-sized overseas argosies shuttling in the Atlantic and the Pacific. Commercial business and commodity exchanges greatly developed. The economic foundation of feudalism had been fundamentally shaken and it eventually went to collapses.

Karl Marx and Frederick Engels once highly appraised the historical significance of the maritime discoveries. They wrote in their co-written brilliant work, Manifesto of the Communist Party:

"The discovery of America, the rounding of the Cape, opened up fresh ground for the rising bourgeoisie. East-Indian and Chinese markets, the colonization of America, trade with the colonies, the increase in the means of exchange and in commodities generally, gave to commerce, to navigation, to industry, an impulse never before known, and thereby, to the revolutionary element in the tottering feudal society, a rapid development."

"The feudal system of industry, under which industrial production was monopolized by closed guilds, now no longer sufficed for the growing wants of the new markets. The manufacturing system took its place. The guild-masters were pushed on the side by the manufacturing middle class; division of labor between the different corporate guilds vanished in the face of division of labor in each single workshop. "

The most direct result of the prosperous development of commerce was the rising of social status of the so-called middle class, merchants. Besides the handicraft workshops and craftsmen who were strongly dependent upon the merchants in their production, almost all the classes in the society depended upon the merchants to some degrees. In a society which exchange relationship generally existed and currency was widely used rent in kind had been replaced by rent in currency since the feudal lords needed more money to buy luxury goods, they were most imported from abroad, directly from markets. That implied peasants must depend upon the merchants to exchange what he harvested into cash in order to hand in rent.

The merchants also played a more important role in life of members of the royal families even for the rule of the sovereignty. The kingdom needed money to hire a great number of officials to manage the state. A large conventional army was required to maintain orders of the society, to defend borders of the nation and to contend for hegemony with the other powers. The soldier's pay and provisions became a very heavy financial burden for the kingdom. When the revenue could not afford the expenditures the Kings or Queens were forced to borrow a lot of money from the merchants. The dependency of the feudal kingdoms on the merchants could be also expressed by the fact that almost all kingdoms in those years employed the leading merchants to be financial advisers of the Kings or officials directly managed affaires of trade and finance for the kingdoms.

As a newly thriving social class with a powerful economic strength the merchants themselves reasonably required the corresponding eminent social political status in the social life of the sovereignty in order to safeguard economic interests of themselves. Based on their personal experiences of carrying out commercial activities the political representatives of the commercial capital taking positions as lawyers, navigators, advisers of the kingdoms, financial officials of the Kings and industrialists or leading merchants, they raised some doctrines about principles of making profits in commercial activities, especially in the overseas trade, and a lot of policies ideas of how to hold the wealth gained from the overseas trade into borders of the sovereignty. Such ideology was what the successors named Mercantilism.

3.1.2 Theory of Mercantilism

3.1.2.1 The Obvious Characteristic of Mercantilism

Compared with the other ideologies the so-called mercantilism has its obvious characteristic. The representatives of mercantilism were not scholars or theorists mainly engaging in academic research. They themselves were enthusiastic activists of commercial business, merchants trading with the long-distant areas, officials of kingdoms managing trade and financial affaires of the sovereignty, famous industrialists of manufacturing, navigators sailing across the Mediterranean even Atlantic and

Pacific, shipbuilders to make ships for the maritime voyages. In one word, the most mercantilists were more like doers rather than scholars. Consequently, their ideas of trade would not be so systematic and theoretic but scattered in their letters, speeches, and of course books. The multifarious opinions and arguments, good or bad, raised by the mercantilists intermingling with each other actually reflected their personal experiences of doing commercial activities on the one hand. On the other hand, mercantilism should be considered as the expression of the innermost thoughts and feelings of commercial capitalists and sometimes the requirements of the rulers who was acquiring great amount of wealth from the overseas trade.

3.1.2.2 The Core Idea of Mercantilism

Mercantilists in the early years differed from the industrial capitalists later in that they did not know how to make money, in somewhat rigidly speaking to acquire surplus value, from commodity production process. But we know that surplus value is the real source of industrial profits. Therefore, mercantilists representing the benefits of commercial capital only inquire the secret of increment of commercial capital. In other word, they were trying to reveal how to make more money in commercial activities. The object of their research was only movement of commercial capital, in other word, circulation currency in commercial activities. That was the formula, "$G - W - G'$". G' here contained the initially input capital in terms of an amount of currency (G_0) and the additional money that was made by a successful merchant. Commercial profits (ΔG). That means $G' = G_0 + \Delta G$.

It was so easy for merchants to grasp the knacks of making money and put those knacks into practice. Their personal experiences told them the following three cardinal principles that must be rigidly followed:

①buying low and selling high;
②buying less and selling more;
③buying nothing and selling everything.

A merchant would be very happy when his business was successful if money acquiring from selling exceeded money paid for buying. By doing so, he could accumulate wealth in his hand and be a rich man. He was so satisfactory because he could use the accumulated money to make more money. From his point of view, money was everything. Money means wealth. As a wealthy man he could have an eminent social status and an enviable luxury life. Gold and silver, mainly gold, was used as currency in most countries at that time. Merchants could naturally conclude that gold implied wealth from their personal experiences of doing commercial business. Therefore, in that society, gold had become the only representative and the avatar of wealth. Thus it would not be difficult to understand why people at that time confused wealth with gold and were striving to acquire gold as much as possible. For gold they would do everything even paying for their lives.

Based on the views on wealth which was commonly accepted by people of all social classes at that time the precursor of the maritime discovery Christopher Columbus once wrote in a letter from Jamaica in 1503: "Gold is a wonderful thing! Whoever possesses it is master of everything he desires. With gold, one can even get souls into paradise."

Some other mercantilists also expressed without any veil their ideas of gold worship.

(1) D. Martin Luther:

Germans are making all the world rich and beggaring themselves by sending their gold and silver to foreign countries. Frankfurt, with its fairs, was the hole through which Germany was losing her treasure.

(2) Serra:

How important it is, both for people and princes, that a kingdom should abundant in gold and silver.

(3) Johann Joachim Becher:

It is always better to sell goods to others than to buy goods from others, for the former brings a certain advantage and latter inevitable damage.

3.1.2.3 Trade Surplus and Currency Surplus

Also based on the views on wealth and from the basic starting point that wealth was only expressed in terms of gold or currency, mercantilism advocated that both for individuals and for sovereignty the purposes of carrying out all sorts of economic activities was nothing but to acquire gold or some other precious metal as much as possible. There is no exception at all! To acquire more gold from commercial business implied to make surplus money. The result of commercial activities of specific merchants showed that such surplus money just arose from buying and selling. But put the overall commercial business of the whole society into consideration it might be true to conclude that the pure selling and buying would create no more money at all, not even a single coin. Therefore, the mercantilists believed just by superficially considering circulation process rather than to have an inquiry into production, in a particular period of time, the total amount of money put into process of commodity circulation seemed to be as the same as the amount of money derived from the circulation by all merchants.

3.2 Government Intervention

Now that we have reviewed the various instruments of trade policy that governments can use, it is time to look at the case for government intervention in international trade. Arguments for government intervention take two paths that are political and economic. Political arguments for intervention are concerned with protecting the interests of certain groups (normally consumers). Economic arguments for intervention are typically concerned with boosting the overall wealth of a nation (to the benefit of all, both producers and consumers).

3.2.1 Political Arguments for Intervention

Political arguments for government intervention cover a range of issues including protecting jobs, protecting industries deemed important for national security, retaliating to unfair foreign competition, protecting consumers from "dangerous" products, furthering the goals of foreign policy and protecting the human rights of individuals in exporting countries.

3.2.1.1 Protecting Jobs and Industries

Perhaps the most common political argument for government intervention is that it is necessary for protecting jobs and industries from foreign competition. Voluntary Export Restraints(VER) that offered some protection to the U.S. mobile, machine tool and steel industries during the 1980s were motivated by such considerations. Similarly, Japan's quotas on imports of rich were aimed at protecting jobs in that country's agricultural sector. The same motive underlay establishment of the Common Agricultural Policy (CAP) by the European Union. The CAP was designed to protect the jobs of Europe's politically powerful farmers by restricting imports and guaranteeing prices. However, the higher prices that resulted from the CAP have cost Europe's consumers dearly. This is true of most attempts to protect jobs and industries through government intervention. As we saw earlier, the VER in the automobile industry raised the price of Japanese imports, at a cost of $1 billion per year to U.S. consumers.

In addition to hurting consumers, trade controls may sometimes hurt the very producers they are intended to protect. The VER agreement in the U.S. machine tool industry turned out to be self-defeating. By limiting Japanese and Chinese Taiwan province machine tool imports, the VER raised the prices of machine tools purchased by U.S. manufacturers to levels above those prevailing in the world market. In turn, this raised the capital costs of the U.S. manufacturing industry in general, thereby decreased its international competitiveness.

3.2.1.2 National Security

Sometimes country argues that it is necessary to protect certain industries because they are important for national security. Defense-related industries often get the kind of attention (e.g. aerospace, advanced electronics, semiconductors, etc.). Although not as common as it used to be, this argument is still made. Those in favor of protecting the U.S. semiconductor industry from foreign competition, for example, argue that semiconductors are now such important components of defense products that it would be dangerous to rely primarily on foreign producers for them. In 1986, this argument helped persuade the federal government to support Sematech, a consortium of 14 U.S. semiconductor companies that accounted for 90 percent of the U.S. industry's revenues. Sematech's mission was to conduct joint research into manufacturing techniques that can be parceled out to members. The government saw the venture as so critical that Sematech was specially protected from antitrust laws. Initially, the U.S. government provided Sematech with $100 million per year in subsidies. By the mid-1990s, however, the U.S. semiconductor industry had regained its leading market position, largely through the personal computer boom and demand for microprocessor chips made by Intel. In 1994, the consortium's board voted to seek an end of federal funding, and since 1996 the consortium has been funded entirely by private money.

3.2.1.3 Protecting Consumers

Many governments have long had regulations in place to protect consumers from "unsafe" products. In 1998, the U.S. government decided to permanently ban imports of 58 types of military-style assault weapons (The United States already prohibited the sale of such weapons in the United States by U.S.-based firms). The ban was motivated by a desire of increasing public safety. It followed on the heels of a rash of random and deadly shootings by deranged individuals using such weapons, including a school-teacher dead.

The conflict over the importation of hormone-treated beef into the European Union may prove to be a taste of things to come. In addition to the use of hormones to promote animal growth and meat production, the science of biotechnology has made it possible to genetically alter many crops so that they are resistant to common herbicides, produce proteins that are natural insecticides, have dramatically improved yields, or can withstand inclement weather conditions. A new breed of genetically modified tomatoes has an antifreeze gene inserted into its genome and can thus grown in colder climates than hitherto possible. Another example is a genetically engineered cotton seed produced by Monsanto. The seed has been engineered to express a protein that provides protection against him three common insect pests: the cotton bollworm, tobacco budworm and pink bollworm. Use of this seed reduces or eliminates the need for traditional pesticide applications for these pests. As enticing as such innovations sound, they have met with intense resistance from consumer groups, particularly in Europe. The fear is that the widespread use of genetically altered seed corn could have unanticipated and harmful effects on human health and may result in "genetic pollution". (An example of genetic pollution would be when the widespread use of crops that produce "natural pesticides" stimulates the evolution of "super-bugs" that is resistant to those pesticides). Such concerns have led Austria and Luxembourg to outlaw the importation, sale or use of genetically altered organisms. Sentiment against genetically altered organisms also runs strongly in several other European countries, most notably Germany and Switzerland. It seems likely, therefore, that the world Trade Organization with drawn into the conflict between those that want to expand the global market for genetically altered organisms, such as Monsanto, and those that want to be limited, such as Austria and Luxembourg.

3.2.1.4 Furthering Foreign Policy Objectives

Governments sometimes use trade policies to support their foreign policy objectives. A government may grant preferential trade terms to a country it wants to build strong relations with. Trade policy has also been used several times to pressure or punish "rogue states" that do not abide by international law or norms. Iraq labored under extensive trade sanctions since the UN coalition defeated the country in the 1991 Gulf War until the 2003 invasion of Iraq by United States-led forces. The theory is that such pressure might persuade the (rogue state) to mend its ways or it might hasten a change of government. In the case of Iraq, the sanctions were seen as a way of forcing that country to comply with several UN resolutions.

Other countries can undermine any unilateral trade sanctions. The U. S. sanctions against Cuba, for example, have not stopped other western countries from trading with Cuba. The U. S. sanctions have done little more than help create a vacuum into which other trading nations, such as Canada and Germany, can have stepped. In an attempt to put a halt to this and further tighting the screws on Cuba, the U. S. Congress passed the *Helms-Burton Act* in 1996. This act allows Americans to sue foreign firms that use property in Cuba confiscated from them after the 1959 revolution. A similar act, the *D'Amato Act*, aimed at Libya and Iran was also passed that year.

The passage of Helms-Burton elicited protests from America's trading partners, including the European Union, Canada and Mexico, all of which claim the law violates their sovereignty and is illegal under World Trade Organization rules. For example, Canadian companies that have been doing business in Cuba for years see no reason they should suddenly be sued in U. S. courts when Canada does not restrict trade with Cuba. They are not violating Canadian law and they are not U. S. companies, so why should they be subject to U. S. law? Despite such protects, the law is still on the books of the United States, although the U. S. government has been less than enthusiasm about enforcing it- probably because it is unenforceable.

3.2.2 Economy Arguments for Intervention

With the development of the new trade theory and strategic trade policy, the economic arguments for government's intervention have undergone a renaissance in recent years. Until the early 1980s, most economists saw little benefit in government intervention and strongly advocated a free trade policy. This position has changed at the margins with the development of strategic trade policy, although as we will see in the next section, these are still strong economic arguments for sticking to a free trade stance.

3.2.2.1 The Infant Industry Argument

The infant industry argument is by far the oldest economic argument for government intervention. Alexander Hamilton first proposed it in 1792. According to this argument, many developing countries have a potential comparative advantage in manufacturing, but new manufacturing industries cannot initially compete with well-established industries in developed countries. To allow to manufacture to get a toehold, the argument is that governments should temporarily support new industries (with tariffs, import quotas and subsidies) until they have grown strong enough to meet international competition.

The argument has had substantial appeal for the governments of developing nations during the past 50 years, and the GATT has recognized the infant industry argument as a legitimate reason for protectionism. Nevertheless, many economists remain very critical of this argument. They have two main points. First, protection of manufacturing from foreign competition does no good unless the protection helps make the industry efficient. In case after case, however, protection seems to have done little more than foster the development of inefficient industries that have little hope of ever competing in the world market. Second, the infant industry argument relies on an assumption that firms are unable to make efficient long-term investments by borrowing money from the domestic or international capital market. Consequently, governments have been required to subsidize long-term investments. Given the development of global capital markets over the past 20 years, this assumption no longer looks as valid as it once did. Today, if a developing country really has a potential comparative advantage in a manufacturing industry, firms in that country should be able to borrow money from the capital markets to finance the required investments. Given financial support, firms based on countries with a potential comparative advantage have an incentive to get through the necessary initial losses in order to make long-run gains without requiring government protection. Many South Korean firms did this in industries such as textiles, semiconductors, machine tools, steel and shipping. Thus, given efficient global capital markets, the only industries that would require government protection would be those that are not worthwhile.

3.2.2.2 Strategic Trade Policy

Some new trade theorists have proposed the strategic trade policy argument. The new trade theory argues that industries where the existence of substantial scale economies implies that the world market will profitably support only a few firms, countries may predominate in the export of certain products simply because they had firms that were able to capture first-mover advantages. The dominance of Boeing in the commercial aircraft industry is attributed to such factors.

The strategic trade policy argument has two components. First, it is argued that by appropriate actions, a government can help raise national income if it can somehow ensure that the firm or firms to gain first-mover advantages in such an industry are domestic rather than foreign enterprises. Thus, according to the strategic trade policy argument, a government should use subsidies to support promising firms that are active in newly emerging industries. Advocates of this argument point out that the substantial R&D grants that the U.S. government gave Boeing in the 1950s and 1960s probably helped tilt the field of competition in the newly emerging market for passenger jets in Boeing's favor (Boeing's 707 jet airliner was derived from a military plane). Similar arguments are now made with regard to Japan's dominance in the production of liquid crystal display screens (used in laptop computers). Although these screens were invented in the United States, Japanese government, in cooperation with major electronics companies, targeted this industry for research support in the late 1970s and early 80s. The result was that Japanese firms, not U.S. firms, subsequently captured the first-mover advantages in this market.

The second component of the strategic trade policy argument is that it might pay government to intervene in an industry if it helps domestic firms overcome the barriers to entry created by foreign firms that have already reaped first-mover advantages. This argument underlies government support of Airbus Industries, Boeing's major competitor. Formed in 1966 as a consortium of four companies from Great Britain, France, Germany and Spain, Airbus had less than 5 percent of the world commercial aircraft market when it began production in the mid-1970s. By 2002, it had increased its share to over 50 percent, threatening Boeing's long-term dominance of the market. How did the Airbus achieve this? According to the U.S. government, the answer is a MYM13.5 billion subsidy from the governments of Great Britain, France, Germany and Spain. Without this subsidy, Airbus would have never been able to break into the world market.

If these arguments are correct, they support a rationale for government intervention in international trade. Governments should target technologies that may be important in the future and use subsidies to support development work aimed at commercializing those technologies. Furthermore, governments should provide export subsidies until the domestic firms have established first-mover advantages in the world market. Government support may also be justified if it can help domestic firms overcome the first-mover advantages enjoyed by foreign competitors and emerge as viable competitors in the world market (as in the Airbus and semiconductor examples). In this case, a combination of home-market protection and export-promoting subsidies may be called for.

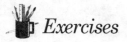
Exercises

1. What's the core idea of mercantilism?

2. What is the infant industry argument for putting up barriers to imports? What are its merits and weaknesses?

3. Tell something about the advantages and disadvantages of government intervention.

Chapter 4　Foreign Trade Policy

4.1　Trade Policy

4.1.1　Basic Concepts and Definitions

The "foreign trade policy" of a country refers to policies and practices that affect and regulate import and export operations. Foreign trade policy includes many laws, decrees, regulations and procedures that are often adopted for different purposes. Such policies will affect foreign exchange, imports, exports, foreign investment and international relations. A foreign trade policy should include trade promotion policy and lead to the design and implementation of successful trade promotion and development programmes.

The "trade promotion policy" of a country is comprised of programmes and measures that promote and develop trade with other countries. It includes all regulations and practices that will increase exports. Trade promotion policies are part of the overall foreign trade policy, and cannot be considered alone. The country's foreign trade policy must make it possible to achieve trade promotion policy objectives.

Other policies will have a significant affect on foreign trade performance, even though they were not intended to directly regulate the country's foreign trade. These policies are part of the framework in which foreign trade policy must be designed and executed. These other policies generally cover the national development plan, monetary policy, fiscal policy and practices, production and price controls and investment policies:

(1) National development plans include planning practices and the scope of state intervention, mechanisms for making the plan cohesive, coordinating the components of the plan, ranking plan priorities and setting overall allocation of resources.

(2) Monetary policy covers policies and management of credit and money and addresses issues of inflation and regulation of foreign borrowing as related to monetary management and control.

(3) Fiscal policy covers all aspects of taxing and spending by the government, the overall fiscal regime, temporary tax holidays and tax exemptions that help achieve other policy objectives.

(4) Production and price controls cover all policies, which regulate or generate production for local use and export, as well as the conditions for carrying out production in all sectors of the economy.

(5) Private investment regimes cover policies, programmes and regulations that affect investment opportunities and decisions, such as incentive schemes, promoting and encouraging selected sectors or industries and lending practices of development banks.

(6) Foreign exchange policy covers policies and regulations designed to manage the exchange rate in line with the national economic policy, for example, making exports more competitive or controlling inflation.

The foreign trade policy in combination with the policies listed above, forming the nation's overall economic strategy. Foreign trade policy will focus on trade promotion, trade development infrastructure and international trade relations.

Trade promotion consists of programmes and measures to promote and develop trade with other countries. The focus is on issues related to exports and imports. Trade development infrastructure concentrates on developing and upgrading the nation's trading ability to develop trade. Areas covered include trade facilitation and administration, trade finance support and development of trading enterprises.

International trade relations involve developing strong trade diplomacy with other countries in order to safeguard a country's commercial interests and ensure market access for its exports. It also involves participating in international and regional trade forums to promote and ensure a fair and more open international trading environment.

4.1.2 Export Promotion Strategies

Export promotion strategies are part of trade promotion and should focus on enterprise, industry and national levels.

4.1.2.1 Enterprise Level

Some parts of the business community in developing countries have been unable to significantly increase export volumes on their own for the following reasons:

(1) A limited number of commodities are available for export, so export sectors depend on international developments affecting the world market. An example is the falling price of cotton and base metals that are a major part of export earnings for Central Asia.

(2) Industrial production of goods is limited by the lack of downstream activities, which does not allow enterprises to produce differentiated products for export or provide some form of export diversification.

(3) There is dependence on one or two key export markets and supply sources, and this does not give enterprises an opportunity to develop products according to the standards of more developed markets. This also results in lack of knowledge about marketing abroad.

(4) Enterprises lack export readiness, which might be due to unwillingness to venture overseas because the domestic market offers comfort and security. However, the transition to a market economy may force enterprises to look beyond the domestic market in order to earn much-needed foreign

exchange and generate employment. International marketing is a much more complicated process than marketing and selling in a domestic economy.

Transitional economies need a leading agency to drive the effort towards becoming exporters.

Industry level: Two kinds of export dimensions to consider are increasing the export of existing products and developing new exportable products.

Increasing the exports of existing products means looking at what industries currently produce for export to the world market. For many transitional and emerging economies, exports are mainly commodity and primary products. Therefore an initial export strategy should focus on enhancing and consolidating the volume of export into existing markets as well as diversifying to other exports markets.

The second dimension involves making an assessment of what new products could be developed for export markets. These new products often originate from spin-offs or downstream activities from existing core industries. For example, the oil industry supports petrochemical industries and oil equipment manufacturing. Therefore, governments could help develop an industry to become ready overall for exporting through industrial cluster planning.

Industry councils or associations can play a major role by advising and working with the government or its designated trade body to develop export strategies. These strategies should be based on comprehensive study of the export potential for select products. This will involve:

(1) Clear identification of what is produced, planned production in the near future and the most suitable markets for such products;

(2) Concurrent study of what is being purchased in foreign markets in order to suggest what could be produced in the country to satisfy the needs and opportunities of foreign markets;

(3) Clear indication of constraints or problems for exports in terms of production or market conditions, which should lead to recommendations about how to solve problems or counteract any constraints.

4.1.2.2 National Level

The government sets the overall economic direction and trade development strategies. Establishing the export dimension of this strategy in terms of appropriate economic instruments and export promotion measures is critical to national export performance. Therefore, the design of relevant trade policies is the key to the successful national export promotion programme.

4.1.3 China Trade Policy

1910-1949: Foreign powers operate in treaty ports located throughout much of coastal and Eastern China. These ports were open to foreign commerce and foreign-administered by the Chinese Maritime Customs Service. The United States, England, France, Germany and Japan were China's main trading partners. More treaty ports opened in the early 20th century, facilitating the growth and spread of trade.

1950-1976: China has a largely closed economy with little trade.

1977: Within the scope of broad economic reforms under Deng Xiaoping, an open-door trade and investment policy was introduced. Special Economic Zones along the coast were set up for foreign investment.

1978-1985: Foreign trade operations were decentralized. By 1985 trade represents 20 percent of Chinese gross national product. Textiles were the nation's leading export, with petroleum and food also strong. Leading imports were machinery, transportation equipment, manufactured goods and chemicals. Japan was China's dominant trading partner, followed by Chinese Hong Kong and the U.S.

1986-1989: Trade becomes increasingly decentralized as China strive to integrate itself into the world trade system.

1990-1998: Foreign investment grows tenfold between 1990 and 1995. Despite unwieldy contractual and legal framework, Chinese billion-plus customers lure many investors, especially from ethnic Chinese in areas near Chinese Hong Kong and Chinese Taiwan.

1999: Chinese global trade totals $353 billion; its trade surplus is $36 billion. Chinese primary trading partners were Japan, the United States, South Korea, Germany, Singapore, Russia and the Netherlands. In November, the United States and China arrived at a bilateral market-access agreement that paved the way for Chinese accession to the World Trade Organization.

2000: China reaches a bilateral WTO agreement with the European Union and other trade partners and begins work on a multilateral WTO accession package. To increase exports, China encouraged the formation of factories that assemble imported components into consumer goods for export. The U.S. approves permanent trade relations with China, and President Clinton signed the *China Trade Relations* Act of 2000.

Asia-Pacific Economic Cooperation

Figure 4.1

2001-2003: In 2001 China serves as the Asia Pacific Economic Group's (APEC, Figure 4.1) chair; Shanghai hosted the annual APEC leaders meeting. After the 2001 World Trade Organization Summit in Qatar, China became a full member of the WTO. Many tariffs and regulations were streamlined or ended, but foreign investors still face procedural obstacles. Trading partners complained that the Chinese currency is undervalued.

4.1.4 Developed Countries' Trade Policies

Developing countries have repeatedly expressed their concern about the U.S. Trade Policy's departures from multilateralism. It has also been a refrain of the EU and some other developed countries. Not that the EU itself is free of blame in this regard. The EU's bilateralism and regionalism is not new. The EU's recent initiatives in the same direction have also attracted similar attention in the WTO. Despite these voiced concerns, there appears to be a general scramble, as it were, to initiate or get on board the preferential trade arrangements. These trends have received attention in academia, and the political, legal and economic implications have been analyzed within theoretical frameworks. The phenomenon of departures from the multilateral principle is, however, not recent, not with standing the fact that multilateralism is reckoned as the very foundation of both tense in 1947, and the more recent agreement establishing the WTO, which was brought into force in 1995.

Those who criticize the departures from the multilateral principle. As well as those who breach it (and the two identities are not always distinct) ritualistically swear their adherence to it. There seems to be an intuitive belief, particularly among the relatively weaker members of the trading system, that the multilateral process by itself would ensure not only the legality but also the fairness or equity of decision making. Once such belief triumphs over experience, it is only a short further step that leads to the proposition that a multilateral system is always desirable. The attention thus gets concentrated on the form rather than the substance, on the "geometry" (the "many-sided"-ness) rather than the "equity" (the norms and the rules, the way they are worked and their relative impact on the unequal sets of participants) of the system. The more basic question of the "power relations" defining the system tends to get obfuscated. Such an environment is conducive to manipulation of multilateralism by the powerful few. The form retains the multilateral character, but the power-equation determines the substance. Some perceptive observers describe the phenomenon as the emergence of "disguised unilateralism" or "new regionalism."

What is the essence of multilateralism? How was multilateralism practiced in GATT/WTO? What accounts for the hiatus between the law and the practice of trade policies? More important, what constitutes the necessary and sufficient conditions for success of multilateralism? This paper proposes to examine these issues conceptually as well as historically so as to explicate what appears to be implicit in the poser raised by the title.

4.2 Pushing Exports

Controversy over export behavior and export policy rivals the perennial fights over import barriers. On the export side, however, the fight takes on a somewhat different form. Here the fight usually centers on the artificial *promotion* of trade rather than on trade barriers. This chapter explores how both businesses and governments may push for more exports than their country would sell under ordinary competition. The underlying policy questions are: Can a country export too much for its own goods or for the goods of the world? Is that happening today? If so, what should an importing country do about another country's apparently excessive exports?

These questions do not arise in a vacuum. Governments, pressured by business and labor lobbies, have long fought over what producers in importing countries consider artificial and excessive exports from other countries. The heat of debate on this issue intensified during the past two decades. U. S. and European producers charged that Japan, Korea, Brazil, China and other rapidly growing industrial powers were engaging in "unfair trade" because exports from these countries were priced too low or subsidized by their governments. These countries were repeatedly accused of violating both the rules of ordinary competition and the rules of the World Trade Organization (WTO).

To address the debate over unfair trade, we turn first to dumping, the most important way in which private firms may export more than competitive supply and demand would lead us to expect. Then we explore how governments push exports with outright or subtle subsidies.

4.2.1 Dumping

Dumping is selling exports at a price that is too low – less than normal value (or "fair market value," as it is often called in the United States). There are two meanings of *normal value*:

(1) The long-standing definition of *normal value* is the price charged to comparable domestic buyers in the home market (or to comparable buyers in other markets). Under this traditional definition, dumping is international price discrimination favoring buyers of exports.

(2) The second definition of *normal value* arose in the 1970s. It is cost-based – the average cost of producing the product, including overhead costs and profit. Under this second standard, dumping is selling exports at a price that is less than the full average cost of the product.

Why would an exporting firm engage in dumping? Why would it sell exports at a price lower than the price it charges with its product in its home market, or lower than its average cost? There are several reasons. To judge whether dumping is good or bad, it is important to understand the full range of reasons why dumping occurs.

Predatory dumping occurs when a firm temporarily charges a low price in the foreign export market, with the purpose of driving its foreign competitors out of business. Once the rivals are gone, the firm will use its monopoly power to raise prices and earn high profits.

Cyclical dumping occurs during periods of recession. During the part of the cycle when demand is low, a firm tends to lower its price to limit the decline in quantity sold. For instance, in a competitive market initially in long-run equilibrium, price equals full average cost (long-run average cost) for the representative firm. If an industry recession or an economy wide recession then causes demand to decline, market price will fall below this full average cost in the short run. A firm continues to produce and sell as long as price exceeds average variable cost. If any of these sales are exports, the firm is dumping.

Seasonal dumping is intended to sell off excess inventories of a product. For instance, toward the end of a fashion season, U.S. clothing manufacturers may decide to sell off any remaining stock of swimsuits at prices that are below full average cost. That is, they have a sale. With production costs sunk, any price above the marginal cost of making the sale is sensible. If some of these low priced sales are to Canada, the U.S. firm is dumping. Perishable agricultural products are also good candidates for seasonal dumping. A big harvest tends to lower the market price and to provide a larger quantity available for export. Similarly, dumping can be a technique for promoting new products in new markets. This is the equivalent of an introductory sale that an exporting firm could use to establish sales of its product in a new foreign market.

Persistent dumping occurs because a firm with market power uses **price discrimination** between markets to increase its total profit. A firm maximizes profits by charging a lower price to foreign buyers if it has less monopoly power (more competition) in the foreign market than it has in its home market, and if buyers in the home country cannot avoid the high home prices by buying the goods abroad and importing it cheaply.

When these conditions hold, the firm can make home-country buyers pay a higher price and thus earn a higher total profit. This is not predatory; it is not intended to drive any other firms out of business. And it can persist for a long time – as long as these market differences continue.

What makes persistent dumping profitable is that the firm faces a less elastic (steeper) demand curve in its home market than in the more competitive foreign market. That is, home-country buyers would not change the quantity they buy very much in response to price, whereas foreign buyers would quickly abandon this firm's product if the firm raised its price much. Sensing this, the firm maximizes profits by equating marginal cost and marginal revenue in each market. In the U.S. market, the profit-maximizing price is \$25. With the \$25 price U.S. consumers buy 150 telephones a year, at which level marginal revenue just equals the marginal cost of \$18. In Japan's home market, where consumers see fewer substitutes for the major Japanese brands, the profit-maximizing price is \$60. With the \$60 price Japanese consumers buy 100 phones a year, and marginal cost equals marginal revenue at this quantity.

Price discrimination is more profitable for the firm than charging the same price in both markets. Charging the same price would yield lower marginal revenues in Japan than in the United States. As long as transport costs and import barriers in Japan make it uneconomical for Japanese consumers to import low priced telephones back from the United States, the firm continues to make greater profits by charging a higher price in Japanese market. Often tariffs or non-tariff barriers to import (back into the exporting the country) are what keeps the two markets separate. These barriers also protect the dumper against foreign competition in the higher-priced home market (Japan, in this example).

4.2.2 Export Subsidies

Governments promote or subsidize exports more often than they restrict or tax exports. Some government efforts to promote exports are not controversial according to international precepts (although there are questions about how effective they are). Government agencies like the Trade Information Center of the U.S. Department of Commerce provide foreign-market research, information on export procedures and foreign government regulations, and help with contacting buyers. Government agencies sponsor export promotion events like trade fairs and organized trips. Governments establish export processing zones that permit imports of materials and components with easier customs procedures and low or non-tariffs.

Governments also provide various forms of financial assistance that benefit their exporters.

These export subsidies are controversial because they violate international norms about fair trade. Our analysis of export subsidies will conclude that export subsidies are usually bad from a world point of view. However, international division of gains and losses turns out to be very different from what you would expect just by listening to who favors export subsidies and who complains about them. Export subsidies are bad for the countries that use them, but are good for the countries that complain about them.

Governments subsidize exports in many ways, some of them deliberately subtle to escape detection. They use taxpayers' money to give low-interest loans to exporters or their foreign customers. An example is the U.S. Export-Import Bank, or Eximbank founded in the 1930s, it has compromised its name by giving easy credit to U.S. exporters and their foreign customers but not to U.S. importers or their foreign suppliers. Governments also charge low prices on inputs (such as raw materials or domestic transport services) that go into production that will be exported. Income tax rules are also twisted to give tax relief based on the value of goods or services each firm exports.

Export subsidies are small on average, but they loom large in certain products and for certain companies. For instance, most Eximbank loans have been channeled toward a few large U.S. firms and their customers. Boeing, in particular, has been helped to extra foreign aircraft orders by cheap Eximbank credit. More broadly, the biggest export subsidies apply to agricultural products.

What are the effects on the country whose government offers the export subsidy?

Let's examine the effects for a *competitive industry*, using our standard supply-and-demand framework. We will reach the following conclusions:

(1) An export subsidy expands export and production of the subsidized product. In fact, the export subsidy can switch the product from being imported to being exported.

(2) An export subsidy lowers the price paid by foreign buyers, relative to the price that local consumers pay for the product. In addition, for the export subsidy to work as intended (the government subsidies only exports, not domestic purchases), something must prevent local buyers from importing the product at the lower foreign price.

(3) The export subsidy reduces the net national well-being of the exporting country. Let's examine three cases to see the validity of these conclusions.

4.2.3 WTO Rules on Subsidies

As a result of the agreements reached in the Tokyo Round and Uruguay Round of trade negotiations, the WTO now has a clear set of rules for subsidies that may benefit exports. The WTO rules divide subsidies into three types:

(1) Subsidies linked directly to exporting are *prohibited*, except export subsidies used by the lowest-income developing countries.

Example: A firm receives a tax break based on the amount that it exports.

(2) Subsidies that are not linked directly to exporting but still have an impact on exports are *actionable*.

Example: Low-priced electricity is provided to assist production by local firms in an industry, and some of this production is exported.

(3) Some subsidies are *non-actionable*. These include subsidies for research and development, assistance to disadvantaged regions, and assistance in meeting environmental regulations.

If an importing country's government believes that a foreign country is using a prohibited subsidy or an actionable subsidy that is harming its industry, the importing country can follow one of two procedures:

(1) File a complaint with the WTO and use its dispute settlement procedure (used occasionally).

(2) Use a national procedure similar to that used for dumping (used more often). If the importing country can show the existence of a prohibited or actionable subsidy and harm to its industry, it is permitted to impose a countervailing duty, a tariff used to offset the price or cost advantage created by the export subsidy.

4.2.4 Trade Policy and Economic Growth

Do countries with lower policy-induced barriers to international trade grow faster, once other relevant country characteristics are controlled for? There exists a large empirical literature providing an affirmative answer to this question. We argue that methodological problems with the empirical strategies employed in this literature leave the results open to diverse interpretations. In many cases, the indicators of "openness" used by researchers are poor measures of trade barriers or are highly correlated with other sources of bad economic performance. In other cases, the methods used to ascertain the link between trade policy and growth have serious shortcomings.

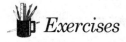

Exercises

1. Define the key terms listed below:
foreign trade policy;
trade promotion policy;
dumping;
export subsidies.
2. What are the promotional measures of trade promotion policy?
3. Tell something about the export promotion strategies.
4. Can you predict the trend of China trade policy after studying the policies from 1910 to 2003?
5. What's the difference between China trade policy and developed countries?
6. What are the WTO rules on subsidies?

Chapter 5 Instruments of Trade Policy

5.1 Tariff Barriers

5.1.1 Tariff

Tariff is a tax levied by the foreign government on goods imported into that country (or import duty). The tariff increases the price at which the goods are sold in the importing country and therefore makes them less competitive with locally produced goods.

5.1.1.1 Types of Tariffs

A tariff may be one of the following four kinds:

①Ad valorem;
②Specific;
③Alternative;
④Compound.

1. Ad Valorem Duty

The kind which most commonly used, is one that is calculated as a percentage of the value of the imported goods – for example, 10, 25 or 35 percent.

This may be based, depending on the country, either on destination (c.i.f.), or on the value of the goods at the port in the country of origin (f.o.b.).

2. Specific Duty

It is a tax of so much local currency per unit of the goods imported (based on weight, number, length, volume or other unit of measurement). Specific duties are often levied on foodstuffs and raw materials.

3. Alternative Duty

It is where both an Ad valorem duty and A Specific duty are prescribed for a product, with the requirement that the more onerous one shall be Ad valorem duty value plus 10 cents per kilo.

4. Compound Duty

It is imposed on manufactured goods contain raw materials that are themselves subject to import duty. The "specific" part of the compound duty (called compensatory duty) is levied as protection for the local raw material industry.

5.1.1.2 Dutiable Weights

Depending on the country, the dutiable weights used to calculate specific import duties may be the gross weight, the legal weight or the net weight.

The dutiable weight is the actual weight upon which duty must be paid.

The gross weight is the weight of the goods and all interior, exterior containers and packing material.

The legal weight (used mainly by Latin American countries) is the weight of the goods and of the immediate interior containers.

The net weight is the weight of the goods without the packing materials. However, in a few countries, it is defined as including the weight of the immediate container.

Very often, there is a fixed percentage allowance (called the tare) used by the customs authorities for determining gross weight from net weight, and vice-versa. Most countries using specific duties employ different types of dutiable weights for difference commodities.

It is essential for an exporter to know what dutiable weight is being used for its product as it may be able to vary its packing accordingly.

In some countries (such as Switzerland, Venezuela and Colombia) most specific duties are levied on gross weight, whatever the nature of the goods.

5.1.1.3 Dutiable Value

For the purpose of calculating Ad Valorem import duties, customs authorities do not always use the stated, or invoice value of the goods.

Some countries use the higher of the export price or the current domestic value of the exporting country or that of another country or the current domestic value in the importing country.

5.1.1.4 Tariff Lists

Most countries have two major tariff lists. Dutiable list for goods subject to customs duties, and a free list for goods permitted to enter free of duty. Depending on the country, goods in the dutiable list may be classified in any one of three different ways.

(1) in alphabetical order of name;

(2) by the height of the duty;

(3) by the attributes of the goods-for example, the raw materials from which they are made, the use to which the product will be put or degree of processing that has been involved.

5.1.1.5 Levels of Import Duty

For each dutiable product, there may be one, two or three different levels of import duty.

(1) Single-Column Tariff Schedule

With this system, there is only one level of import duty for each product wherever the country of origin.

(2) Double-Column Tariff Schedule

Below are two levels of import duty for each export.

1) Maximum-Minimum Form

This is where both levels of tariff are set autonomously by the foreign country, without modification by international agreement.

The higher or "maximum" level is the one that applies to imports from countries that have signed reciprocal tariff reduction agreements with the country employing this tariff system.

2) General and Conventional Form

Here, the higher level of duty is established autonomously.

But the lower level of duty comprises all the reduced duties granted to other countries as a result of tariff negotiations.

The higher level is the normal rate of duty. The lower level, the rate charged on imports from countries that have signed reciprocal agreements with importing country.

This lower level of tariff may also apply to products from third countries, which may be entitled by treaty to most-favored-nation treatment – that is, not having their products subject to higher import duties than those of any other country.

This system is used by, for example, the United States and Japan. With the U.S. tariff system, column-two rates apply to products from most socialist countries, and column-one rates (negotiated rates) to all other countries.

5.1.1.6 Triple-Column Tariff Schedule

Countries which have close political ties with other countries or which have colonial possessions may have a lower level of tariffs for goods from their affiliated countries.

This preferential system is used by, for example, the members of the British Commonwealth.

5.1.1.7 Customs Nomenclature

Since 1950, over 120 countries have agreed to use the Brussels Tariff Nomenclature (BTN) established in that year, which classifies products according to their physical substance.

Another customs nomenclature, the Standard International Trade Classification (SITC), was developed by the United Nations, but had been adopted for only a few various products.

An item-by-item correspondence has been worked out between the two tariff classifications.

Because many thousands of different products entering into international trade, more and more countries are switching to the already-widely-used Brussels Tariff Nomenclature.

A Customs Cooperation's Council, located in Brussels, with membership of over 120 countries, is promoting this trend towards greater customs uniformity by preparing drafts for new customs conventions and by offering technical assistance in customs administration.

Below are some of the many benefits arising from greater uniformity of customs nomenclature:

(1) It would assure exporters and importers of a uniform classification of their goods, whatever countries.

(2) It facilitates the negotiation and administration of tariff agreements as the participating coun-

tries would classify their products in the same way.

(3) It removes many of the trade obstructions and distortions that result from the administration of dissimilar nomenclatures.

(4) It is essential for any country planning to enter into regional trade pacts.

In many countries, there are Bonded Warehouses in which dutiable imports may be temporarily stored. Import duty needs to be paid only as and when the goods are removed for domestic sale.

If the goods are re-exported, no import duty is collected. Bonded Warehouses offer an exporter the opportunity to defer payment of import duty and so ease its cash flow requirements.

5.1.2 Case Study

5.1.2.1 A Case for Lower Tariffs

After a three-year study of eight tariff-protected U.S. industries, economist Percy W. Bidwell concluded last week that gradual but deep tariff cuts would not hurt U.S. industry as a whole and would damage only the marginal producers in import-sensitive industries. "Most of these industries," he wrote, "have been in long-term declines and are characterized by weak financial situations, severe seasonal or cyclical unemployment and wages below the national levels." Bringing down the tariff walls could channel U.S. capital and labor into more productive endeavor.

Bidwell's book *What the Tariff Means to American Industries* was sponsored by the nonpartisan Council on Foreign Relations. To get the facts on both sides of the tariff story, Bidwell assembled a standing team of 28 top bankers, educators, editors, businessmen, government officials and had them scrimmage in round-table discussions with leaders of the eight industries: iron and steel, synthetic chemicals, electrical equipment, watches, bicycles, chinaware, glassware and woolens. Represented were both ardent protectionists and advocates of free trade.

Foreign Scapegoats Tariffs have been halved in the past generation, Bidwell acknowledged, and an increasing majority of U.S. businessmen favor still more slicing. However, Bidwell observed, "when business is bad, American firms are tempted to make a scapegoat of foreign competition, although their difficulties may have arisen principally from domestic causes."

Tariffs only encouraging sliding, and inefficient manufacturers to continue in uneconomic industries that require federal protection, said the study. In effect, they are subsidized by consumers. In the mass-production industries, where U.S. wages are far above world scales, Bidwell found that the U.S. worker usually so outproduces low-paid foreign workers that most tariffs and other import restrictions can be safely eliminated. Even in handwork industries, where the cost of labor makes up a large share of the product cost, he concluded that the tariff does little more than bail out the marginal producer.

In the U.S. China-tableware industry, Bidwell noted, labor is 60% of the wholesale price of the final product. Long protected by a high tariff, this industry never got even a 5% toehold in the domestic market until World War II blocked imports. Now it demands continuing protection to keep output at wartime levels.

Defense Dogma that what about the industry that insists that it is vital to national defense? The watch manufacturers won tariff increases up to 50% in 1954 on the argument that the U. S. has to maintain at least 4000 watchmakers to turn out military timing devices in case of war. Yet Bidwell found that domestic production of sensitive jeweled watches continued to slump even after the tariff rise, and "it is doubtful whether the present level of import duties will guarantee that watches will be produced at a level which defense authorities would consider adequate." In any case, he said, a high tariff is not the best way to protect the industry. In its place the U. S. should choose the lesser evil of paying government subsidies to makers, just as some airlines and ship owners are subsidized as a defense necessity. Thus watch prices would drop to the world-market level, and the cost of supporting a defense industry would be placed where it belongs – with the taxpayers, not watch buyers.

5.1.2.2 The Indisputable Case for Keeping Steel Tariffs

President Bush's upcoming decision on maintaining steel tariffs is usually described as a classic case of good economics clashing with good politics. Eliminate or gut the tariffs, and the president pleases Wall St. , the media, steel-using industries, and economists nearly everywhere. But keeping the tariffs can help keep Bush in the White House by catering to voters in key 2004 battleground states like Pennsylvania and Ohio.

In fact, preserving the tariffs is a no-brainer for Bush economically as well as politically. For the recent debate on this issue makes clear that the tariff opponents don't have a leg to stand on.

Foreign steel producers are among the loudest critics of the steel tariffs, but the case for their removal centers on their alleged costs to the American economy. In particular, steel-consuming U. S. industries – which have a major short-term interest in getting steel as cheaply as possible – have complained that by restricting imports, the tariffs have jacked up steel prices and harmed their competitiveness vis-a-vis foreign firms.

Economists and editorialists, meanwhile, have charged that the harm done to steel users and American consumers has greatly outweighed the tariffs' benefits to the nation's steel industry and its relatively small workforce – not only lost sales and profits, but lost jobs for the steel users' employees.

These arguments sound powerful in principle, but the facts overwhelmingly refute them. According to an authoritative September report from the independent U. S. International Trade Commission (Figure 5.1), steel prices in America did increase after the tariffs' onset in March, 2002, and remained relatively high for several months. By last May, however, the ITC reported that "prices in the U. S. market may be higher, lower, or about the same as those in foreign markets depending on the markets being compared."

Figure 5.1

What's the reason for the price drop? It is simple economics. Thanks to the tariffs, the restructuring domestic steel industry started to re-attract investment. This trend in turn enabled shuttered plants to re-open and start making steel again. As more U.S. supply came on to the market, prices predictably fell.

Even when steel prices were raising, however, steel-consuming industries and their workers generally enjoyed better times than before the tariffs were imposed. The ITC found, for example, that "Overall sales and profits increased, while capital investment fell, for most steel-consuming industries in ... (the year following the imposition of the safeguard measures), compared with ... (the year preceding the safeguard measures)." Employment levels in these steel-using industries "generally fell or remained flat" after the tariffs as opposed to before, but "productivity and wages increased over the three-year period."

The tariffs so far seem to have depressed returns on capital and labor for the U.S. economy as a whole, but by utterly trivial levels. Steel-consuming industries' earnings, for example, fell by a grand total of 0.01 percent.

According to the International Trade Commission, "A majority of steel-consuming firms indicated that neither continuation nor termination of the safeguard measures would change employment, international competitiveness, or capital investment. Purchaser responses were split over whether profitability would increase or decrease if the safeguards continued..." Translation: Whatever ails U.S. steel-consuming industries – and plenty are ailing – it ain't the steel tariffs. These sectors should look instead to the NAFTA-style trade expansion of the last decade and its cumulative effects.

Nor is the ITC alone in these conclusions. Pricing data from the consultants CRU International show that, as of June, 2003, prices of hot-rolled, cold-rolled, and galvanized steel were all lower in the United States than in other major steel-producing regions. Indeed, according to CRU, prices of flat-rolled steel in the United States today are actually lower today relative to Asian and European prices than they were before the tariffs were imposed.

In addition to these short-term issues, however, the steel-using industries and other steel tariff opponents need to think about long-term issues. Steel is hardly the only product in the global economy today whose production is heavily subsidized and then dumped into the U.S. market. Rescinding or lowering the steel tariffs under consuming-industry pressure would broadcast loud and clear to foreign governments and other dumpers that it's open season on U.S. domestic manufacturing. All our trade partners would need to do is to continue dividing and conquering American industry.

But the domestic disputes opened by the steel tariffs should not be ignored by Washington. In particular, when dealing with goods like steel, which are industrial inputs, not final products, and U.S. responses to predatory foreign trade practices should indeed reflect the needs of consuming industries as well. But if tariffs do increase consuming industries' prices, the way to help these sectors is to grant them tariffs as well, especially if they can show they are using mainly domestically made parts, components and materials.

Of course, this kind of comprehensive approach to preserving and strengthening American industry will require a wholly new mindset in the White House and the rest of the U.S. government. Washington will have to begin thinking strategically about trade and manufacturing, not reactively. The jury is out on whether President Bush is capable of such growth. Maintaining the steel tariffs would be a great place to start.

5.2 Non-Tariff Barriers

5.2.1 Definition

The various types of non-tariff barriers (or NTB) that impede the flow of international trade consist of: import quotas, exchange controls, customs delays, government purchasing policies, subsidies, customs calculation procedures, boycotts, technical barriers, bribes and voluntary restraints.

Additional steps are continuously being taken through the General Agreement on Tariffs and Trade or GATT(Figure 5.2) or now referred to as WTO World Trade Organization since 1995, to reduce trade barriers to imports from non-members.

5.2.2 Characteristics of Non-Tariff Barriers

Compared with tariffs and quotas, NTBs have several advantages. With the development of the world economy and technology, NTBs tend to be more varied and unpredictable with the same result of tariffs and quotas.

NTBs are more flexible and pertinent: While tariff barrier settings must be agreed to by legislation, usually over a drawn-out period of time, NTBs can be carried out by an administrative process very quickly, and it is much more convenient in urgent cases where the importing country needs to take a quick action on one importing item from one certain country. For example, Tara Materials Inc. (Tara) U.S. company, applied for an anti-dumping appeal to the United States Department of Commerce (DOC) and International Trade Commission (ITC) regarding painting fabric imported from China on 31st March 2005 with a request to levy an anti-dumping tariff on certain painting fabric made in China. ITC accepted the appeal from Tara on 21st April and judged the painting fabric from China injured the existing same industry in the U.S., according to the progress; DOC launched an investigation and levied a 244% import tax (currently, it is only 6%). The entire process took only three weeks.

Figure 5.2

More efficient on limiting importing: Tariff barriers indirectly restrict importing by weakening the rival's competition with higher tariff collection to increase the cost and price of importing product. At the same time, if an export country has tax refund for stimulation exports, such as China, or exporting country uses dumping sales strategies to decrease the cost and price, then high taxation will not have the desired effect. NTBs, however, can have an immediate effect on this situation.

More concealable: Tariffs, once set are not easily changed and are usually not difficult to understand. For NTBs however, prior notification is not required and given their arbitrary nature, it can be very difficult to understand what is being restricted. NTBs vary from year to year and from country to country and can often be quite contradictory making a concentrated response difficult and frustrating.

5.2.3 Classification of Non-Tariff Barriers

5.2.3.1 Environmental Issues

One allowance to regulate imports is the concern that such product will have a detrimental affect on the environment of the importing country. As there is no international standard on what qualifies as harmful, countries are free to make up their own standards such as certain AZO-free fabrics, nickel-free buttons or zippers and so on. Exporters have been responsible for abiding by these requirements and as such have had to assume the cost. The cost of such regulations has proved more than many suppliers can handle. In 2001, one garment company in Jiangsu province was punished with USD $160000 by the Germany importing company, for a failure to abide by ecological standards. Another company in Zhejiang Province was informed that the buyer in Belgium would return 300000 jackets because the jacket zippers contained a banned chemical content nickel that would have endangered the public health and environment.

5.2.3.2 Social Issues

Major concerns being focused on child labors, forced labors, health and safety, disciplinary practices, working hours and remuneration, which are currently being addressed in such voluntary standards/certification schemes as SA8000, Worldwide Responsible Apparel Production (WRAP) certification scheme, and Compliance and Supply Chain Management (CSM) system. Attached 2 pages regarding the detail of SA8000 (appendix 1). According to the research done in the province of Guangdong, not one of the thousands of manufactures in Shanshui city would be qualified to produce such products in accordance with SA8000. This will result in substantial difficulties for manufacturers who wish to export to U.S. and EU markets if they should require such a certification for export.

5.2.3.3 Anti-Dumping Actions

Dumping happens when a company sells a product in an aboard country at a price lower than the one in its own home market or under cost. To prove dumping a country needs to establish three things:

①Dumping test: that imported goods are being sold at "below the normal price";

②Injury test: that a domestic firm is being injured by these exports;

③Causality test: that dumping is causing injury.

During the 1990's the number of anti-dumping regulations implemented against China increased by 10%-20% each year, totaling 467 times by the end of April 2002. This is a 3000% increase from the number of cases in the early 1990's. China today is the subject of more anti-dumping legislation than any other country in the world.

5.2.3.4 Safeguard Measures

While both safeguard and anti-dumping measures are aimed at import surges, safeguard measures act in a blanket non-discriminatory manner, whereas anti-dumping measure is against a specific company in the exporting country. When a safeguard measure is applied, the country applying the measure shall endeavor to maintain a substantially equivalent level of concession through mutual agreement with the countries affected. As opposed to anti-dumping actions, no compensation is required.

Upon its accession, China agreed two provisions that would allow the U.S. and all other WTO members to invoke safeguard measures against its textile and clothing products. These are special textile safeguards and product-specific safeguards. The special textile safeguard will last until the end of 2008, and stipulates that the importing country can invoke the restraints if imports from China cause market disruption. China will have no right to retaliate against these restraints.

The product-specific safeguard will be in effect for 12 years until December 2013. Similarly, the importing country can invoke restrictions if imports from China cause market disruption, but it will require a public hearing before the invocation of such safeguard. Both safeguards cannot be applied to the same product at the same time. In addition to these two safeguards, China will continue to be subject to simpler rules for invocation of anti-dumping restraints until 2016. These restrictions have been described as conditions of the "post quota era", as garment companies still must deal with quotas for certain items, such as woven trousers, knitted wear, woven skirts.

Despite the foreseeable opportunities that the post-quota era would bring, these "China-specific" safeguards will certainly put limits on the predicted wider expansion of the textile industry. Even before full non-quota status had been reached, the U.S. and EU textile manufacturers had already petitioned their governments to impose these safeguards on China.

One case in point is the U.S. textile industry's attempt to seek protection against Chinese imports. On 24 July 2003, the U.S. textile industry coalition, including cotton, man-made fiber, yarn spinners and fabric manufacturers, submitted to the Committee for the Implementation of Textile Agreements (CITA) the first petitions under the special textile safeguard contained in Chinese WTO accession agreement. This safeguard may be used to impose quotas on textiles and clothing products covered by the ATC, including those that have already been integrated into the GATT. The coalition wants the U.S. government to impose quotas on Chinese knit fabric, dressing gowns, brassieres and gloves. A similar petition regarding socks is rumored to be the next target for safeguard request.

Preferential Rules of Origin: Preferential rules of origin under various free trade agreements and customs unions could be used by countries to discriminate between imports from different countries. They allow a country to deny the benefits of an agreement to countries that have not signed up to a treaty or agreement [e. g. NAFTA, CAFTA(Figure 5.3), EU, etc.]. This discrimination can operate in a positive or negative manner; positive for countries that are members of an agreement or treaty, and negative if they are not. China is not a party to any of these trading blocks and there is little momentum in East Asia to build one.

Figure 5.3   CAFTA: China-ASEAN Free Trade Area

5.2.4   Types of Non-Tariff Barriers

5.2.4.1   Anti-Dumping Duties

Dumping is the sale of a product abroad at a price lower than that usually charged in the home country. This may be profitable for a manufacturing firm because it enables it:

(1) to engage in longer production per unit of output;

(2) to sell goods that would otherwise remain unsold;

(3) to sell goods at a price that covers the variable or "incremental" cost of production and marketing of each unit and also makes some contribution – however small, to the cost of plant overhead.

Exchange dumping means a country manipulates its exchange rates to lower the selling price of its products when calculated in terms of the foreign currency.

Since these practices are naturally considered to be unfair competition by manufacturers in the country in which the goods are being dumped, the government of the foreign country will be asked to impose "anti-dumping" duties.

Anti-dumping are special duties additional to the normal ones, designed to match the difference between the price in the home country and the price abroad.

5.2.4.2   Countervailing Duties

These special additional import duties that a government may levy on goods exported from their country of origin, have been encouraged by the payment of an export bounty or subsidy.

The purpose of the duty is to offset, or "countervail" the county or subsidy so that the goods cannot be sold at an artificially low price in the foreign country and thereby provide unfair competition for local manufacturers.

In addition to customs duty, an exporter may sometimes have to pay one or more extra charges in order to get its goods into the foreign country. These include:

1) Taxes

(1) An import surtaxt – calculated as a percentage of import duty.

(2) A package tax – that is, a small tax on each package in a shipment.

(3) An import surcharge – this is calculated as a percentage of the value of the shipment, it is usually levied on selected items, notable luxury goods, to discourage their import.

The exporter may also be required to pay various internal taxes (such as sales taxes, excise taxes, purchase taxes, and value added taxes) before its goods reach the final customer.

2) Prior Deposit

Some countries, particularly in Latin America, require importers to deposit local funds of up to 100 per cent of the value of shipment before they are permitted to import any goods. These deposits are then held, interest-free, by the Central Bank of that country, for various lengths of time before being refunded.

3) Consular Fees

Another, and often substantial, additional charge on imports is the consular fee required to legalize shipping documents.

This fee may be collected by the consular authorities in the exporting country or by the customs officials at the port of entry.

5.2.4.3 Import Quotas

An exporter may find that the foreign country mostly restrict imports not only by means of tariffs but also by qualitative measures.

These usually take the form of import quotas for each particular product. Once the quota for the period has been filled, no more import licenses are issued.

There are three main types of import quota in use today:

(1) unilateral quotas;

(2) negotiated bilateral or multilateral quotas;

(3) tariffs quotas.

1) Unilateral Quotas

These are quotas set by a country without pervious consultation or negotiation with others. Such a quota may be global or allocated. If it is global, the total volume of goods that may be imported is set regardless of the countries of origin or the importers and exporters involved. If it is allocated, the permitted volume of imports is allocated among countries of origin and private traders in accordance with some previous patterns.

2) Negotiated Quotas

In this case, the importing country, after negotiations with the government of each exporting country or with groups of its exporters, allots shares of the quota to each country. Often, with a bilateral negotiated quota, the exporting country is given the responsibility for issuing licenses to its exporter. Sometimes a negotiated bilateral quota goes under the guise of a voluntary export quota – for example, the "voluntary" quotas that Japan places on its exports of man-made textiles to the United States. With a multilateral quota, the restriction is placed on the total amount of imports only, with no restriction as to source.

3) Tariff Quotas

With this type of quota, a country allows a certain amount of a product to enter at a given rate of import duty or even duty free. Any excess amount is subjected to a much higher rate of duty.

5.2.4.4   Voluntary Restraints

Sometimes, when one of its domestic industries is being badly hurt by foreign imports, a government will undertake to persuade the exporting countries to voluntarily restrict their exports.

The government usually obtains co-operation for such a program of voluntary restraint by making explicit or implicit their intention to impose quotas or increase tariffs.

Voluntary restrain, as far as the exporting country is concerned, is the less disagreeable alternative. Canada and the EEC have used this policy to reduce imports of Japanese goods.

France, for example, once required that all imports of Japanese video players be cleared through a tiny Customs office in the inland town of Poitiers.

5.2.4.5   Exchange Controls

Some countries restrict imports by limiting the amount of "exchange" or foreign currency, available to pay for them. Often, imports are classified into essential and non-essential or luxury goods.

Foreign currency is made available at one rate of exchange for essential imports while a more limited amount of foreign currency is made available at a much higher rate of exchange for the luxury items such as foreign cars.

This restricts the imports of luxury goods and is taxed more heavily than essential goods through the sale of foreign currency at a "free market" rate of exchange rather than at the official one.

Other countries achieve the same effect by levying exchange taxes at various rates according to the priority attached to the product to be imported.

With exchange control, anyone wishes to obtain foreign exchange must secure permission from the government. Such a system permits the government to restrict the demand for scare foreign exchange and to ration it out among different needs.

This rationing of foreign exchange also applies to importers: they must obtain a foreign exchange permit before they can import any goods and must pay a higher rate of exchange for imports of **"luxury"** or **"non-essential"** goods.

Exchange control, like import quotas, is therefore another very effective way of restricting imports as well as other types of foreign exchange spending.

5.2.4.6 Customs Delays

Exporters sometimes find that their goods are held up at foreign ports because of inexplicable delays by Customs Officials. These are sometimes the result of a deliberate government policy to restrict imports.

The customs authorities may argue that the documentation or marking of the goods is not exactly as required.

Exporter documentation should try to give as little excuse as possible for such delays. However, should the customs authorities decide to inspect thoroughly each item imported, rather than just a sample, there will always be horrendous delays.

Canada once used this technique in the port of Vancouver to pressure Japan into agreeing to place "voluntary restraints" on auto exports to Canada.

5.2.4.7 Government Purchasing Policies

In some countries, government departments and agencies are required, officially or unofficially to buy locally made goods rather than imports. Japan, for example, has been accused of this practice.

In the United States, "Buy American" legislation requires that all or most goods bought by government departments and agencies be produced in that country.

5.2.4.8 Customs Valuation Procedures

Not all countries use the same method to assess the import duty on the value of goods imported. By using one method rather than another, an importing country can set a higher value on the goods and therefore levy a larger Ad Valorem duty.

One guilty country of such practice was Canada. Its previous customs code allowed it to impose duty levels not directly related to the price paid for the goods but to what is termed "fair market value". This was branded by other countries, particularly the United Stated, as a non-tariff barrier and an unfair protective device.

It was defended by Canada as a necessary measure to prevent predatory export pricing by foreign firms and the setting of artificially low transfer prices on goods sold to Canadian subsidiaries by foreign multinational parent corporations.

Canada agreed to adopt in 1984 the standardized GATT customs valuation procedure. This has involved a switch from "fair market value" to "international transaction price" as the basis for assessment of import duties, at the Tokyo round of GATT trade negotiations that ended in 1979.

5.2.4.9 Technical Barriers

Measures referring to product characteristics such as quality, safety or dimensions including the applicable administrative provisions, terminology symbols, testing and test methods, packaging, marking and labelling requirements as they apply to a product. The implementation of these measures by sensitive product categories can result in the application of one of the measures listed under codes ending in 71 to 79.

1) Technical Regulations

Regulations that provide technical requirements, either directly or by referring to or incorporating the content of a standard, technical specification or code of practice, in order to protect human life or health or to protect animal life or health (sanitary regulation); to protect plant health (phytosanitary regulation); to protect the environment and to protect wildlife; to ensure human safety; to ensure national security; to prevent deceptive practices.

The regulation may be supplemented by technical guidance that outlines some means of compliance with the requirements of the regulation, including administrative provisions for customs clearance, such as prior registration of the importer or obligation to present a certificate issued by relevant governmental services in the country of origin of the goods. In certain cases, a prior recognition of the exporter or certificate issuing service by the importing country is also required.

2) Product Characteristics Requirements

Technical specifications prescribe technical requirements to be fulfilled by a product.

3) Marking Requirements

Measures defining the information for transport and customs, that the packaging of goods should carry (country of origin, weight, special symbols for dangerous substances, etc.)

4) Labelling Requirements

Measures regulating the kind and size of printing on packages and labels and defining the information that may or should be provided to the consumer.

5) Packaging Requirements

Measures regulating the mode in which goods must be or cannot be packed, in conformity with the importing country handling equipment or for other reasons, and defining the packaging materials to be used.

6) Testing, Inspection and Quarantine Requirements

Compulsory testing of product samples by a designated laboratory in the importing country, inspection of goods by health authorities prior to release from customs or a quarantine requirement in respect of live animals and plants.

7) Pre-Shipment Inspection

Compulsory quality, quantity and price control of goods prior to shipment from the exporting country, affected by an inspecting agency mandated by the authorities of the importing country. Price control is intended to avoid under invoicing and over invoicing, so that customs duties are not evaded or foreign exchange is not being drained.

8) Special Customs Formalities

Formalities which are not clearly related to the administration of any measure applied by the given importing country such as the obligation to submit more detailed product information than normally required on the basis of a customs declaration, the requirement to use specific points of entry, etc.

5.2.4.10 Green Trade Barriers

Green Trade Barrier, simply Green Barrier or Environment Barrier, comes into being at the late

1980s and begins to develop in every country all over the world in the 90s. It concludes those measures either directly or indirectly taken to restrict or even ban on import trade by the importing country during the international trade activities in order to protect its environment, natural resources and human beings' health. It is a new type of non-tariff barriers which is actually used by developed countries as a tool of restricting developing countries' importing and exporting trade in the name of environmental protection under the condition of the fierce conflict between environment and trade. For example, American refused to import the petrol of Venezuela because the Pb content in it has been beyond the standard of this country; European countries ban imports on the refrigerators which content Freon; The USDA bans imports on the beef from countries that have had cases of mad cow disease.

Objectively speaking, there are two general kinds of Green Barrier, namely Kind Green Barrier and Vicious Green Barrier, which is classified according to its own motives. If the importing countries establish and implement their policies, law and technical standards to restrict the import with the purpose of protecting ecology, people's health and developing sustainably, it is a Kind Green Barrier. However, the Vicious Green Barrier is actually a way of trade protectionism, which is aimed at making use of the domestic technical advantages to stop developing countries from entering its home market. Such kind of green barrier should be resisted and prevented. They have different or even opposite influence on the international trade. The former can keep our society developing in a sustainable and harmonious order, whereas the latter fails to do it like that. Therefore, we should keep this problem in prospective.

1) Reasons of the Rise

(1) Green Trade Barrier is more elusive and safer than other non-tariff barriers.

Compared with import quotas, import license, import ban and many other non-tariff barriers, the Green Trade Barrier has fewer problems in the unreasonable distribution and varieties of discriminations hence it is much easier to avoid trade friction. Besides, the modern inspection standards based on the scientific technology are so stringent and complicated that it is difficult for the export countries to deal with and adjust to.

(2) The deterioration of the worldwide environment has changed our human value.

With the fast growth of the industrialization and the world economy, the pollution and disruption of environment and natural recourses have become more and more serious, such as global warming, ozone depletion, bio-diversity reduction and many other environmental problems. And they have brought out great changes in people's value and consuming behaviors. Going for good life quality and creating green civilization have taken the dominant place in their mind. Therefore, there is an increasing demand in environmentally friendly and healthy green products. The preference for green products in the developed countries is one of forming reasons of this barrier.

(3) The decrease of traditional non-tariff barriers has given a good chance for the rise of the Green Trade Barrier.

With the implement of The GATT and the World Trade Organization and the constant decrease of duties, the non-tariff barriers have been more restricted stringently and the traditional trade barriers do not work as well as before. In this case, the developed countries have to find out and conduct new trade-protection measures standing in their own shoes. So the Green Trade Barrier happens.

(4) The environmental standards in every country are different.

It cannot be denied that the level of social productive forces and the awareness of protecting environment in the developed countries are far higher than them in the developing ones. Though the stipulation and implement of environmental standards in which they are very strict mean little to the homemade product competitive, they will have great impact on lots of developing countries. Consequently, for protecting their own trade, the Green Barriers are built with restricting the import of developing countries.

(5) The existence of all kinds of green organizations and its influence on the national policy are one of the major factors.

Since 1970s, there have been many green organizations establishing all over the world. They are an increasingly important kind of political power which has directly great impact on the government policy as well as the official status and their political career. Therefore lots of parties have politicalized the environmental problems by setting about adding the environment protection policy into their policy system, which unavoidably involves the economy and trade areas. At the same time, under the pressure given by the domestic manufacturers, the governments in developed countries have to establish some green barriers to protect their benefits.

(6) Another rise of the trade protectionism in developed countries and the loophole of WTO rules are the fundamental factors for the rise of Green Trade Barrier.

Under the pressure of the slow growth of domestic economy, the increasing unemployment and the lack of superior industry, the developed countries, on one hand, strongly advocate Free Trade Theory within WTO for developing and expanding service trading market, especially in the superior industry and knowledge-based economy. On the other hand, they adopt new trade protectionism measures in their relatively inferior areas by establishing some unattainable standards for the import products of the developing countries. It is not surprising that the Green Trade Barrier is adopted.

2) The basic characteristics of Green Trade Barrier

(1) It is nominally reasonable.

Outwardly speaking, Green Trade Barrier is set with the purpose of preserving our natural resources, environment and maintaining our health. However, it is actually used by developed countries as a tool of restricting developing countries' importing and exporting trade.

(2) It is formally lawful.

Green Trade Barrier belongs to non-tariff barriers. However, it is based on a series of international and domestic public law and regulations, which is totally different form the other non-tariff barriers. It is lawfully allowable that the developed countries conduct the stringent green barriers measures towards the import according to the Agreement on Technical Barriers to Trade.

(3) It is extensive in the content of protecting.

It not only makes provisions and restrictions in producing and selling of many products involved with environmental protection and human beings' health, but also lays great pressure in the industrial manufactured goods which have to commit to the safety, health, antifouling and many other environmental standards.

(4) It is elusive in the ways of protecting.

Compared with import quotas, import license, import ban and many other non-tariff barriers, the Green Trade Barrier has fewer problems in the unreasonable distribution and varieties of discriminations hence it is much easier to avoid trade friction. Besides, the modern inspection standards based on the scientific technology are so stringent and complicated that it is difficult for the export countries to deal with and adjust to.

(5) It needs high technology.

It has great demand in high technology in the process of products' producing, using, consuming and use-after handling.

5.3 Case Study

5.3.1 Abstract

The measures and the loss: case study on non-tariff barriers related to veterinary export certificates in Dutch exports.

Case study research into the mandatory veterinary requirements on Dutch exports of live animals and animal products provide empirical evidence on the trade effects of non-tariff measures (NTMs). The paper discusses the analytical approach to assess how veterinary health attestation may create (temporary) obstacles for Dutch exports, what these obstacles are, and whether competing exporters in EU countries have encountered similar barriers. We have a dataset on 166 cases in June, 2004 where the process of issuing veterinary certificates for Dutch exports to non-EU destinations was disrupted. Products covered are animal-based products, live animals and feed. We use a sample of 30 cases that continued after 2006, the "long lasting problems", and 39 cases that came up and got solved between 2004 and 2006, the temporary problems.

The main challenge is to link the available record of recognition problems to the disruptions in exports. In order to assess trade disruptions, statistical tests of outliers and trend breaches are performed on detailed monthly trade data, and the issue of not-observed trade needs to be addressed. This raises the need to address disruption patterns around the imposition of measures in trade. The alternative patterns under examination are:

①measures that have an immediate trade impact;
②measures due to which trade gradually expands or reduces;
③measures that divert trade to alternative export destinations.

Finally, we want to examine whether the impact of veterinary health attestation on trade can be specified towards the type of trade barrier. For that, we suggest introducing a distinction between three different types of barriers, based on whether obstacles relate to the non-conformity of products to import requirements or a failure in the conformity assessment or both.

5.3.2 Keywords – Non-Tariff Measures, Conformity Assessment, Animal Products

5.3.2.1 Introduction

Governments use various measures ranging from import bans, quarantine to food safety requirements as import conditions in order to minimise food safety and health risks associated with imports of agri-food products. Such risks relate to the possible health hazards caused by foreign products, including the importation of invasive species or diseases that are harmful or perceived harmful from a health point of view and can cause damage for domestic producers.

While protecting health of humans, animals and plants in the importing country, food safety requirements also help to globally manage and eradicate infectious diseases, thereby contributing to a global public goods.

These motives provide rationale for governments to require that both domestic and foreign products satisfy certain food safety and health standards.

As opposed to traditional trade policy measures, food safety requirements are non-tariff measures (NTMs), and their potentially trade-restricting effect is often emphasized. Trade impediments are likely to occur if the requirements of importing countries are tighter than national ones and vary across importing countries such that exporters have to meet several different requirements to supply foreign markets.

However, the trade effect is difficult to ascertain, and it has only recently been acknowledged that requirements for exporting agri-food products can also promote trade. Opening the door for controlled imports, they can be considered to facilitate the exchange of agri-food products, and in their absence, quarantine measures and import bans are the only alternative to effectively reduce or rather eliminate food safety and health risks.

Import requirements play a particularly important role in trade of products of animal origin that can present serious health hazards. In international trade of meat, dairy products and live animals, import requirements refer to the health status of the herd, handling as well as processing of raw animal products into consumer goods. While meeting additional quality specifications according to the demand and preferences of buyers, firms dealing with animal products apply sanitary control and monitoring measures so as to satisfy the food safety and health requirements necessary. For exporting, firms usually have to obtain official certificates that attest compliance with the respective governmental requirements. This paper focuses on trade impediments that Dutch exporters of animal products face with regard to export certificates. The Dutch case study presented refers to on-going work on the quantitative analysis of the trade effect of NTMs. With empirical evidence by large missing, the goal of the paper is to discuss the analytical approach to measure the trade effect of NTMs and its application to the Dutch case study of export certificates for products of animal origin.

5.3.2.2 Export Certificates in Trade of Animal Products

The regulatory framework to control food safety and health issues can generally be divided into the main elements of requirements, conformity assessment and enforcement. Export certificates can be considered to involve all three elements. That is export certificates contain requirements, and for those consignments of products that satisfy the necessary tests of requirements exporters receive export certificates.

With the border checks, exports products have to be accompanied by valid export certificates in order to be allowed on the market of the importing country. This paper thus uses the regulatory framework presented in order to elaborate on export certificates in the international trade of animal products.

Export certificates refer to both product and process standards, including management and monitoring systems along the entire food supply chain that is increasingly implemented and aim at reducing the probability that the production and consumption of products result in hazard for humans, animal and plant health. The requirements stated in export certificates can be those of the importing country, the exporting country or a mixture of both. Most importantly, export certificates stipulate that the exporting country must be free of certain infectious animal diseases, such as foot and mouth disease, Rinderpest or BSE in order to protect the disease-free status in the importing country, or to accommodate other animal health and food safety objectives. This makes export certificates specific to pairs of trading partners, and exporters may have to qualify for several different export certificates according to their export destinations.

While negotiated by the respective authorities of importing and exporting country, the contents and format of certificates are mainly determined by the importing country, and thus reflect the domestic requirements of the importing country. According to the WTO trade rules, import requirements are not to exceed domestic requirements. However, importing countries can impose further reaching and different food safety and health standards under the Sanitary and Phytosanitary Agreement, and include them in the respective export certificates. Based on scientific information and international agreement, the World Organisation for Animal health (OIE) provides guidelines for devising export certificates for animal products. The OIE's Terrestrial Animal Health Code, for example, recommends procedures to prepare, formulate and implement veterinary and health certificates required for exporting. The OIE also provides templates of model certificates for different types of animal products that trading partners can adapted to their specific agreement on requirements.

Conformity assessment verifies compliance with respective food safety and health requirements that either do not show in product characteristics or are difficult to ascertain without specific testing. In order to obtain the necessary export certificate, firms who wish to export may have to undergo additional tests if the requirements of the importing county are different from those in the exporting country. The governmental veterinary service in the exporting country or other competent authorities, sometimes involving approved third party conformity assessment, conduct the necessary tests and subsequently issue export certificates on consignments of compliant products.

Alternatively, firms may be approved for exporting, and receive general export licenses via certification or pre-listing. While both export certificates and licenses mean costs for exporters, obtaining export certificates seems to be more expensive due to the batch-wise system.

Officials in the exporting country usually sign the export certificates, and thus assume the responsibility for the claims of compliance made. For the importing country, the governmental stamp supplies the certificate with the necessary trustworthiness and signals the integrity of the foreign product. Export certificates thus enable trust between both the respective governmental authorities and firms in the exporting and importing country, thereby facilitating trade. In comparison to other food safety and health control measures applied in international trade, export certificates may also be trade promoting since they bundle the information necessary for controlled imports. Based on negotiations between country pairs, they on the one hand involve two-way information flows and reduce transaction costs for governments in both the importing and exporting country. On the other hand, export certificates also lead to lower transaction costs of firms that wish to export and do not separately have to proof compliance with import requirements.

5.3.2.3 The Dutch Case Study

The specific aim is to assess how veterinary health attestation may create (temporary) obstacles for Dutch exports, what these obstacles are, and whether competing exporters in EU countries have encountered similar barriers. We have a dataset on 166 cases where the process of issuing veterinary certificates for Dutch exports to non-EU destinations was disrupted. The data is derived from the proceedings of the Veterinary Export (VEX) committee of the Dutch ministry of agriculture, nature and food quality (LNV), for June, 2004.

Products covered are animal-based products, live animals and genetic material and feed. Interestingly, the data record a strong overrepresentation of live animals and genetic material. This is particularly striking in relation to the small share of live animals and genetic material in total exports that require veterinary export certificates.

Out of the total of 166 cases we select two samples for further analysis: a sample of 30 cases that continued after 2006, the "long-lasting problems", and 39 cases that came up and got solved between 2004 and 2006, the "temporary" problems.

The information reported on Dutch exports shows that two types of problems exist. At the firm level, problems occur in the compliance of the respective requirements of the export certificate, and they could be related to compliance costs, including the fees for obtaining the export certificate. Less important in the Dutch case, expected that recognition failure – langue of certificate, finding agreement and lack of recognizing testing methods – much more important and time-consuming. Problems relate to governmental level.

5.3.2.4 Analytical Approach to Measure Trade Effect

With the use of statistical and econometric analysis the dataset is analyzed to answer the following questions:

(1) To what extent have the recognition problems related to veterinary export certificates impeded Dutch exports to third countries?

(2) For problems related to export certificates that affected not only Dutch trade but also several other EU exporters, were Dutch exports more or less impeded by problems than their EU competitors?

The main challenge is to link the available record of recognition problems to the disruptions in exports. In order to assess trade disruptions, statistical tests of outliers and trend breaches are performed on detailed monthly trade data, and the issue of not-observed trade needs to be addressed. This raises the need to address disruption patterns around the imposition of measures in trade. The following alternative patterns are under examination:

(1) measures that have an immediate trade impact;

(2) measures due to which trade gradually expands or reduces;

(3) measures that divert trade to alternative export destinations.

The patterns themselves are important contributions to the NTM literature. Finally, we want to examine whether the impact of veterinary health attestation on trade can be specified towards the type of trade barrier. For that, we introduce a distinction between three different types of barriers, based on whether obstacles relate to the non-conformity of products to import requirements or a failure in the conformity assessment or both.

5.3.3 Case study: Tariffs and Non-tariff Barriers of China

Since entering the World Trade Organization (WTO) in December 2001, China has taken measures to comply with its WTO trade commitments. These commitments include lowering tariffs, reducing non-tariff barriers, expanding market access for foreign firms and improving transparency. Although China has implemented progressive reforms in certain areas (most notably import tariff reductions), exporters perceive that a variety of non-tariff trade barriers still remain which impedes access to the China market.

The Australian Federal Government is currently conducting Free Trade Agreement (FTA) negotiations with China to eliminate or reduce tariffs and non-tariff trade barriers for Australian exports. For further information, please refer to the Australia-China Free Trade Agreement Negotiations.

5.3.3.1 Import Tariff

Chinese import tariff rates are calculated based on the Harmonised System (HS) of Classification Codes. There are two columns of tariffs according to the Most Favoured Nation (MFN) Rates and the General Rates. The MFN Rates applied to those countries that have concluded trade treaties or a reciprocal agreement for preferential treatment with China, or more broadly speaking are member countries of the WTO. (Australia is included in this group.) The General Rate is applied to those countries that have not concluded a reciprocal agreement with China. Please refer to the APEC Tariff Database for Chinese tariff rates.

Import tariff rates also vary according to the type of product, components and the intended use of the products. Most import tariff rates are ad valorem, assessed as a percentage of the CIF value.

Average tariff rates on imports have dropped to 9.8 per cent, with agricultural products at an average of 15.3 per cent and industrial products at an average of 8.95 per cent (at 2007). China has also adopted a policy of tariff exemption on certain imported equipment and machinery that encourages scientific research and technology development, and investment in key hi-tech industries.

Foreign exporters sometimes experience difficulties with inconsistent application of customs classifications, tariff rates and import controls by local customs officials.

5.3.3.2 Non-Tariff Barriers

The Chinese authorities divide imports into three categories:

(1) Contraband goods, which are prohibited from import. Prohibited imports include weapons, poisons and toxic chemicals.

(2) Restricted goods that require an import licence or quota.

(3) Permitted goods under which most imports are categorised.

The Chinese government issues "Public Information Notices" to inform of actual or impending policy changes and categories of goods. Many of these notices are issued in Chinese and are not translated into English. Information on policy releases in English can be found on China Ministry of Commerce website.

The Chinese government administers an "import licence" system on the importation of certain restricted goods, in order to strictly monitor the content or volume. On 1st April 2007, the Chinese government relaxed the import licensing requirement on 338 categories of products, requiring Chinese importers to apply for an "automatic import license".

China Ministry of Commerce and the General Administration of Customs are responsible for determining the products included in the Merchandise Catalogue of Permitted Automatic Import Goods. Products in this catalogue are free from import restriction, however are still recorded by the Ministry of Commerce.

China has a wide range of tariff rate quotas (TRQs) that are based on a two-tiered tariff system. Global access is granted for a specific import quota at a low rate, and then excess imports are charged at a higher rate. Given that Chinese tariff rate quotas are placed on certain sensitive agricultural products, this creates a non-tariff barrier to trade for many Australian exporters. The following are some of the items that operate under tariff rate quotas:

(1) raw wool/wool tops;

(2) sugar;

(3) wheat;

(4) cotton;

(5) rice;

(6) diammonium phosphate;

(7) urea imports;

(8) NPK compound fertiliser.

Other non-tariff barriers that may restrict trade are covered under the respective content headings for "Doing Business" in China.

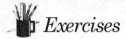 Exercises

1. Define the key terms listed below:

Ad Valorem duty;

a Specific duty;

compound duties;

countervailing duties;

import quotas;

voluntary restraints;

exchange controls;

customs delays;

technical barriers.

2. How many types do the tariff barriers have? And talk about something about them.

3. Why do some governments use import quotas instead of just using tariffs to restrict imports by the same amounts? Is it because quotas bring a bigger national gain than tariffs?

4. What are voluntary export restraint (VER) agreements? Why do some governments force foreign exporters into them instead of just using quotas or tariffs to restrict imports by the same amounts? Is it because VER bring the importing country a bigger national gain than quotas or tariffs?

5. Under what conditions could an import quota and a tariff have exactly the same effect on price, and bring the same gains and losses (given a tariff level that restricts imports just as the quota would)?

6. The United States is considering adopting a regulation that foreign apples can be imported only if they are grown and harvested using the same techniques that are used in the United States. These methods are used in the United States to meet various government standards about worker safety and product quality.

(1) As a representative of the U.S. government, you are asked to defend the new import regulation before the WTO. What will you do?

(2) As a representative of foreign apple growers, you are asked to present the case that this regulation is an unfair restriction on trade. What will you do?

Chapter 6　Economic Integration

6.1　Economic Integration: Overview

For a variety of reasons it often makes sense for nations to coordinate their economic policies. Coordination can generate benefits that are not possible otherwise. There it is shown that if countries cooperate and set zero tariffs against each other, then both countries are likely to benefit relative to the case when both countries attempt to secure short-term advantages by setting optimal tariffs. This is just one advantage of cooperation. Benefits may also accrue to countries that liberalize labor and capital movements across borders, who coordinate fiscal policies and resource allocation towards agriculture and other sectors and who coordinate their monetary policies.

Any type of arrangement in which countries agree to coordinate their trade, fiscal and/or monetary policies is referred to as economic integration. Obviously, there are many different degrees of integration.

6.1.1　Preferential Trade Agreement

A preferential trade agreement(PTA) is perhaps the weakest form of economic integration. In a PTA countries would offer tariff reductions, though perhaps not eliminations, to a set of partner countries in some product categories. Higher tariffs, perhaps non-discriminatory tariffs, would remain in all remaining product categories. This type of trade agreement is not allowed among WTO members who are obligated to grant most-favored nation status to all other WTO members. Under the most-favored nation (MFN) rule countries agree not to discriminate against other WTO member countries. Thus, if a country's low tariff on bicycle imports, for example, is 5%, then it must charge 5% on imports from all other WTO members. Discrimination or preferential treatment for some countries is not allowed. The country is free to charge a higher tariff on imports from non-WTO members, however. In 1998 the U.S. proposed legislation to eliminate tariffs on imports from the nations in sub-Sahara Africa. This action represents a unilateral preferential trade agreement since tariffs would be reduced in one direction but not the other.

Note: a PTA is also used, generally, to describe all types of economic integration since they all incorporate some degree of "preferred" treatment.

6.1.2　Free Trade Area

A free trade area(FTA) occurs when a group of countries agree to eliminate tariffs between themselves, but maintain their own external tariff on imports from the rest of the world. The North American Free Trade Area is an example of a FTA. When NAFTA is fully implemented, tariffs of automobile imports between the U. S. and Mexico will be zero. However, Mexico may continue to set a different tariff than the U. S. on auto imports from non-NAFTA countries. Because of the different external tariffs, FTAs generally develop elaborate "rules of origin". These rules are designed to prevent goods from being imported into the FTA member country with the lowest tariff and then transshipped to the country with higher tariffs. Of the thousands of pages of text that made up the NAFTA, most of them described rules of origin.

6.1.3 Customs Union

A customs union occurs when a group of countries agree to eliminate tariffs between themselves and set a common external tariff on imports from the rest of the world. The European Union represents such an arrangement. A customs union avoids the problem of developing complicated rules of origin, but introduces the problem of policy coordination. With a customs union, all member countries must be able to agree on tariff rates across many different import industries.

6.1.4 Common Market

A common market establishes free trade in goods and services, setting common external tariffs among members and also allowing for the free mobility of capital and labor across countries. The European Union was established as a common market by the Treaty of Rome in 1957, although it took a long time for the transition to take place. Today, EU citizens have a common passport, can work in any EU member country and can invest throughout the union without restriction.

6.1.5 Economic Union

An economic union typically will maintain free trade in goods and services, set common external tariffs among members, allow the free mobility of capital and labor, and will also relegate some fiscal spending responsibilities to a supra-national agency. The European Union's Common Agriculture Policy (CAP) is an example of a type of fiscal coordination indicative of an economic union.

6.1.6 Monetary Union

Monetary union establishes a common currency among a group of countries. This involves the formation of a central monetary authority which will determine monetary policy for the entire group. The Maastricht treaty signed by EU members in 1991 proposed the implementation of a single European currency (the Euro) by 1999. The degree of monetary union that will arise remains uncertain in 1998.

Perhaps the best example of an economic and monetary union is the United States. Each U. S. state has its own government which sets policies and laws for its own residents. However, each state cedes control, to some extent, over foreign policy, agricultural policy, welfare policy, and monetary policy to the federal government. Goods, services, labor and capital can all move freely, without restrictions among the U. S. states and the nations sets a common external trade policy.

6.1.7 Multilateralism vs. Regionalism

In the post World War II period, many nations have pursued the objective of trade liberalization. One device used to achieve this was the GATT and its successor, the WTO. Although the GATT began with less than 50 member countries, the WTO claimed 132 members by 1997. Since GATT and WTO agreements commit all member nations to reduce trade barriers simultaneously, it is sometimes referred to as a *multilateral* approach to trade liberalization.

An alternative method used many countries to achieve trade liberalization includes the formation of preferential trade arrangements, free trade areas, customs unions and common markets. Since many of these agreements involve geographically contiguous countries, these methods are sometimes referred to as a *regional* approach to trade liberalization.

The key question of interest concerning the formation of preferential trade arrangements is whether these arrangements are a good thing. If so, what conditions? If not, why not?

One reason supporters of free trade may support regional trade arrangements are because they are seen to represent movements towards free trade. Indeed, Section 24 of the original GATT allows signatory countries to form free trade agreements and customs unions despite the fact that preferential agreements violate the principle of non-discrimination. When a free trade area or customs union is formed between two or more WTO member countries, they agree to lower their tariffs to zero between each other but will maintain their tariffs against other WTO countries. Thus, the free trade area represents discriminatory policies. Presumably the reason these agreements are tolerated within the WTO is because they represent significant commitments to free trade, which is another fundamental goal of the WTO.

However, there is also some concern among economists that regional trade agreements may make it more difficult, rather than easier, to achieve the ultimate objective of global free trade.

The fear is that although regional trade agreements will liberalize trade among its member countries, the arrangements may also increase incentives to raise protectionist trade barriers against countries outside the area. The logic here is that the larger the regional trade area, relative to the size of the world market, the larger will be that region's market power in trade. The more market power, the higher would be the region's optimal tariffs and export taxes. Thus, the regional approach to trade liberalization could lead to the formation of large "trade blocs" which trade freely among members but choke off trade with the rest of the world. For this reason some economists have argued that the multilateral approach to trade liberalization, represented by the trade liberalization agreements in successive WTO rounds, is more likely to achieve global free trade than the regional or preferential approach.

In what follows here we present the economic argument regarding trade diversion and trade creation. These concepts are used to distinguish between the effects of free trade area or customs union formation that may benefit from those that are detrimental. As mentioned above, preferential trade arrangements are often supported because they represent a movement in the direction of free trade. If free trade is economically the most efficient policy, it would seem to follow that any movement towards free trade should be beneficial in terms of economic efficiency. It turns out that this conclusion is wrong. Even if free trade is most efficient, it is not true that a step in that direction necessarily raises economic efficiency. Whether a preferential trade arrangement raises a country's welfare and raises economic efficiency depends on the extent to which the arrangement causes trade diversion versus trade creation.

6.2 Trade Creation and Trade Diversion

With the growth of regional trading blocs such as COMESA, the European Union and Mercosur, the question arises; do such arrangements benefit world trade and increase overall welfare? The answer depends upon the difference between trade creation effect and trade diversion effects.

The trade creation effect is caused by the extra output produced by the member countries. This extra output is generated due to the freeing up of trade between them. Increased specialisation and economies of scale should increase productive efficiency within member countries.

The trade diversion effect exists because countries within trading blocs, protected by trade barriers, will now find they can produce goods more cheaply than countries outside the trade bloc. Production will be diverted away from those countries outside the trade bloc that has a natural comparative advantage to those within the trading bloc.

The diagram below shows the trade creation and trade diversion effects. Zambia has a domestic supply curve for maize S_z. If it forms a trading bloc with South Africa then the supply curve for maize is S_z/s_a. The world output of maize is shown by the horizontal supply curve S_w. The Zambian demand curve for maize is D_z (Shown in Figure 6.1).

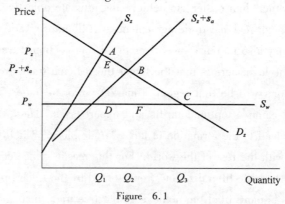

Figure 6.1

Assuming no trade the domestic price of maize in Zambia would be P_z and the quantity would be Q_1. By forming a trade bloc with South Africa the price of maize would fall to $P_z + s_a$ and the quantity produced to Q_2. The triangle AEB represents the resulting welfare gain or trade creation effect. If Zambia trade freely on the world market, quantity Q_3 of maize could be purchased at the world price of P_w. This has been prevented from happening by the formation of the trade bloc with South Africa, and the imposition of some form of trade barrier. There has therefore been a welfare loss of BFC. This is the trade diversion effect.

A comparison of the two effects enables the overall welfare gain or loss of the formation of the trading bloc to be assessed. The welfare implication of the trade creation and trade diversion effect are summarised in the Table 6.1 below:

Table 6.1

	With no trade	With trade bloc	With free trade
Price and Quantity	P_z, Q_1	$P_z + s_a, Q_z + s_a$	P_w
Trade Creation	—	EAB	DAC
Trade Diversion	ADC	BFC	—

From the point of view of LDCs the existence of trading blocs depends rather on firstly whether the country is in the trading bloc and secondly which other countries are also members.

Being outside a trading bloc will often mean that a country loses out through the trade diversion effect. Zambian textile producers will face trade barriers such as tariffs into the European Union and consequent disadvantage.

Forming a trade bloc with other LDCs may result in only a small trade creation effect as the share of world trade involving LDCs is so small, that the trade bloc has limited influence on the market price and quantity. If the country joins a trade bloc to a MDC then there may be real advantages to the LDC as resources flow within the bloc to the countries where there are cost advantages and the potential market for exports is significantly expanded.

6.3 Regional Economic Integration

6.3.1 Introduction

Regional economic integration occurs when countries come together to form free trade areas or customs unions, offering members preferential trade access to each others' markets. The article reviews the economic effects of such agreements on member countries and on the world trading system. Effects on member countries include the benefits and costs of trade creation and trade diversion, as well as gains from increased scale and competition. "Deeper" integration can be pursued by going beyond abolition of import tariffs and quotas, to further measures to remove market segmentation and promote integration. Effects on the world trading system are not clear-cut. There is little evidence that regionalism has retarded multilateral liberalization, but neither is there support for the view that continuing expansion of regional agreements will obviate the need for multilateral liberalization efforts.

6.3.2 Regional Economic Integration

Regional integration agreements (RIAs) are groupings of countries formed with the objective of reducing barriers to trade between members. They have long historical antecedents, sometimes being a stage to nation building (most famously in the Zollverein of nineteenth century Germany), and sometimes as part of colonial trading arrangements.

In the post-war period, developments were led by the European Union (EU, originally the European Economic Communities, founded in 1958), and in the 1960s and 1970s there was a number of rather inward looking (and largely unsuccessful) RIAs between developing countries. Since the mid-1980s there has been a dramatic increase in regional integration activity. Of the 194 RIAs notified to the General Agreement on Trade and Tariffs/ World Trade Organization (GATT/WTO) at the beginning of 1999, 87 were notifications since 1990. Now almost all countries are members of at least one RIA, and more than one third of world trade takes place within such agreements. The new developments include the expansion and deepening of the EU; the construction of new and more open RIAs between developing countries and the advent of RIAs in which both high income and developing countries are equal partners, lead by the North American Free Trade Area (NAFTA) which, in 1994, extended the Canadian-U.S.A free trade agreement to Mexico.

RIAs come in many shapes and sizes. They vary in income levels, in openness to trade, and in the share of trade that takes place within the RIA, (60% for the fifteen members of the EU, but just 10% for the eight members of the West African Economic and Monetary Union). Structures vary, from the loose agreements to facilitate trade of the African Cross-Border Initiative and Asia Pacific Economic Cooperation (APEC) forum, through to the deep integration of the EU, involving the construction of shared executive, judicial and legislative institutions. The focus of this article, in common with most of the economics literature, is on RIAs as mechanisms for trade liberalization, not addressing the integration of factor markets, monetary systems, or political institutions.

Even with this focus, RIAs differ widely in structure. "Free trade areas" remove internal tariff and non-tariff barriers, but permit members to retain independent external tariff policies. "Customs unions" go further, in fully harmonizing external trade policy. And it is increasingly recognized that effective integration of markets requires more than reducing tariffs and quotas. Many other barriers – such as differing national product standards and a host of minor border frictions – impede trade and support market segmentation, and some RIAs are now pursuing "deep integration" policies to eliminate these barriers.

6.3.3 Economic Effects on Member Countries

6.3.3.1 Trade Creation and Diversion

The modern analysis of RIAs originates from Viner (1950), who drew the distinction between the trade creating and trade diverting effects of RIA formation. The classical source of gains from trade is that global free trade allows consumers and firms to purchase from the cheapest source of supply, hence ensuring that production is located according to comparative advantage. In contrast, trade barriers discriminate against foreign supply, inducing domestic import competing producers to expand even though they have higher costs than imports. This, in turn, starves domestic export sectors of resources and causes them to be smaller than they otherwise would be. Since a RIA liberalizes trade, reducing at least some of the barriers, doesn't it follow that it too will generate gains from trade? Viner's contribution was to show that the answer is: not necessarily. The gains from trade argument applied if all trade barriers are reduced, but need not apply to a partial – and discriminatory – reduction in barriers, as in a RIA. This is because discrimination between sources of supply is not eliminated, it is just shifted. If partner country production displaces higher cost domestic production then there will be gains – trade creation. But it is possible that partner country production may displace lower cost imports from the rest of the world, and this is welfare reducing trade diversion.

The analysis of trade creation and trade diversion constitutes one of the first formal analyses of the more general problem of "second-best welfare economics". Given that distortions remain in place in some activities in the economy, it is not necessarily the case that removing just some of the distortions (e.g. eliminating trade barriers on partner countries and leaving them in place on external countries) is welfare improving. In the literature on regional integration, the response to the fundamental ambiguity created by the second-best took three main forms.

First, authors established circumstances under which there is no interaction between formation of the RIA and external trade flows, so no possibility of trade diversion. Meade (1955) pointed out that if trade barriers with non-members take the form of fixed quantitative restrictions, then a RIA must raise the total welfare of member countries since there is no possibility that imports from the rest of the world are displaced. Ohyama (1972) and Kemp and Wan (1976) showed how, when external trade barriers take the form of tariffs, it is possible to adjust these to hold external trade volumes constant, so preventing trade diversion from occurring.

Second, researchers identified conditions, in terms of changes in endogenous variables, for welfare gain. For example, welfare increases if the initial-tariff weighted change in trade volume is positive (Meade 1955). If internal tariffs are close to zero, then reducing them to zero raises welfare if it increases tariff revenues earned on external trade (Ethier and Horn, 1984).

The third approach is to identify features of economies (in terms of their underlying exogenous characteristics) under which they are more or less likely to gain or lose from RIA membership. Lipsey (1957) argued that joining with countries that are already one's largest trading partners is unlikely to lead to diversion, since the fact that the countries were originally the largest trading partners suggests that they are the lowest cost source of supply. Similar reasoning, including transport costs in the costs of supply, leads to the "natural trading bloc" argument (Wonnacott and Lutz 1989, Summers 1991).

Venables (2000) shows that those members of a RIA with comparative advantage most different from the world average are most likely to lose from trade diversion, as their trade is diverted to partner countries with comparative costs between theirs and the world average.

Empirical work on trade creation and trade diversion has taken two main forms: econometric studies of changes in trade flows, and computer simulation studies of the full general equilibrium effects of RIA membership.

Econometric studies seek to quantify the changes in trade flows attributable to membership of a RIA, and thereby identify trade creation and diversion. A variety of different econometric models have been developed, the most common being based on the gravity model which estimates bilateral trade between countries as a function of their GDPs, populations, the distance between them and physical factors such as sharing a land border, and being landlocked or an island. Dummy variables capture whether or not countries are in a particular RIA, their estimated effect indicating whether countries in a RIA trade more or less than would otherwise be expected. Using this technique, Bayoumi and Eichengreen (1997) found that the formation of the EEC reduced the annual growth of member trade with other industrial countries by 1.7 percentage points, with the major attenuation occurring over 1959-1961, just as trade preferences were phased in. Soloaga and Winters (1998) looked at a wide range of RIAs, producing a mixed picture with little evidence of widespread trade diversion. Overall, there appears to be weak evidence that external trade is smaller than it otherwise might have been in at least some of the blocs that have been researched, but the picture is sufficiently mixed that it is not possible to conclude that trade diversion has been a major problem. Furthermore, it cannot be inferred that trade diversion has been economically damaging without information on relative costs and tariff structures, variables that are not revealed in this sort of aggregate exercise.

The second empirical approach is based on computable equilibrium modeling.

This involves construction of a full computer model of the economies under study and use of the model to simulate the effects of the policy changes associated with the RIA. Such a model typically contains a great deal of microeconomic details, so can be used to predict changes in production in each sector, and changes in factor prices and real incomes. In models that assume a perfectly competitive environment, the combined effects of trade diversion and trade creation typically give very small welfare gains – just a fraction of 1% of GDP (see Baldwin and Venables 1997 for a survey). The strength of these models is that they have sufficient micro-economic structure for the effects of a policy change to be traced out in detail, and its real income effects to be calculated. They are also often used for prediction – to estimate the likely effects of a policy change before it is implemented. But they have the major weakness that they are not usually fitted to data as carefully, or subject to the same statistical testing, as econometric models. The cost of the micro-economic detail is a complexity that makes rigorous econometric estimation impossible.

Although the focus of the trade creation and diversion literature has been on the changes in trade flows induced by regional integration, two consequent effects are important. The first is that changes in trade flows may change world prices, possibly improving the terms of trade of member countries, although this gain arises at the expense of outside countries. For example, if trade diversion occurs then RIA imports from outside countries are reduced, and any reduction in import prices that this cause is a terms of trade gain. Empirical work on this issue by Winters and Chang (2000) shows that Brazil's membership in Mercosur has been accompanied by a significant decline in the relative prices of imports from non-member countries.

The second is that changes in tariffs and trade volumes will lead to loss of government tariff revenue. This can occur directly (as intra-RIA tariffs are cut) and as a consequence of trade diversion (as imports are diverted away from external, tariff inclusive, sources of supply). Its cost depends on the social cost of raising funds by alternative means, and can be severe in some developing countries. For example, in the South African Development Community, where some countries are quite heavily dependent on trade with South Africa, substantial amounts of revenue are involved, amounting to perhaps 5.6% and 9.8% of government revenue for Zambia and Zimbabwe respectively. Cambodia derived 56% of its total tax revenues from customs duties prior to its entry into the Association of South East Asian Nations (ASEAN, Figure 6.2), and Fukase and Martin (1999) argue that entry into ASEAN provided a powerful stimulus for the introduction of a value added tax.

Figure 6.2 ASEAN: Association of Southeast Asian Nations (Malaysia, Philippines, Thailand, Vietnam)

6.3.3.2 Scale and Competition Effects

A second mechanism through which member countries are affected by RIA membership derives from the fact that countries may be too small to support, separately, activities that are subject to large economies of scale. Regional cooperation offers a route to overcome the disadvantages of smallness, by pooling resources or combining markets.

These scale benefits can arise in public projects (see World Bank 2000) and also at the level of the private firm, where they typically interact with imperfectly competitive market structures. These considerations are absent from the trade creation and trade diversion approach outlined above, which is based on the perfect competition and constant returns to scale paradigm of traditional trade theory. It was only in the 1970s and 1980s that formal analysis of the interaction between trades, economies of scale and imperfect competition began with the "new trade theory", and these techniques have now been extensively applied to regional integration.

The basic argument is that there is a trade-off between the extent to which firms can achieve economies of scale, and the intensity of competition in the market. For a given size market, larger firms means fewer firms and hence more monopolistic outcomes. If regional integration combines markets, then it shifts this trade-off, potentially allowing firms to be bigger and markets to be more competitive (Smith and Venables 1988). For example, there might be an initial situation in which two economies each have two firms in a particular industry, and these firms exploit their "duopoly" power, setting prices well above marginal cost. After formation of the RIA, this becomes four firms in one combined RIA market. This increases the intensity of competition, and possibly induces merger (or bankruptcy), perhaps leaving only the three most efficient firms. The net effect is increased competition, increased firm scale, and lower costs. "Triopoly" competition is likely to be more intense than the original duopolies, and surviving firms are larger and more efficient, so can better exploit economies of scale. A further source of gains comes from possible reductions in internal inefficiencies that firms are induced to make. If the RIA increases the intensity of competition, it may induce firms to eliminate internal inefficiencies (X-inefficiency) and raise productivity. Since competition raises the probability of bankruptcy and hence layoffs, it also generates stronger incentives for workers to improve productivity, and increases labor turnover across firms within sectors.

Although these are significant potential sources of gain, they have been difficult to achieve in many RIAs. This is addressed further in section 2.1.

6.3.3.3 Winners and Losers

A continuing concern is with the distribution of the costs and benefits of regional integration between member countries. Do central regions gain at the expense of peripheral ones, and do poor countries tend to catch up or get left behind? The evidence is, broadly, that RIAs composed of developed countries tend to show convergence (for example the narrowing of per capita income differentials observed in the EU, see Ben-David, 1993). However, the picture for RIAs composed of developing countries is more mixed, with some examples of divergent performance (World Bank, 2000).

The analytical literature on these questions is quite sparse, but provides several clues why this might occur. First, as mentioned above, trade diversion is more likely for countries with "extreme" comparative advantage, suggesting that in a RIA amongst developing countries it might be the lowest income countries that experience diversion.

For example, their imports of manufactures might be diverted from non-member countries to a partner that has a comparative advantage in manufactures within the RIA, but not relative to the world at large. Second, industries might tend to cluster in locations that have relatively good market access, or that are well supplied with business services or provision of other intermediate goods. This is more likely to occur in developing countries than in developed ones, partly because of their sparser provision of business infrastructure, and partly because the small size of their manufacturing sectors mean that clustering is less likely to run into congestion and other sources of diminishing returns. The clustering may lead to wages being bid up in one member country at the expense of others.

6.3.4 Policy Making

6.3.4.1 The Depth of Integration

The simplest form of regional integration is the elimination of tariffs (or quotas) between member countries. Beyond this there is a wide range of policy options open to countries considering integration, many of which turn on the "depth" of integration sought by member countries – ranging from modest trade liberalization, through full economic integration, to the formation of shared institutions.

The distinction between a free trade area and a customs union, in which a common external tariff is set, has already been made. The latter involves greater sharing of sovereignty and requires establishing procedures for revenue sharing, but in return can yield much greater market integration. In a free trade area where countries set different external tariffs the free internal circulation of goods is impossible; border formalities have to be maintained to ensure that external imports do not all enter through the member with the lowest external tariff, for re-export to other member countries. Since these imports include intermediate goods that are further processed in member countries, in practice this involves enforcing complicated "rules of origin" governing trade flows within the RIA. These rules are not necessary in a customs union, enabling simplification – or elimination – of internal border formalities.

It is increasingly recognized that tariffs and quotas alone may be just a small part of the overall barriers to trade created by an international border. Rules of origin create frictions, and so too does contingent protection (such as anti-dumping rules, known to have a "trade chilling" effect even when not used), duplicative customs procedures, differing national product standards and simple border red tape. The cost of border formalities on intra-EU trade in the early 1990s has been estimated to more than one percent of the gross value of internally trade, despite implementation of procedures to cut these costs; in many RIAs the costs of border formalities are much larger. Furthermore, relatively minor border frictions may constitute large real trade barriers because it can be in the interests of firms to try and limit effective cross-border competition in order to maintain collusive market sharing arrangements. This will prevent the "scale and competition" effects discussed in section 1.2 from being achieved.

Recognition of the importance of these barriers – and of the failure of more than 25 years tariff-free trade to truly integrate markets – was a motivation behind the "deep integration" of the EU's 1992 Single Market Program, (Flam 1992). The program involved adoption of almost 300 measures falling into the following five main types.

(1) Simplification and in some cases abolition of intra-EC border controls, involving, e.g. replacing border paper-work by an EU wide system of administering value added tax on cross-border transactions.

(2) Adoption of the "mutual recognition" principle for product standards, under which a product that can be legally sold in any EU country can be legally sold in all, thereby removing the need for expensive re-testing and re-certification of products.

(3) Progress towards deregulation of the transport sectors of EU countries, including measures to reduce restrictions on truckers from one country accepting loads in another.

(4) Opening of public procurement in EU countries to effective competition from suppliers in all EU countries.

(5) Deregulation of service sector activities, including opening financial services to competition and giving service providers and professionals the right of establishment in other EU countries. Estimates of the gains from these measures range up to as much as 5% of EU GPD, although these are based largely on computable equilibrium studies rather than an actual survey of outcomes (see Baldwin and Venables, 1997).

6.3.4.2 Policy Reform and Commitment

Trade policy reforms – and other sorts of reform – are often hampered by the expectation that they may be reversed. Adjusting to reform typically involves investments, but these investments will not be made unless investors are confident that the reform will persist. These problems are mitigated if a country has a "commitment mechanism" guaranteeing that the reform will be durable, and membership of a RIA can, in some circumstances, provide such a mechanism (Fernandez and Portes, 1998).

The commitment mechanism operates most obviously for trade policy – membership requires that tariffs with member countries be cut, and reneging on agreed internal liberalization is likely to bring swift retaliation by partner countries. However, it has been argued that RIAs are valuable as commitment mechanisms for a much wider range of measures. Although NAFTA was ostensibly about trade policy, an important part of its motivation was the desire on the part of both the Mexican and U.S. governments to lock in the broad range of economic reforms that the Mexican government had undertaken in the preceding years. The EU Articles of Agreement with eastern European accession candidates are explicit in promoting "full integration into the community of democratic nations". And the intervention of other Mercosur countries is credited with having averted a military coup in Paraguay in 1996 (Survey on Mercosur, *The Economist*, October 12, 1996). Paradoxically, it is even suggested that the value of a RIA as a commitment mechanism is greatest in areas other than trade policy, because there is already a way committing to tariff reductions – the tariff bindings of the GATT/WTO.

6.3.5 Regional Integration Agreements and the World Trading System

The effect of regionalism on the world trading system as a whole has been the subject of extensive recent debate. Is the growth of regionalism part of a process towards global free trade, or is it a substitute for it, damaging to multilateral negotiations and likely to lead to a situation of protected trading blocs? It is noteworthy that RIAs go against the fundamental principle of the GATT/WTO, the "most favored nation" principle under which trade policy must be non-discriminatory. They are permitted only via Article XXIV of the GATT, which requires that they cover "substantially all trade" of member countries and lead to external tariffs that "shall not on the whole be higher or more restrictive".

There are essentially three questions. First, does a given structure of RIAs creates a force for more or less liberal external trade policy? Second, is there an inherent dynamic of RIA formation which will lead to ever larger RIAs – perhaps even a RIA of the whole world, giving global free trade? And third, is there evidence that the presence of RIAs has assisted or retarded progress in the multi-lateral trade system?

An insight into the effect of the number of RIAs on incentives to set external tariffs was provided by Krugman (1993) who noted that if tariffs are set to improve member countries' terms of trade, and then they will be lowest – and consequently world income greatest – in two opposite circumstances. One is when there is a single world trade bloc containing all countries, i.e. global free trade, the other is when trade policy is set by many small independent jurisdictions, each so small as to have no market power and no reason to deviate from free trade. Between these extremes each trading bloc has an incentive to use external tariffs to try and improve its terms of trade, suggesting that a situation of relatively few large trading blocs might be the worst possible outcome.

This line of argument has been criticized from a number of different angles.

From the theory side, it should be recognized that tariff setting is a repeated game, so the incentives to cooperate, or to deviate from cooperation, need to be taken into account (Bond and Syropoulos, 1996; Winters, 1998). From the institutional side, it has been pointed out that article XXIV of the GATT expressly forbids RIAs from raising external tariffs. And from the empirical side, no evidence has been found to suggest that RIAs are in fact prone to set higher external tariffs than separate countries (Foroutan, 1998).

What of the dynamics of RIA formation? Does adding a member country to a RIA increase the incentives for further countries to join, and will existing members be willing to permit unrestricted entry? A number of researchers have argued that the incentives to join increase as RIAs become larger – a phenomenon termed "domino regionalism" by Baldwin (1995). This may be because of perception of growing benefits of membership, or because of increasing costs of being outside. These costs can arise as outsiders terms of trade may decline (the other side of the members improving terms of trade referred to in section 1.1). Perhaps more importantly, countries fear that firms may relocate, in search of the benefits of a larger market (evidence of foreign direct investment flows in Europe at the time of the Single Market Program suggests that this occurred, Baldwin, Forslid and Haaland, 1996). Another source of loss from nonmembership of RIAs is the risk of being isolated if a trade war occurs (Whalley, 1996).

Although these arguments suggest a growing demand for membership of RIAs, it is less clear that this will be matched by a willingness to accommodate new members, at least within existing RIAs. The most important trade-off here is between the benefits of "deeper" integration, and the difficulty of achieving this with larger memberships. Thus, while the EU has continued to enlarge, worries about the difficulty of accommodating new entrants impedes progress. An important contribution to the ideas on regionalism was made when the Asia Pacific Economic Cooperation (APEC) forum announced the principle of "open regionalism". Although this term has been given a number of quite different meanings, the key idea is that of open access, whereby the RIA announces that any country willing to abide by its rules may join. However, at time of writing, the idea remains to be put to the test, since APEC itself has yet to develop as a RIA. Overall, then, it seems that regional integration does create its own dynamic, attracting further countries to want to join. But there is no reason to believe that all such requests should be successful or that the end of the process is more likely to be a single world free trade area than it is to be a number of competing trade blocs.

Finally, are there any reasons to believe that the presence of RIAs has facilitated or impeded progress in multilateral trade negotiations? The argument for impedance hinges mainly on finite government capacity. Investment of time and effort in regionalism reduces the capacity of governments to invest in multilateral negotiation. On the other side, it is argued that regionalism can help, by reducing the number of separate negotiators (since members of a customs union negotiate as a single body) – an argument that begs the question of how members formulate their common position. Also, it is suggested that regionalism has proved valuable by providing "laboratories" for trying new approaches to issues of trade reform, particularly on more difficult issues. As for the track record of RIAs and multilateral negotiations, views are again divided, although there is a view that fears of fragmentation into regional blocs provided a spur for successful completion of the Uruguay round of trade negotiations (WTO, 1995).

6.3.6 Conclusions

Joining a RIA is a major "one-off" event for a country. It affects all aspects of the economy – goods prices, the structure of production and income flows to different economic agents. Generalizing about the implications of such occasional and large changes is inevitably difficult. Nevertheless, research has established the circumstances under which gains or losses are more or less likely, and drawn out the implications of this for the design of agreements (World Bank, 2000). Future research needs to pay greater attention to strategies for developing countries, and the role of RIAs in assisting them to participate effectively in the world trading system.

6.4 Trading Blocs

6.4.1 Regional Economic Integration in Europe

Figure 6.3

Europe has two trade blocs – the European Union and the European Free Trade Association (Figure 6.3). Of the two, the EU is by far the more significant, not just in terms of membership (the EU currently has 28 members; the EFTA has 6), but also in terms of economic and political influence in the world economy. Many now see the EU as an emerging economic and political superpower of the same order as the United States and Japan. Accordingly, we will concentrate our attention on the EU.

6.4.1.1　Evolution of the European Union

The EU is the product of two political factors:

①the devastation on Western Europe of two world wars and the desire for a lasting peace, and;

②the European nations' desire to hold their own on the world's political and economic stage.

In addition, many Europeans were aware of the potential economic benefits of closer economic integration of the countries.

The original forerunner of the EU, the European Coal and Steel Community, was formed in 1951 by Belgium, France, West Germany, Italy, Luxembourg and the Netherlands. Its objective was to remove barriers to intragroup shipments of coal, iron, steel and scrap metal. With the signing of the Treaty of Rome in 1957, the European Community was established. The name changed again in 1994 when the European Community became the European Union following the ratification of the Maastricht Treaty (discussed later).

The Treaty of Rome provided for the creation of a common market. Article 3 of the treaty laid down the key objectives of the new community, calling for the elimination of internal trade barriers and the creation of a common external tariff and requiring member states to abolish obstacles to the free movement of factors of production among the members. To facilitate the free movement of goods, services and factors of production, the treaty provided for any necessary harmonization of the member states' laws. Furthermore, the treaty committed the EC to establish common policies in agriculture and transportation.

6.4.1.2　Political Structure of the European Union

The economic policies of the EU are formulated and implemented by a complex and still-evolving political structure. The five main institutions in this structure are the European Council, the Council of Ministers, the European Commission, the European Parliament, and the Court of Justice.

The European Council is composed of the heads of state of the EU's member nations and the president of the European Commission. Each head of state is normally accompanied by a foreign minister to these meetings. The European Council meets at least twice a year and often resolves major policy issues and sets policy directions.

The European Commission is responsible for proposing EU legislation, implementing it, and monitoring compliance with EU laws by member states. Headquartered in Brussels, Belgium, the commission has more than 10000 employees. It is run by a group of 20 commissioners appointed by each member country for four-year renewable terms. Most countries appoint only one commissioner, although the most populated states – Great Britain, France, Germany, Italy, and Spain – appoint two each, A president and six vice presidents are chosen from among these commissioners for two-year renewable terms. The commission has a monopoly in proposing European Union legislation. The commission starts the legislative ball rolling by making a proposal, which goes to the Council of Ministers and then to the European Parliament.

The Council of Ministers cannot legislate without a commission proposal in front of it. The commission is also responsible for implementing aspects of EU law, although in practice much of this must be delegated to member states. Another responsibility of the commission is to monitor member stares to make sure they are complying with EU Claws. In this prejudicial role, the commission will normally ask a state to comply with any EU laws that are being broken. If this persuasion is not sufficient, the commission can refer a case to the Court of Justice.

The European Commission's role in competition policy has become increasingly important to business in recent years. Since 1990 when the office was formally assigned a role of competition policy, the EU's competition commissioner has been steadily gaining influence as the chief regulator of competition policy in the member nations of the EU. As with antitrust authorities in the United States, which include the Federal Trade Commission and the Department of Justice, the role of the competition commissioner is to ensure that no one enterprise uses its market power to drive out competitors and monopolize markets. The commissioner also reviews proposed mergers and acquisitions to make sure they do not create a dominant enterprise with substantial market power.

The Council of Ministers represents the interests of member states. It is clearly the ultimate controlling authority within the EU since draft legislation from the commission can become EU law only if the council agrees. The council is composed of one representative from the government of each member state. The membership, however, varies depending on the topic being discussed. When agricultural issues are being discussed, the agriculture ministers from each state attend council meetings; when transportation is being discussed, transportation ministers attend and so on. Before 1993, all council issues had to be decided by unanimous agreement between member states. This often led to marathon council sessions and a failure to make progress or reach agreement on commission proposals, as an attempt to clear the resulting logjams, the Single European Act formalized the use of majority voting rules on issues "which have as their object the establishment and functioning of a single market." Most other issues, however, such as tax regulations and immigration policy, still require unanimity among council members if they are to become law.

The European Parliament, which now has about 630 members, is directly elected by the populations of the member states. The parliament, which meets in Strasbourg, France, is primarily a consultative rather than legislative body. It debates legislation proposed by the commission and forwarded to it by the council. It can propose amendments to that legislation, which the commission and ultimately the council are not obliged to take up but often will. The power of the parliament recently has been increasing, although not by as much as parliamentarians would like. The European Parliament now has the right to vote on the appointment of commissioners as well as veto some laws (such as the EU budget and single-market legislation). One major debate now being waged in Europe is whether the council or the parliament should ultimately be the most powerful body in the EU. There is concern in Europe over the democratic accountability of the EU bureaucracy. Some think the answer to this apparent democratic deficit lies in increasing the power of the parliament, while others think that true democratic legitimacy lies with elected governments, acting through the Council of Ministers.

The Court of Justice, which is comprised of one judge from each country, is the supreme appeals court for EU law. Like commissioners, the judges are required to act as independent officials, rather than as representatives of national interests. The commission or a member country can bring other members to the court for failing to meet treaty obligations. Similarly, member countries, companies, or institutions can bring the commission or council to the court for failure to act according to an EU treaty.

6.4.1.3 The Single European Act

Two revolutions occurred in Europe in the late 1980s. The first was the democratization waves in Eastern Europe. The second revolution was much quieter, but its impact on Europe and the world may have been just as profound as the first. It was the adoption of the Single European Act by the member nations of the EC in 1987. This act committed the EC countries to work toward establishment of a single market by December 31, 1992.

The Single European Act was born of a frustration among EC members that the community was not living up to its promise. By the early 1980s, it was clear that the EC had fallen short of its objectives to remove barriers to the flee flow of trade and investment between member countries and to harmonize the wide range, of technical and legal standards for doing business. Against this background, many of the EC's prominent businesspeople mounted an energetic campaign in the early 1980s to end the EC's economic divisions, The EC responded by creating the Delors Commission. Under the chairmanship of Jacques Delors, the former French finance minister and president of the EC Commission, the Delors Commission produced a discussion paper in 1985. This proposed that all impediments to the formation of a single market be eliminated by December 31, 1992. The result was the Single European Act, which was independently ratified by the parliaments of each member country and became EC law in 1987.

6.4.1.4 The Objectives of the Act

The purpose of the Single European Act was to have one market in place by December 31, 1992. The act proposed the following changes:

Remove all frontier controls between EC countries, thereby abolishing delays and reducing the resources required for complying with trade bureaucracy. Apply the principle of "mutual recognition" to product standards. A standard developed on one EC country should be accepted in another, provided it meets basic requirements in such matters as health and safety.

Open public procurement to non-national suppliers, reducing costs directly by allowing lower-cost suppliers into national economies and indirectly by forcing national suppliers to compete.

Lift barriers to competition in the retail banking and insurance businesses, which should drive down the costs of financial services, including borrowing, throughout the EC.

Remove all restrictions on foreign exchange transactions between member countries by the end of 1992.

Abolish restrictions on cabotage – the tight of foreign truckers to pick up and deliver goods within another member state's borders – by the end of 1992. Estimates suggested this would reduce the cost of haulage within the EC by 10 to 15 percent.

All those changes were predicted to lower the costs of doing business in the EC, but the single market program was also expected to have more complicated supply side effects.

6.4.1.5 Impact

It is clear that the Single European Act has had a significant impact on the EU economy. The act provided the impetus for the restructuring of substantial sections of European industry. Many firms have shifted from national to pan-European production and distribution systems in an attempt to realize scale economies and better compete in a single market. The results have included faster economic growth than would otherwise have been the cause.

However, 10 years after the formation of a single market it is clear that the reality still falls someway short of the ideal. As documented in the opening case, as of 2002 there was still not a fully functioning single market for automobiles in the EU (although that may ultimately change given the new rules introduced in November 2002). The same is true in a number of other industries. The financial services industry for example, still remains segmented on a national basis due to the presence of different rules in different member nations. Currently, regulations prohibit banks in Britain from selling mortgages to consumers living in Germany, investment specialists in Finland from selling mutual funds in Spain and French financial institutions from making loans to Italian firms. According to economists, if the barriers between EU nations were removed and a single integrated EU market for financial services created, the EU's economic output would be 0.5 percent to 0.7 percent higher. Thus, although the EU is undoubtedly moving toward a single marketplace, established legal, cultural and language differences between taxations mean that implementation has been uneven. As in the case of the automobile industry however, progress is being made toward the adoption of a single market.

6.4.1.6 The Establishment of the Euro

In December 1991, leaders of the EC member states met in Maasnicht, the Netherlands, to discuss the next steps for the EC. The results of the Maastricht meeting surprised both Europe and the rest of the world. The EC countries had been fighting for months over the issue of common currency. Although many economists believed a common currency was required to cement a closer economic union, deadlock had been predicted. The British, in particular, had opposed any attempt in establish a common currency. But instead of deadlock, the 12 members signed a treaty that committed them to adopting a common currency by January 1, 1999, and paved the way for closer political cooperation.

The treaty laid down the main elements, if only in embryo, of a future European government: a single currency, the euro; a common foreign and defense policy; a common citizenship; and an EU parliament with teeth, it is now just a matter of waiting, some believe, for a "The United States of Europe" to emerge. Of more immediate interest are the implications for business of the establishment of a single currency.

The euro is a currency unit now used by 12 of the 15 member states of the European Union; these 12 states are now members of what is often referred to as the euro zone. The establishment of the euro has rightly been described an amazing political feat with few historical precedents. Establishing the euro required the participating national governments not only to give up their own currencies, but also to give up control over monetary policy. Governments do not routinely sacrifice national sovereignty for the greater goods, indicating the importance that the Europeans attach to the euro. By adopting the euro, the EU has created the second largest currency zone in the world after that of the U.S. dollar. Some believe that ultimately the euro could come to rival the dollar as the most important currency in the world.

Three EU countries, Britain, Denmark and Sweden are still sitting on the sidelines. The 12 countries agreeing to the euro locked their exchange rates against each other January 1st, 1999. Euro notes and coins were not actually issued until January 1st, 2002. In the interim, national currencies circulated in each of the 12 countries. However, in each participating state, the national currency stood for a defined amount of euros. After January 1st, 2002, euro notes and coins were issued and the national currencies were taken out of circulation. By mid-2002, all prices and routine economic transactions within the cure zone were in cures.

6.4.1.7 Enlargement of the European Union

One major issue facing the EU over the past few years has been that of enlargement. Enlargement of the EU into Eastern Europe has been a possibility ever since the collapse of communism at the end of the 1980s, and by the end of the 1990s, 13 countries had applied to become EU members. To qualify for EU membership the applicants had to privatize state assets, deregulate markets, restructure industries, and tame inflation. They also had to enshrine complex EU laws into their own systems, establish stable democratic governments and respect human rights. In December 2002, the EU formally agreed to accept the applications of 10 countries. Only the Mediterranean island nations of Malta and Cyprus are not in Eastern Europe. They include the Baltic States, the Czech Republic and the larger nations of Hungary and Poland. Their inclusion in the EU will expand the union to 25 states, stretching from the Atlantic to the borders of Russia; add 23 percent to the landmass of the EU; bring 75 million new citizens into the EU, creating an EU with a population of 450 million people; and create a single continental economy with a GDP of MYM9.3 trillion that rivals the United States in size.

Before this occurs, however, a number of things have to happen. First, voters in each applicant nation will have their saying on joining, and passage is by no means certain. If the referendums are approved, the nations will formally join the EU May 1st, 2004. The new members will not be able to adopt the euro until 2007, and free movement of labor between the new and existing members will not be allowed until 2007. Consistent with theories of free trade, the enlargement should create added benefits for all members. However, given the small size of the Eastern European economies (together they only amount to 5 percent of the GDP of current EU members) the initial impact will probably be small. The biggest notable change might be in the EU bureaucracy and decision-making processes, where budget negotiations among 25 nations are bound to prove more problematic than negotiations among 15 nations.

6.4.2 Regional Economic Integration in America

No other attempt at regional economic integration comes close to the BU in its boldness or its potential implications for the world economy, but regional economic integration is on the rise in America, the most significant attempt is the North American Free Trade Agreement. In addition to NAFTA, several other trade blocs are in the offing in America, the most significant of which appear to be the Andean Group and MERCOSUR. There are also plans to establish a hemisphere-wide Free Trade Area of America (FTAA) by late 2005.

The North American Free Trade Agreement. The governments of the United States and Canada in 1988 agreed to enter into a free trade agreement, which took effect January 1, 1989. The goal of the agreement was to eliminate all tariffs, on bilateral trade between Canada and the United States by 1998. This was followed in 1991 by talks among the United States, Canada and Mexico aimed at establishing a North American Free Trade Agreement for the three countries. The talks concluded in August 1992 with an agreement in principle, and the following year the agreement was ratified by the governments of all three countries.

6.4.2.1 NAFTA's Contents

The agreement became law January 1st, 1994. The contents of NAFTA (Figure 6.4) include the following:

Abolition within 10 years of tariff on 99 percent of the goods traded between Mexico, Canada and the United States.

Figure 6.4

Removal of most barriers on the cross-border flow of services, allowing financial institutions, for example, unrestricted access to the Mexican market by 2000.

Protection of intellectual property rights. Removal of most restrictions on foreign direct investment among three member countries, although special treatment (protection) will be given to Mexican energy and railway industries, American airline and radio communications industries and Canadian culture.

Application of national environmental standards, provided such standards have a scientific basis lowering of standards to lure investment is described as being inappropriate.

Establishment of two commissions with the power to impose fines and remove trade privileges when environmental standards or legislation involving health and safety, minimum wages, or child labor are ignored.

6.4.2.2 NAFTA: The First Decade

Studies of NAFTA's early impact suggest that its initial effects were at best muted, and both advocates and detractors may have been guilty of exaggeration, the most comprehensive early study was undertaken by researchers at the University of California, Los Angeles and funded by various departments of the U.S. government. This study focused on the effects of NAFTA in its first three and a half years. The authors conclude that the growth in trade between Mexico and the United States began to change nearly a decade before the implementation of NAFTA when Mexico unilaterally started to liberalize its own trade regime to conform to GATT standards. The initial period since NAFTA took effect had little impact on trends already in place. The study found that trade growth in those sectors that underwent tariff liberalization in the first two and a half years of NAFTA was only marginally higher than trade growth in sectors not yet liberalized. For example, between 1993 and 1996, U.S. exports to Mexico in sectors liberalized under NAFTA grew by 5.83 percent annually, while exports in sectors not liberalized under NAFTA grew by 5.35 percent. In short, the authors argue that NAFTA had only a marginal impact on the level of trade between the United States and Mexico.

As for NAFTA's much-debated impact on jobs in the United States, the study concluded the impact was positive but very small. The study found that while NAFTA created 31158 new jobs in the United States, 28168 jobs were lost due to imports from Mexico, for a net job gain of about 3000 in the first two years of the NAFTA regime. However, as the report's authors point out, trade flows anti employment in 1995 anti 1996 were significantly affected by an economic crisis that gripped Mexico in early 1995. Given this, it may have been too early to draw conclusion about the true impact of NAFTA on trade flows and employment.

More recent surveys indicate that NAFTA's overall impact has been small but positive. From 1993 to 2001, trade between NAFTA's partners grew from $297 billion to $622 billion, an increase of 109 percent. Canada and Mexico are, now the number one and two trade partners of the United States, suggesting that the economies of the three NAFTA nations have become more closely integrated, there has also been strong productivity growth in all three countries over this period. In Mexico, labor productivity has increased by 50 percent since 1993, and the passage of NAFTA may bare contributed to this. However, estimates suggest that employment effects of NAFTA have been small. Perhaps the most significant impact of NAFTA has not been done economically, but politically. Many observers credit NAFTA with helping to create the background 1or increased political stability in Mexico. Mexico is now viewed as a stable democratic nation with a steadily growing economy, something that is beneficial to the United States, which shares a 2000-mile border with the country.

6.4.2.3 Enlargement

One issue confronting NAFTA is that of enlargement. A number of other Latin American countries have indicated their desire to eventually join NAFTA. The governments of both Canada and the United States are adopting a wait-and-see attitude with regard to most countries. Getting NAFTA approved was a bruising political experience, and neither government is eager to repeat the process soon. Nevertheless, the Canadian, Mexican and U.S. governments began talks in 1995 regarding Chile's possible entry into NAFTA. As of 2002, however, these talks had yielded little progress, partly because of political opposition in the U.S. Congress to expanding NAFTA. In December 2002, however, the United States and Chile did sign a bilateral free trade pact.

6.4.3 The Andean Pact

The Andean Pact was formed in 1969 when Bolivia, Chile, Ecuador, Colombia and Peru signed the Cartagena Agreement. The Andean Pact was largely based on the EU model, but it has been far less successful at achieving its stated goals. The integration steps begun in 1969 included an internal tariff reduction program, a common external tariff, a transportation policy, a common industrial policy, special concessions for the smallest members, Bolivia and Ecuador. By the mid-1980s, the Andean Pact had all but collapsed and had failed to achieve any of its stated objectives. There was no tariff-free trade between member countries, no common external tariff, and no harmonization of economic policies. Political and economic problems seem to have hindered cooperation between member countries. The countries of the Andean Pact have had to deal with low economic growth, hyperinflation, high unemployment, political unrest and crushing debt burdens. In addition, the dominant political ideology in many of the Andean countries during this period tended toward the radical/socialist end of the political spectrum. Since such an ideology is hostile to free market economic principles on which the Andean Pact was based, progress toward closer integration could not be expected.

The tide began to turn in the late 1980s when, after years of economic decline, the governments of Latin America began to adopt free market economic policies. In 1990, the heads of the five current members of the Andean Pact Bolivia, Ecuador, Peru, Colombia and Venezuela met in the Gab/pages Islands. The resulting Galapagos Declaration effectively relaunched the Andean Pact. The declaration's objectives included the establishment of a free trade area by 1992, a customs union by 1994, and a common market by 1995.

This last milestone has not been reached. However, there are some grounds for cautious optimism. For the first time, the controlling political ideology of the Andean countries is at least consistent with the free market principles underlying a common market. In addition, since the Galapagos Declaration, internal tariff levels have been reduced by all five members, and a customs union with a common external tariff was established in mid-1994, six months behind schedule.

Significant differences between member countries still exist which may make harmonization of policies and close integration difficult. For example, Venezuela's GNP per person is four times that of Bolivia's, and Ecuador's tiny production-line industries cannot compete with Colombia's and Venezuela's more advanced industries. Such differences are a recipe for disagreement and suggest that many of the adjustments required to achieve a true common market will be painful, even though the net benefits will probably outweigh the costs. To complicate matters even further, in recent years, Peru and Ecuador have fought a border war, Venezuela has remained aloof during a banking crisis, and Colombia has suffered from domestic political turmoil and problems related to its drug trade. This has led some to argue that tile pact is more "formal than real." The outlook for the Andean Pact started to change in 1998 when the group entered into negotiations with MERCOSUR to establish a South American free trade area. However, these negotiations broke down in 1999, and there has been no progress since then.

6.4.3.1 MEREOSUR

MERCOSUR originated in 1988 as a free trade pact between Brazil and Argentina.

The modest reductions in tariffs and quotas accompanying this pact reportedly helped bring about an 80 percent increase in trade between the two countries in the late 1980s. This success encouraged the expansion of the pact in March 1990 to include Paraguay and Uruguay. The initial aim was to establish a full free trade area by the end of 1994 and a common market sometime thereafter. The firm countries of MERCOSUR have a combined population of 200 million. With a market of this size, MERCOSUR could have a significant impact on the economic growth rate of the four economies. In December 1995, MERCOSUR's members agreed to a five-year program under which they hoped to perfect their free trade area and move toward a full customs union.

For its first eight years or so, MERCOSUR seemed to be making a positive contribution to the economic growth rates of its member states. Trade between MERCOSUR's tour core members quadrupled between 1990 and 1998. The combined GDP of the four member states grew at an annual average rate of 3.5 percent between 1990 and 1996, a performance that is significantly better than the four attained during the 1980s.

However, MERCOSUR has its critics, including Alexander Yeats, a senior economist at the World Bank, who wrote a stinging critique of MERCOSUR that was "leaked" to the press in October 1996. According to Yeats, the trade diversion effects of MERCOSUR outweigh its trade creation effects. Yeats points out that the fastest growing items in intra-MERCOSUR trade are cars, buses, agricultural equipment and other capital-intensive goods that are produced relatively inefficiently in the four member countries. In other words, MERCOSUR countries, insulated from outside competition by tariffs that run as high as 70 percent of value on motor vehicles, are investing in factories that build products that are too expensive to sell to anyone but themselves. The result, according to Yeats, is that MERCOSUR countries might not be able to compete globally once the group's external trade barriers come down. In the mean time, capital is being drawn away from more efficient enterprises. At the near term, countries with more efficient manufacturing enterprises lose because MERCOBUR's external trade barriers keep them out of the market.

The leak of the Yeats report caused a storm at the World Bank, which typically does not release reports that are critical of member states (the MERCOSUR countries are members of the World Bank). It also drew strong protests from Brazil, one of the primary targets of the critique. Still, in tacit admission that at least some of the arguments have merit, a senior MERCOSUR diplomat let it be known that external trade barriers will gradually be reduced, forcing member countries to compete globally. Many external MERCOSUR tariffs, which average 14 percent, are lower than they were before the group's creation, and there are plans for a hemispheric Free Trade Area of the Americas to be established by 2005 (which will combine MERCOSUR, NAFTA and other American nations). If that occurs, MERCOSUR will have no choice but to reduce its external tariffs further.

MERCOSUR hit a significant roadblock in 1998, when its member states slipped into recession and intrablock trade slumped. Trade fell further in 1999 following a financial crisis in Brazil that led to the devaluation of the Brazilian real, which immediately made the goods of other MERCOSUR members 40 percent more expensive in Brazil, their largest export market. At this point, progress toward establishing a full customs union all but came to a halt. Things deteriorated further in 2001 when Argentina, beset by economical stresses, suggested that the customs union be temporarily suspended.

Argentina wanted to suspend MERCOSUR's tariff so that it could abolish duties on imports of capital equipment, while raising those on consumer goods to 35 percent (MERCOSUR had established a 14 percent import tariff on both sets of goods). Brazil agreed to this request, effectively halting MERCOSUR's quest to become a fully functioning customs union. Hope for a revival in the importance of MERCOSUR rose in 2003 when new Brazilian President Lula da Silva announced his support for a revitalized and expanded MERCOSUR modeled after the EU with a larger membership, a common currency, and a democratically elected MERCOSUR parliament.

6.4.3.2 Central American Common Market end CARIEOM

Two other trade pacts in the Americas have not made much progress yet. In the early 1960s, Costa Rica, El Salvador, Guatemala, Honduras and Nicaragua attempted to set up a central American common market, it collapsed in 1969 when war broke out between Honduras and El Salvador after a riot at a soccer match between teams from the two countries. Since then the five countries have made some progress toward reviving their agreement, and the proposed common market was given a boost in 2003 when the United States signaled its intention to enter into bilateral free trade negotiations with the group.

A customs union was to have been created in 1991 between the English-speaking Caribbean countries under the auspices of the Caribbean Community. Referred to as CARICOM, it was established in 1973. However, it has repeatedly failed to progress toward economic integration. A formal commitment to economic and monetary union was adopted by CARICOM's member states in 1984, but since then little progress has been made. In October 1991, the CARICOM governments failed, for the third consecutive time, to meet a deadline for establishing a common external tariff.

6.4.3.3 Free Trade Area of the Americas

At a hemisphere-wide "Summit of the Americas" in December 1994, a Free Trade Area of the Americas (FTAA) was proposed. It took more than three years for the talks to start, but in April 1998, 34 heads of state traveled to Santiago, Chile, for the second Summit of the Americas where they formally inaugurated talks to establish an FTAA by 2005. The continuing talks have addressed a wide range of economic, political and environmental issues related to cross-border trade and investment. Although the United States was an early advocate of the FTAA, support from the United States seems to be mixed at this point. Because the United States has by far the largest economy in the region, strong the U.S. support is a precondition for establishment of the free trade area. Canada is chairing the crucial first stage of negotiations and hosted the second summit of the Americas in early 2001. If the FTAA is established, it will have major implications for cross-border trade and investment flows within the hemisphere. The FTAA would open a free trade umbrella over nearly 800 million people who accounted for more than \$11 trillion in GDP in 2000.

At this point, however, any definitive agreement is still several years away.

6.4.4 Regional Economic Integration Elsewhere

Numerous attempts at regional economic integration have been tried throughout Asia and Africa. However, few exist in anything other than name. Perhaps the most significant is the Association of Southeast Asian Nations (ASEAN). In addition, the Asia Pacific Economic Cooperation (APEC) forum has recently emerged as the seed of a potential free trade region.

6.4.4.1 Association of Southeast Asian Nations

Formed in 1967, ASEAN includes Brunei, Indonesia, Laos, Malaysia, Myanmar, Philippines, Singapore, Thailand, Vietnam. Laos, Myanmar and Vietnam have all joined recently, and their inclusion complicates matters because their economies are so far behind those of the original members. The basic objectives of ASEAN are to foster freer trade between member countries and to achieve cooperation in their industrial policies. Progress has been very limited, however, for example, only 5 percent of intra-ASEAN trade currently consists of goods whose tariffs have been reduced through an ASEAN preferential trade arrangement. Future progress seems limited because the financial crisis that swept through Southeast Asia in 1997 bit several ASEAN countries particularly hard, most notably Indonesia, Malaysia and Thailand.

Until these countries can get back on their economic feet, it is unlikely that much progress will be made.

6.4.4.2 Asia Pacific Economic Cooperation

Asia Pacific Economic Cooperation (APEC) was founded in 1990 at the suggestion of Australia. APEC currently has 21 member states including such economic power houses as the United States, Japan and China Collectively the 18 member states account for half of the world's GNP, 40 percent of world trade, and most of the growth in the world economy. The stated aim of APEC is to increase multilateral cooperation in view of the economic rise of the Pacific nations and the growing interdependence within the region. The U. S. support for APEC was also based on the belief that it might prove a viable strategy for heading off any moves to create Asian groupings from which it would be excluded.

Interest in APEC was heightened considerably in November 1993 when the heads of APEC member states met for the first time at a two-day conference in Seattle. Debate before the meeting speculated on the likely future role of APEC. One view was that APEC should commit itself to the ultimate formation of a free trade area. Such a move would transform the Pacific Rim from a geographical expression into the world's largest free trade area. Another view was that APEC would produce no more than hot air and lots of hot opportunities for the leaders involved. As it turned out, the APEC meeting produced little more than some vague commitments from member states to work together fur greater economic integration and a general lowering of trade barriers. However, significantly, member states did not rule out the possibility of closer economic cooperation in the future.

The heads of stare met again in November they agreed to take more concrete steps, and the joint statement at the end of the meeting formally committed APEC's industrialized members to remove their trade and investment barriers by 2010 and for developing economies to do so by 2020. They also called for a detailed blueprint charting how this might be achieved. This blueprint was presented and discussed at the next APEC summit, held in Osaka, Japan, in November 1995. This was followed by further annual meetings. At the 1997 meeting, member states formally endorsed proposals designed to remove trade barriers in 15 sectors, ranging from fish to toys. However, the plan is vague and commits APEC to doing no more than holding further talks. Commenting on the vagueness of APEC pronouncements, the influential Brookings Institution, an U. S. -based economic policy institution, noted that APEC "is in grave danger of shrinking into irrelevance as a serious forum."

Despite the slow progress, APEC is worth watching. If it eventually does transform itself into a free trade area, it will probably be the world's largest.

6.4.4.3 Regional Trade Blocs in Africa

African countries have been experimenting with regional trade blocs for half a century. There are now nine trade blocs on the African continent. Many countries are members of more than one group. Although the number of trade groups is impressive, progress toward the establishment of meaningful trade blocs has been slow.

Many of these groups have been dormant for years. Significant political turmoil in several African nations has persistently impeded any meaningful progress. Also, deep suspicion of free trade exists in several African countries. The argument most frequently heard is that because these countries bare less developed and less diversified economies, they need to be "protected" by tariff barriers from unfair foreign competition. Given the prevalence of this argument, it has been hard to establish free trade areas or customs unions.

The most recent attempt to reenergize the free trade movement in Africa occurred in early 2001, when Kenya, Uganda and Tanzania, member states of the East African Community (EAC), committed themselves to relaunching their bloc, 24 years after it collapsed. The three countries, with 80 million inhabitants, intend to establish a customs union, regional court, legislative assembly, and eventually, a political federation. Their program includes cooperation on immigration, road and telecommunication networks, investment and capital markets. However, while local business leaders welcomed the relaunch as a positive step, they were critical of the EAC's failure in practice to make progress on free trade.

6.4.5 Implications

Currently the most significant developments in regional economic integration are occurring in the EU and NAFTA. Although some of the Latin American trade blocs, APEC, and the proposed FTAA may have economic significance in the future, at present the EU and NAFTA have more profound and immediate implications for business practice. Accordingly, in this section we will concentrate on the business implications of those two groups. Similar conclusions, however, could be drawn with regard to the creation of a single market anywhere in the world.

6.4.5.1 Opportunities

The creation of a single market offers significant opportunities because markets that were formerly protected from foreign competition are opened. For example, in Europe before 1992 the large French and Italian markets were among the most protected. These markets are now much more open to foreign competition in the form of both exports and direct investment. Nonetheless, to fully exploit such opportunities, it may pay non-EU firms to set up EU subsidiaries many major U.S. firms have long had subsidiaries in Europe. Those that do not would be advised to consider establishing them now, lest they run the risk of being shut out of the EU by non-tariff barriers. Non-EU firms have rapidly increased their direct investment in the EU in anticipation of the creation of a single market. Between 1985 and 1989, for example, approximately 37 percent of the FDI inflows into industrialized countries were directed at the EC. By 1991, this figure had risen to 66 percent, and FDI inflows into the EU have been substantial ever since.

Additional opportunities arise from the inherent lower costs of doing business in a single market — as opposed to 15 national markets in the case of the EU or 3 national markets in the case of NAFTA. Free movement of goods across borders, harmonized product standards and simplified tax regimes make it possible for firms based in the EU and the NAFTA countries to realize potentially significant cost economies by centralizing production in those EU and NAFTA locations where the mix of factor costs and skills is optimal rather than producing a product in each of the 15 EU countries or the 3 NAFTA countries, a firm may be able to serve the whole EU or north American market from a single location. This location must be chosen carefully, of course, with an eye on local factor costs and skills.

For example, in response to the changes created by EU after 1992, the St. Paul-based 3M Company has been consolidating its European manufacturing and distribution facilities to take advantage of economies of scale. Thus, a plant in Great Britain now produces 3M's printing products and a German factory its reflective traffic control materials for the entire EU. In each case, 3M chose a location for centralized production after carefully considering the likely production costs in alternative locations within the EU. The ultimate goal of 3M is to dispense with all national distinctions, directing R&D, manufacturing, distribution and marketing for each product group from an EU headquarters. Similarly, Unilever, one of Europe's largest companies, began rationalizing its production in advance of 1992 to attain scale economies. Unilever concentrated its production of dishwashing powder for the EU in one plant, bath soap in another, and so on.

Even after the removal of barriers to trade and investment, enduring differences in culture and competitive practices often limit the ability of companies to realize cost economies by centralizing production in key locations and producing a standardized product for a single multi-country market. Consider the case of Atag Holdings NV, a Dutch maker of kitchen appliances. Due to enduring differences between nations within the EU's single market, A tag still has to produce various "national brands," which clearly limits the company's ability to attain scale economies.

6.4.5.2 Threats

Just as the emergence of single markets in the EU and America creates opportunities for business, it also presents a number of threats, for one thing, the business environment within each grouping will become more competitive.

The lowering of barriers to trade and investment between countries is likely to lead to increased price competition throughout the EU and NAFTA. For example, before 1992 a Volkswagen Golf cost 55 percent more in Great Britain than in Denmark and 29 percent more in Ireland than in Greece. Over time, such price differentials will vanish in a single market. This is a direct threat to any firm doing business in EU or NAFTA countries. To survive in the tougher single-market environment, firms must take advantage of the opportunities offered by the creation of a single market to rationalize their production and reduce their costs. Otherwise, they will be severely disadvantaged.

A further threat to firms outside these trading blocs arises from the likely long term improvement in the competitive position of many firms within the areas. This is particularly relevant in the EU, where many firms are currently limited by a high cost structure in their ability to compete globally with North American and Asian firms. The creation of a single market and the resulting increased competition in the EU is beginning to produce serious attempts by many EU firms to reduce their cost structure by rationalizing production. This could transform many EU companies into efficient global competitors. The message for non EU businesses is that they need to prepare for the emergence of more capable European competitors by reducing their own cost structures.

Another threat to firms outside of trading areas is the threat of being shut out of the single market by the creation of a "trade fortress." The charge that regional economic integration might lead to a fortress mentality is most often leveled at the EU. Although the free trade philosophy underpinning the EU theoretically argues against the creation of any fortress in Europe, there are occasional signs that the EU may raise barriers to imports and investment in certain "politically sensitive" areas, such as autos. Non-EU firms might be well advised, therefore, to set up their own EU operations as quickly as possible. This could also occur in the NAFTA countries, but it seems less likely.

Finally, the emerging role of the European Commission in competition policy suggests the EU is increasingly willing and able to intervene and impose conditions on companies proposing mergers and acquisitions. This is a threat insofar as it limits the ability of firms to pursue the corporate strategy of their choice.

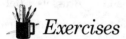

Exercises

1. Define the key terms listed below:

PTA (Preferential Trade Agreement);

FTA (Free Trade Area);

Customs Union;

Common Market;

Economic Union;

Monetary Union;

Regional Economic Integration.

2. What are the economic effects of Regional Economic Integration on member countries?

3. Tell something about the Regional Economic Integration in Europe.

4. What are the opportunities and threats of Regional Economic Integration?

Chapter 7 GATT and WTO

7.1 Brief History

Much of the history of those 47 years was written in Geneva. But it also traces a journey that spanned the continents, from that hesitant start in 1948 in Havana (Cuba), via Annecy (France), Torquay (UK), Tokyo (Japan), Punta del Este (Uruguay), Montreal (Canada), Brussels (Belgium) and finally to Marrakesh (Morocco) in 1994. During that period, the trading system came under GATT, salvaged from the aborted attempt to create the ITO. GATT helped establish a strong and prosperous multilateral trading system that became more and more liberal through rounds of trade negotiations. But by the 1980s the system needed a thorough overhaul. This led to the Uruguay Round, and ultimately to the WTO.

7.1.1 GATT: "Provisional" for almost Half a Century

From 1948 to 1994, the General Agreement on Tariffs and Trade (GATT) provided the rules for many of world trade and presided over periods that saw some of the highest growth rates in international commerce. It seemed well-established, but throughout those 47 years, it was a provisional agreement and organization.

The original intention was to create a third institution to handle the trade side of international economic cooperation, joining the two "Bretton Woods" institutions, the World Bank and the International Monetary Fund. Over 50 countries participated in negotiations to create an International Trade Organization (ITO) as a specialized agency of the United Nations. The draft ITO Charter was ambitious. It extended beyond world trade disciplines, to include rules on employment, commodity agreements, restrictive business practices, international investment, and services. The aim was to create the ITO at an UN Conference on Trade and Employment in Havana, Cuba in 1947.

Meanwhile, 15 countries had begun talks in December 1945 to reduce and bind customs tariffs. With the Second World War only recently ended, they wanted to give an early boost to trade liberalization, and to begin to correct the legacy of protectionist measures which remained in place from the early 1930s.

This first round of negotiations resulted in a package of trade rules and 45000 tariff concessions affecting $10 billion of trade, about one fifth of the world's total. The group had expanded to 23 by the time the deal was signed on 30 October, 1947. The tariff concessions came into effect by 30

June 1948 through a "Protocol of Provisional Application". And so the new General Agreement on Tariffs and Trade was born, with 23 founding members (officially "contracting parties").

The 23 were also part of the larger group negotiating the ITO Charter. One of the provisions of GATT says that they should accept some of the trade rules of the draft. This, they believed, should be done swiftly and "provisionally" in order to protect the value of the tariff concessions they had negotiated. They spelt out how they envisaged the relationship between GATT and the ITO Charter, but they also allowed for the possibility that the ITO might not be created. They were right.

The Havana conference began on 21 November 1947, less than a month after GATT was signed. The ITO Charter was finally agreed in Havana in March 1948, but ratification in some national legislatures proved impossible. The most serious opposition was in the U. S. Congress, even though the U. S. government had been one of the driving forces. In 1950, the United States government announced that it would not seek congressional ratification of the Havana Charter, and the ITO was effectively dead. So, the GATT became the only multilateral instrument governing international trade from 1948 until the WTO was established in 1995.

For almost half a century, the GATT's basic legal principles remained much as they were in 1948. There were additions in the form of a section on development added in the 1960s and "plurilateral" agreements (i. e. with voluntary membership) in the 1970s, and efforts to reduce tariffs further continued. Much of this was achieved through a series of multilateral negotiations known as "trade rounds"- the biggest leaps forward in international trade liberalization have come through these rounds which were held under GATT's auspices.

In the early years, the GATT trade rounds concentrated on further reducing tariffs. Then, the Kennedy Round in the mid-sixties brought about a GATT Anti-Dumping Agreement and a section on development. The Tokyo Round during the seventies was the first major attempt to tackle trade barriers that do not take the form of tariffs, and to improve the system. The eighth, the Uruguay Round of 1986-1994, was the last and highest extensive of all. It led to the WTO and a new set of agreements.

7.1.2 The Tokyo Round: First Try to Reform the System

The Tokyo Round lasted from 1973 to 1979, with 102 countries participating. It continued GATT's efforts to progressively reduce tariffs. The results included an average one-third cut in customs duties in the world's nine major industrial markets, bringing the average tariff on industrial products down to 4.7%. The tariff reductions phased in over a period of eight years, and involved an element of "harmonization"- the higher the tariff, the larger the cut, proportionally.

In other issues, the Tokyo Round had mixed results. It failed to come to grips with the fundamental problems affecting farm trade and also stopped short of providing a modified agreement on "safeguards" (emergency import measures). Nevertheless, a series of agreements on non-tariff barriers did emerge from the negotiations, in some cases interpreting existing GATT rules, in others breaking entirely new ground. In most cases, only a relatively small number of (mainly industrialized) GATT members subscribed to these agreements and arrangements. Because they were not accepted by the full GATT membership, they were often informally called "codes".

They were not multilateral, but they were a beginning. Several codes were eventually amended in the Uruguay Round and turned into multilateral commitments accepted by all WTO members. Only four remained "plurilateral"— those on government procurement, bovine meat, civil aircraft and dairy products. In 1997, WTO members agreed to terminate the bovine meat and dairy agreements, leaving only two.

7.1.3 Did GATT Succeed

GATT was provisional with a limited field of action, but its success over 47 years in promoting and securing the liberalization of many of world trade is incontestable. Continual reductions in tariffs alone helped spur very high rates of world trade growth during the 1950s and 1960s — around 8% a year on average. And the momentum of trade liberalization helped ensure that trade growth consistently out-paced production growth throughout the GATT era, a measure of countries' increasing ability to trade with each other and to reap the benefits of trade. The rush of new members during the Uruguay Round demonstrated that the multilateral trading system was recognized as an anchor for development and an instrument of economic and trade reform.

But all was not well. As time passed new problems arose. The Tokyo Round in the 1970s was an attempt to tackle some of these but its achievements were limited. This was a sign of difficult times to come.

GATT's success in reducing tariffs to such a low level, combined with a series of economic recessions in the 1970s and early 1980s, drove governments to devise other forms of protection for sectors facing increased foreign competition. High rates of unemployment and constant factory closures led governments in Western Europe and North America to seek bilateral market-sharing arrangements with competitors and to embark on a subsidies race to maintain their holds on agricultural trade. Both these changes undermined GATT's credibility and effectiveness.

The problem was not just a deteriorating trade policy environment. By the early 1980s the General Agreement was clearly no longer as relevant to the realities of world trade as it had been in the 1940s. For a start, world trade had become far more complex and important than 40 years before: the globalization of the world economy was underway, trade in services — not covered by GATT rules — was of major interest to more and more countries, and international investment had expanded. The expansion of services trade was also closely tied to further increases in world merchandise trade. In other respects, GATT had been found wanting. For instance, in agriculture, loopholes in the multilateral system were heavily exploited, and efforts at liberalizing agricultural trade met with little success. In the textiles and clothing sector, an exception to GATT's normal disciplines was negotiated in the 1960s and early 1970s, leading to the Multifiber Arrangement. Even GATT's institutional structure and its dispute settlement system were causing concern.

These and other factors convinced GATT members that a new effort to reinforce and extended the multilateral system should be attempted. That effort resulted in the Uruguay Round, the Marrakesh Declaration, and the creation of the WTO.

7.1.4 The Uruguay Round

It took seven and a half years, almost twice the original schedule. By the end, 123 countries were taking part. It covered almost all trade, from toothbrushes to pleasure boats, from banking to telecommunications, from the genes of wild rice to AIDS treatments. It was quite simply the largest trade negotiation ever, and most probably the largest negotiation of any kind in history.

At times it seemed doomed to fail. But in the end, the Uruguay Round brought about the biggest reform of the world's trading system since GATT was created at the end of the Second World War. And yet, despite its troubled progress, the Uruguay Round did see some early results. Within only two years, participants had agreed on a package of cuts in import duties on tropical products – which are mainly exported by developing countries. They had also revised the rules for settling disputes, with some measures implemented on the spot. And they called for regular reports on GATT members' trade policies, a move considered important for making trade regimes transparent around the world.

A Round to End All Rounds:

The seeds of the Uruguay Round were sown in November 1982 at a ministerial meeting of GATT members in Geneva. Although the ministers intended to launch a major new negotiation, the conference stalled on agriculture and was widely regarded as a failure. In fact, the work programme that the ministers agreed formed the basis for what was to become the Uruguay Round negotiating agenda.

Nevertheless, it took four more years of exploring, clarifying issues and painstaking consensus-building, before ministers agreed to launch the new round. They did so in September 1986, in Punta del Este, Uruguay. They eventually accepted a negotiating agenda that covered virtually every outstanding trade policy issue. The talks were going to extend the trading system into several new areas, notably trade in services and intellectual property, and to reform trade in the sensitive sectors of agriculture and textiles. All the original GATT articles were up for review. It was the biggest negotiating mandate on trade ever agreed, and the ministers gave themselves four years to complete it.

Two years later, in December 1988, ministers met again in Montreal, Canada, for what was supposed to be an assessment of progress at the round's half-way point. The purpose was to clarify the agenda for the remaining two years, but the talks ended in a deadlock that was not resolved until officials met more quietly in Geneva the following April.

Despite the difficulty, during the Montreal meeting, ministers did agree a package of early results. These included some concessions on market access for tropical products – aimed at assisting developing countries – as well as a streamlined dispute settlement system, and the Trade Policy Review Mechanism which provided for the first comprehensive, systematic and regular reviews of national trade policies and practices of GATT members. The round was supposed to end when ministers met once more in Brussels, in December 1990. But they disagreed on how to reform agricultural trade and decided to extend the talks. The Uruguay Round entered its bleakest period.

Despite the poor political outlook, a considerable amount of technical work continued, leading to the first draft of a final legal agreement. This draft "Final Act" was compiled by the then GATT director-general, Arthur Dunkel, who chaired the negotiations at officials' level. It was put on the table in Geneva in December 1991. The text fulfilled every part of the Punta del Este mandate, with one exception – it did not contain the participating countries' lists of commitments for cutting import duties and opening their services markets. The draft became the basis for the final agreement.

Over the following two years, the negotiations lurched between impending failure, to predictions of imminent success. Several deadlines came and went. New points of major conflict emerged to join agriculture: services, market access, anti-dumping rules and the proposed creation of a new institution. Differences between the United States and European Union became central to hopes for a final, successful conclusion.

In November 1992, the U.S. and EU settled most of their differences on agriculture in a deal known informally as the "Blair House accord". By July 1993 the "Quad" (The U.S., EU, Japan and Canada) announced significant progress in negotiations on tariffs and related subjects ("market access"). It took until 15 December 1993 for every issue to be finally resolved and for negotiations on market access for goods and services to be concluded (although some final touches was completed in talks on market access a few weeks later). On 15 April 1994, the deal was signed by ministers from most of the 123 participating governments at a meeting in Marrakesh, Morocco.

The delay had some merits. It allowed some negotiations to progress further than would have been possible in 1990: for example some aspects of services and intellectual property, and the creation of the WTO itself. But the task had been immense, and negotiation-fatigue felt in trade bureaucracies around the world. The difficulty of reaching agreement on a complete package containing almost the entire range of current trade issues led some to conclude that a negotiation on this scale would never again be possible. Yet, the Uruguay Round agreements contain timetables for new negotiations on a number of topics. And by 1996, some countries were openly calling for a new round early in the next century. The response was mixed; but the Marrakesh agreement did already include commitments to reopen negotiations on agriculture and services at the turn of the century. These began in early 2000 and were incorporated into the Doha Development Agenda in late 2001.

7.1.5 What Happened to GATT

The WTO replaced GATT as an international organization, but the General Agreement still exists as the WTO's umbrella treaty for trade in goods, updated as a result of the Uruguay Round negotiations. Trade lawyers distinguish between GATT 1994, the updated parts of GATT, and GATT 1947, the original agreement which is still the heart of GATT 1994. Confusing? For most of us, it's enough to simply refer to "GATT".

The post-Uruguay Round built-in agenda. Many Uruguay Round agreements set timetables for future work. Part of this "built-in agenda" started almost immediately. In some areas, it included new or further negotiations, in other areas, it included assessments or reviews of the situation at specified times. Some negotiations were quickly completed, notably in basic telecommunications, financial services. (Member governments also swiftly agreed a deal for freer trade in information technology products, an issue outside the "built-in agenda".)

The agenda originally built into the Uruguay Round agreements has seen additions and modifications. A number of items are now part of the Doha Agenda, some of them updated.

There were well over 30 items in the original built-in agenda. This is a selection of highlights:

(1)1996.

①Maritime services: market access negotiations to end (30 June 1996, suspended to 2000, now part of Doha Development Agenda);

②Services and environment: deadline for working party report (ministerial conference, December 1996);

③Government procurement of services: negotiations start.

(2)1997.

①Basic telecoms: negotiations end (15 February);

②Financial services: negotiations end (30 December);

③Intellectual property, creating a multilateral system of notification and registration of geographical indications for wines: negotiations start, now part of Doha Development Agenda.

(3)1998.

①Textiles and clothing: new phase begins 1 January;

②Services (emergency safeguards): results of negotiations on emergency safeguards to take effect (by 1 January 1998, deadline now March 2004);

③Rules of origin: Work programme on harmonization of rules of origin to be completed (20 July 1998);

④Government procurement: further negotiations start, for improving rules and procedures (by end of 1998);

⑤Dispute settlement: full review of rules and procedures (to start by end of 1998).

(4)1999.

Intellectual property: certain exceptions to patentability and protection of plant varieties: review starts.

(5)2000.

①Agriculture: negotiations start, now part of Doha Development Agenda;

②Services: new round of negotiations start, now part of Doha Development Agenda;

③Tariff bindings: review of definition of "principle supplier" having negotiating rights under GATT Art 28 on modifying bindings;

④Intellectual property: first of two-yearly reviews of the implementation of the agreement.

(6)2002.

Textiles and clothing: new phase begins 1st January.

(7)2005.

Textiles and clothing: full integration into GATT and agreement expires 1st January.

7.2 WTO

7.2.1 Overview

The World Trade Organization (WTO) deals with the rules of trade between nations at a global or near-global level. But there is more to it than that.

There are a number of ways of looking at the WTO. It's an organization for liberalizing trade. It's a forum for governments to negotiate trade agreements. It's a place for them to settle trade disputes. It operates a system of trade rules. (But it's not Superman, just in case anyone thought it could solve – or cause – all the world's problems!)

Above all, it's a negotiating forum... Essentially, the WTO is a place where member governments go, to try to sort out the trade problems they face with each other. The first step is to talk. The WTO was born out of negotiations, and everything the WTO does is the result of negotiations. The bulk of the WTO's current work comes from the 1986-1994 negotiations called the Uruguay Round and earlier negotiations under the General Agreement on Tariffs and Trade (GATT). The WTO is currently the host to new negotiations, under the "Doha Development Agenda" launched in 2001.

Where countries have faced trade barriers and wanted them lowered, the negotiations have helped to liberalize trade. But the WTO is not just about liberalizing trade, and in some circumstances its rules support maintaining trade barriers – for example to protect consumers or prevent the spread of disease.

It's a set of rules... At its heart are the WTO agreements, negotiated and signed by the bulk of the world's trading nations. These documents provide the legal ground-rules for international commerce. They are essentially contracts, binding governments to keep their trade policies within agreed limits. Although negotiated and signed by governments, the goal is to help producers of goods and services, exporters and importers conduct their business, while allowing governments to meet social and environmental objectives.

The system's overriding purpose is to help trade flow as freely as possible – so long as there are no undesirable side-effects – because this is important for economic development and well-being. That partly means removing obstacles. It also means ensuring that individuals, companies and governments know what the trade rules are around the world, and giving them the confidence that there will be no sudden changes of policy. In other words, the rules have to be "transparent" and predictable.

And it helps to settle disputes... This is a third important side to the WTO's work. Trade relations often involve conflicting interests. Agreements, including those painstakingly negotiated in the WTO system, often need interpreting. The most harmonious way to settle these differences is through some neutral procedures based on an agreed legal foundation. That is the purpose behind the dispute settlement process written into the WTO agreements.

Born in 1995, but not so young ... The WTO began life on 1st January 1995, but its trading system is half a century older. Since 1948, the General Agreement on Tariffs and Trade (GATT) had provided the rules for the system. (The second ministerial meeting of WTO held in Geneva in May 1998, including a celebration of the 50th anniversary of the system.)

It did not take too long for the General Agreement to give birth to an unofficial, *de facto* international organization, also known informally as GATT. Over the years GATT evolved through several rounds of negotiations.

The last and largest GATT round, was the Uruguay Round which lasted from 1986 to 1994 and led to the WTO's creation. Whereas GATT had mainly dealt with trade in goods, the WTO and its agreements now cover trade in services, and in traded inventions, creations and designs (intellectual property).

7.2.2 Principles of the Trading System

The WTO agreements are lengthy and complex because they are legal texts covering a wide range of activities. They deal with: agriculture, textiles and clothing, banking, telecommunications, government purchases, industrial standards and product safety, food sanitation regulations, intellectual property and much more. But a number of simple, fundamental principles run throughout all of these documents. These principles are the foundation of the multilateral trading system.

A closer look at these principles.

7.2.2.1 Trade without Discrimination

1) Most-Favoured-Nation (MFN): Treating Other People Equally

Under the WTO agreements, countries cannot normally discriminate between their trading partners. Grant someone a special favour (such as a lower customs duty rate for one of their products) and you have to do the same for all other WTO members.

This principle is known as most-favoured-nation (MFN) treatment. It is so important that it is the first article of the General Agreement on Tariffs and Trade (GATT), which governs trade in goods. MFN is also a priority in the General Agreement on Trade in Services (GATS) (Article 2) and the Agreement on Trade-Related Aspects of Intellectual Property Rights (TRIPS) (Article 4), although in each agreement the principle is handled slightly differently. Together, those three agreements cover all three main areas of trade handled by the WTO.

Some exceptions are allowed. For example, countries can set up a free trade agreement that applies only to goods traded within the group-discriminating against goods from outside. Or they can give developing countries special access to their markets. Or a country can raise barriers against products that are considered to be traded unfairly from specific countries. And in services, countries are allowed, in limited circumstances, to discriminate. But the agreements only permit these exceptions under strict conditions. In general, MFN means that every time a country lowers a trade barrier or opens up a market, it has to do so for the same goods or services from all its trading partners — whether rich or poor, weak or strong.

2) National Treatment

Treating foreigners and locals equally imported and locally-produced goods should be treated equally— at least after the foreign goods have entered the market. The same should apply to foreign and domestic services, and to foreign and local trademarks, copyrights and patents. This principle of "national treatment" (giving others the same treatment as one's own nationals) is also found in all the three main WTO agreements (Article 3 of GATT, Article 17 of GATS and Article 3 of TRIPS), although once again the principle is handled slightly differently in each of these.

National treatment only applies once a product, service or item of intellectual property has entered the market. Therefore, charging customs duty on an import is not a violation of national treatment even if locally-produced products are not charged an equivalent tax.

(1) Freer Trade: gradually, through negotiation.

Lowering trade barriers is one of the most obvious means of encouraging trade. The barriers concerned include customs duties (or tariffs) and measures such as import bans or quotas that restrict quantities selectively. From time to time other issues such as red tape and exchange rate policies have also been discussed.

Since GATT's creation in 1947-1948 there have been eight rounds of trade negotiations. A ninth round, under the Doha Development Agenda, is now underway. At first these focused on lowering tariffs (customs duties) on imported goods. As a result of the negotiations, by the mid-1990s industrial countries' tariff rates on industrial goods had fallen steadily to less than 4%.

But by the 1980s, the negotiations had expanded to cover non-tariff barriers on goods, and to the new areas such as services and intellectual property.

Opening markets can be beneficial, but it also requires adjustment. The WTO agreements allow countries to introduce changes gradually, through "progressive liberalization". Developing countries are usually given longer to fulfil their obligations.

(2) Predictability: through binding and transparency.

Sometimes, promising not to raise a trade barrier can be as important as lowering one, because the promise gives businesses a clearer view of their future opportunities. With stability and predictability, investment is encouraged, jobs are created and consumers can fully enjoy the benefits of competition-choice and lower prices. The multilateral trading system is an attempt by governments to make the business environment stable and predictable.

In the WTO, when countries agree to open their markets for goods or services, they "bind" their commitments. For goods, these bindings amount to ceilings on customs tariff rates. Sometimes countries tax imports at rates that are lower than the bound rates. Frequently this is the case in developing countries. In developed countries the rates actually charged and the bound rates tend to be the same.

A country can change its bindings, but only after negotiating with its trading partners, which could mean compensating them for loss of trade. One of the achievements of the Uruguay Round of multilateral trade talks was to increase the amount of trade under binding commitments (see table). In agriculture, 100% of products now have bound tariffs. The result of all this: a substantially higher degree of market security for traders and investors.

The system tries to improve predictability and stability in other ways as well. One way is to discourage the use of quotas and other measures used to set limits on quantities of imports – administering quotas can lead to more red-tape and accusations of unfair play. Another is to make countries' trade rules as clear and public ("transparent") as possible. Many WTO agreements require governments to disclose their policies and practices publicly within the country or by notifying the WTO. The regular surveillance of national trade policies through the Trade Policy Review Mechanism provides a further means of encouraging transparency both domestically and at the multilateral level.

7.2.2.2 Promoting Fair Competition

The WTO is sometimes described as a "free trade" institution, but that is not entirely accurate. The system does allow tariffs and, in limited circumstances, other forms of protection. More accurately, it is a system of rules dedicated to open, fair and undistorted competition.

The rules on non-discrimination – MFN and national treatment – are designed to secure fair conditions of trade. So too are those on dumping (exporting at below cost to gain market share) and subsidies. The issues are complex, and the rules try to establish what is fair or unfair, and how governments can respond, in particular by charging additional import duties calculated to compensate for damage caused by unfair trade.

Many of the other WTO agreements aim to support fair competition: in agriculture, intellectual property, services, for example. The agreement on government procurement (a "plurilateral" agreement because it is signed by only a few WTO members) extends competition rules to purchases by thousands of government entities in many countries. And so on.

7.2.2.3 Encouraging Development and Economic Reform

The WTO system contributes to development. On the other hand, developing countries need flexibility in the time they take to implement the system's agreements. And the agreements themselves inherit the earlier provisions of GATT that allow for special assistance and trade concessions for developing countries.

Over three quarters of WTO members are developing countries and countries in transition to market economies. During the seven and a half years of the Uruguay Round, over 60 of these countries implemented trade liberalization programmes autonomously. At the same time, developing countries and transition economies were much more active and influential in the Uruguay Round negotiations than in any previous round, and they are even more so in the current Doha Development Agenda.

At the end of the Uruguay Round, developing countries were prepared to take on most of the obligations that are required of developed countries. But the agreements did give them transition periods to adjust to the more unfamiliar and perhaps difficult WTO provisions – particularly so for the poorest, "least-developed" countries. A ministerial decision adopted at the end of the round says better-off countries should accelerate implementing market access commitments on goods exported by the least-developed countries, and it seeks increased technical assistance for them. More recently, developed countries have started to allow duty-free and quota-free imports for almost all products from least-developed countries. On all of these, the WTO and its members are still going through a learning process. The current Doha Development Agenda includes developing countries' concerns about the difficulties they face in implementing the Uruguay Round agreements.

7.2.3 Case Study: the Timetable in Practice

On 23 January 1995, Venezuela complained to the Dispute Settlement Body that the United States was applying rules that discriminated against gasoline imports, and formally requested consultations with the United States. Just over a year later (on 29 January 1996) the dispute panel completed its final report. (By then, Brazil had joined the case, lodging its own complaint in April 1996. The same panel considered both complaints.) The United States appealed and the Appellate Body completed its report, and the Dispute Settlement Body adopted the report on 20th May 1996, one year and four months after the complaint was first lodged.

The United States and Venezuela then took six and a half months to agree on what the United States should do. The agreed period for implementing the solution was 15 months from the date the appeal was concluded (20th May 1996 to 20th August 1997).

The case arose because the United States applied stricter rules on the chemical characteristics of imported gasoline than it did for domestically-refined gasoline. Venezuela (and later Brazil) said this was unfair because U.S. gasoline did not have to meet the same standards – it violated the "national treatment" principle and could not be justified under exceptions to normal WTO rules for health and environmental conservation measures. The dispute panel agreed with Venezuela and Brazil. The appeal report upheld the panel's conclusions (making some changes to the panel's legal interpretation). The United States agreed with Venezuela that it would amend its regulations within 15 months and on 26 August 1997 it reported to the Dispute Settlement Body that a new regulation had been signed on 19 August (see Table 7.1).

Chapter 7 GATT and WTO

Table 7.1

Time (0 = start of case)	Target/Actual period	Date	Action
−5 years		1990	U. S. Clean Air Act amended
−4 months		September 1994	U. S. restricts gasoline imports under Clean Air Act
0	"60 days"	23 January 1995	Venezuela complains to Dispute Settlement Body, asks for consultation with U. S.
+1 month		24 February 1995	Consultations take place. Fail
+2 months		25 March 1995	Venezuela asks Dispute Settlement Body for a panel
+2½ months	"30 days"	10 April 1995	Dispute Settlement Body agrees to appoint panel. U. S. does not block. (Brazil starts complaint, requests consultation with U. S..)
+3 months		28 April 1995	Panel appointed. (31 May, panel assigned to Brazilian complaint as well)
+6 months	9 months (target is 6-9)	10~12 July and 13~15 July 1995	Panel meets
+11 months		11 December 1995	Panel gives interim report to U. S., Venezuela and Brazil for comment
+1 year		29 January 1996	Panel circulates final report to Dispute Settlement Body
+1 year, 1 month		21 February 1996	U. S. appeals
+1 year, 3 months	"60 days"	29 April 1996	Appellate Body submits report
+1 year, 4 months	"30 days"	20 May 1996	Dispute Settlement Body adopts panel and appeal reports
+1 year, 10½ months		3 December 1996	U. S. and Venezuela agree on what U. S. should do (implementation period is 15 months from 20 May)
+1 year, 11½ months		9 January 1997	U. S. makes first of monthly reports to Dispute Settlement Body on status of implementation
+2 years, 7 months		19-20 August 1997	U. S. signs new regulation (19th). End of agreed implementation period (20th)

7.2.4 Analysis

Background: Congress in 1963 passed the Clean Air Act, which is supposed to prevent air pollution in the United States. As part of the implementation of the act, the U. S. Environmental Protection Agency regulates the composition of gasoline in an effort to reduce vehicle emissions of toxic air pollutants. In 1994, the EPA decided to establish a baseline cleanliness level for each domestic refiner, and then the future products of those refiners would be compared to their individual baseline. For foreign refiners, because of concern about the quality of foreign data, the EPA decided to use as a baseline standard the average of the domestic baselines.

How the WTO got involved: Venezuela and Brazil in 1995 went to the World Trade Organization and challenged the standards the EPA had adopted for regulating gasoline composition. The countries argued that under certain circumstances, the U.S. rules would require that imported gasoline be cleaner than domestically produced gasoline.

What the WTO said: The panel found that the U.S. rule was discriminatory against foreign refineries.

Result: The EPA rewrote its regulations for foreign refineries, which can now accept the average U.S. baseline standard or can apply for their own individual baseline standards if they agree to allow the United States to audit their data.

How the United States sees it: The Clinton administration insists that they have been able to comply with the WTO ruling without weakening standards for gasoline cleanliness.

How environmental groups see it: Environmental groups say the EPA adopted a weaker method for regulating gasoline that the agency had previously considered unenforceable.

Postscript: An environmental group and the oil industry sued the federal government over the gasoline rules. The federal government won. The EPA says air quality monitoring shows no negative impact from the rule change prompted by the WTO decision.

7.3 China and WTO

Affordable luxury was probably the first benefit most Chinese imagined they would enjoy when the country joined the World Trade Organization (WTO) four years ago.

But there are many other positive changes that have taken place since China joined the global trading club.

There are great choices of services, more job opportunities and a greater desire to learn English.

WTO membership has brought cheaper, diversified foreign products to supermarkets, improvements in the services offered by banks, and chances to attend all sorts of training courses with a view to securing better positions with different employers.

But when we review the changes that have taken place in China since 2001, we have to say the impact of the WTO on Chinese people reaches far beyond mere material comfort.

An even more profound change has taken place in many people's mindset, no matter whether they are civil servants, the employees of businesses or farmers.

New concepts such as market economy, fair competition, transparency, win-win, the rule of law and international practice are no longer just buzzwords, but have seeped into everyday thinking and become part of daily life.

The broader opening up has widened horizons, ushered in social changes, enriched knowledge about international practices, and increased eagerness for integration in the world arena. Many have abandoned old ideas and working habits formed under the rigid planned economy.

What is really behind these changes is the transformation of the whole country from an inward-looking, planned economy to a more market-oriented powerhouse, and the reform of domestic enterprises that are adopting modern management systems.

The past four years have witnessed Chinese integration with the world economy in which China has become a fully-fledged player.

At home, laws and regulations have been revised so as to gradually open the market to foreign companies according to its commitments.

China has become a critical part of the global economy, contributing 12 percent to world trade growth and 10 percent to world economic growth last year.

Over the four years, China has attracted investment from the world's major multinationals, grown into a dominant manufacturer of goods, and became the third largest trader with foreign trade topping USMYM1.1 trillion last year.

For domestic enterprises, the impact of WTO membership is even more obvious. One needs only to observe how hot competition is in some sectors such as retailing, insurance and banking.

Pressure imposed by the market entry of multinationals has triggered sweeping reforms among domestic enterprises.

To narrow the gap with foreign rivals, they are striving to become modern enterprises applying advanced management and marketing skills.

The wider access to the world market has also encouraged a global perspective among enterprises when positioning themselves and their products in the market.

Reforms, as well as changes in overall economic performance, have inevitably influenced individuals.

More and more people have realized that Chinese integration with the world economy is an irreversible trend, and have been preparing in different ways.

To play the WTO game, firms have to learn international rules, refresh their ideas and abide by the new regulations.

In addition to its role as an administrator of society, the government has been striving to provide more services for the market economy making efforts to increase awareness of good service, fairness and efficiency among civil servants.

WTO protocols on transparency, and in particular WTO supervision of government performance, have put government departments under more pressure to deliver, leading to changes in their working style.

That explains government departments' simplified procedures and improved efficiency and more smiling civil servants.

Market-oriented reforms at domestic enterprises have also catalyzed changes in ideas and activities among employees. Fearing they may lose their jobs, many workers have been striving to improve their efficiency, acquire new skills and provide better services to make themselves, as well as their companies, more competitive.

In the past, a job at one of Chinese "big four" banks was described as a golden bowl meaning a high salary, rights to grant loans, a light workload and almost no chance of being laid-off.

But staffs are facing tough times as banks launch massive market-oriented reform programmes in preparation for competition when China fully opens its banking sector in 2006.

An important part of reform is setting higher standards for business performance and service provision. To meet the new challenges, staffs have to embrace concepts such as good service and efficiency, and improve their working habits.

WTO commitments have facilitated increased competition in many other industries, which in turn have motivated individuals to try to adapt to the new environment.

Another change in mindset is the increasing awareness of rights.

With China implementing its WTO commitments to foster the highest degree of transparency possible and the rule of law throughout society, citizens have learned to ask for better government services, to be treated equally, and call for greater government efforts to implement international rules and practices. That was rarely seen before 2001.

This process is not a flash in the pan. Only when new ideas, rules and practices are embodied in the actions of everyone in society will we really be able to claim that we are fully integrated with the world.

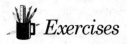
Exercises

1. Define the key terms listed below:
MFN (Most-Favored-Nation);
National Treatment.
2. What are the principles of the trading system?
3. How much do you know about the transition from GATT to WTO?
4. Tell something about the relationship between China and WTO.

Chapter 8　Foreign Direct Investment and Transnational Corporations

8.1　Case Study: Starbucks' Foreign Direct Investment

Thirty years ago, Starbucks was a single store in Seattle's Pike Place Market selling premium roasted coffee. Today, it is a global roaster and retailer of coffee with more than 6000 stores, an increasing proportion of which are to he found outside the United States Starbucks Corporation set out on its current course in the 1980s when the company's director of marketing, Howard Schultz, came back from a trip to Italy enchanted with the Italian coffee house experience Schultz, who later became CEO, persuaded the company's owners to experiment with the coffeehouse format and the Starbucks experience was born. The basic strategy was to sell the company's own premium roasted coffee, along with freshly brewed espresso style coffee beverages, a variety of pastries, coffee accessories, teas and other products, in a taste fully designed coffeehouse setting the company also stressed providing superior customer service. Reasoning that motivated employees provide the best customer service, Starbucks executives devoted much attention to employee hiring and training programs and progressive compensation policies that gave even part time employees stock option grants and medical benefits. The formula met with spectacular success in the United States, where Starbucks went from obscurity to one of the best known brands in the country in a decade.

In 1995, with almost 700 stores across the United States, Starbucks began exploring foreign opportunities. Its first target market was Japan. Although Starbucks had resisted a franchising strategy in North America, where its stores are company owned, Starbucks initially decided to license its format in Japan. However, the company also realized that a pure licensing agreement would not give Starbucks the control needed to ensure that the Japanese licensees closely followed Starbucks' successful formula. So the company established a joint venture with a local retailer, Sazaby Inc, each company held a 50 percent stake in the venture, Starbucks Coffee of Japan. Starbucks initially invested $10 million in this venture, its first foreign direct investment. The Starbucks format was then licensed to the venture, which was charged with taking over responsibility for growing Starbucks' presence in Japan.

To make sure Japanese operations replicated the North American "Starbucks experience", Starbucks transferred some employees to the Japanese operation. The licensing agreement required all

Japanese store managers and employees to attend training classes similar to those given to U. S. employees. The agreement also required that stores adhere to the design parameters established in the United States. In 2001, the company introduced a stock option plan for all Japanese employees, making it the first company in Japan to do so. Skeptics doubted that Starbucks would be able to replicate its North American success overseas, but by early 2003, Starbucks had more than 310 stores in Japan and plans to continue opening them at a brisk pace.

After getting its feet wet in Japan, the company embarked on an aggressive foreign investment program. In 1998, it purchased Seattle Coffee, a British coffee chain with 60 retail stores, for $84 million. An American couple, originally from Seattle, had started Seattle Coffee with the intention of establishing a Starbucks like chain in Britain, in the late 1990s, Starbucks opened stores in China, Singapore, Thailand, New Zealand, South Korea and Malaysia.

In Asia, Starbucks' most common strategy was to license its format to a local operator in return for initial licensing fees and royalties on store revenues Starbucks licensees, who then resold them to customers. As in Japan, Starbucks insisted on an intensive employee training program and strict specifications regarding the format and layout of the store. However, Starbucks became disenchanted with some of the straight licensing arrangements and converted several into joint venture arrangements or wholly owned subsidiaries. In Thailand, for example, Starbucks initially entered into a licensing agreement with Coffee Partners, a local Thai company under the terms of the licensing agreement, Coffee Partners was required to open at least 20 Starbucks coffee stores in Thailand within five years, However, Coffee Partners found it difficult to raise funds from Thai banks to finance this expansion. In July 2000, Starbucks acquired Coffee Partners for about $12 million. Its goal was to gain tighter control over the expansion strategy in Thailand A similar development occurred in South Korea, where Starbucks initially licensed its format to ESCO Korea Ltd. in 1999. Although bucks felt that ESCO would not be able to achieve the company's aggressive growth targets, so in December 2000 it converted its licensing arrangement into a joint venture with Shinsegae, the parent company of ESCO; the joint venture enabled Starbucks to exercise greater control over the growth strategy in South Korea and to help fund that operation, while gaining the benefits of a local operating partner.

By October 2000, Starbucks had invested some $52 million in foreign joint ventures. By the end of 2002, Starbucks had more than 1200 stores in 27 countries outside of North America and was initiating aggressive expansion plans into Europe. The company's plans called for opening of some 650 stores in six European countries, including the coffee cultures of France and Italy by 2005. As its first eats/point on the European Continent (Starbucks had 150 stores in Great Britain), Starbucks chose Switzerland Drawing on its experience in Asia, the company entered into a joint venture with a Swiss company, Bon Appetit Group, Switzerland's largest food service company. Bon Appetit was to hold a majority stake in the venture, and Starbucks would license its format to the Swiss company using an agreement similar to those it had used successfully in Asia.

In May 2008, a loyalty program was introduced for registered users of the Starbucks Card (previously simply a gift card) offering perks such as free Wi-Fi Internet access, no charge for soy milk and flavored syrups, and free refills on brewed drip coffee, iced coffee or tea. In 2009, Starbucks began beta testing its mobile app for the Starbucks card, a stored value system in which consumers access pre-paid funds to purchase products at Starbucks. Starbucks released its complete mobile platform in January 2011.

In November 2012, Starbucks announced the purchase of Teavana for U. S. $ 620 million in cash and the deal was formally closed on December 31, 2012.

In February 2013, Starbucks opened its first store in Ho Chi Minh City, Vietnam, and this was followed by an announcement in late August 2013 that the retailer will be opening its inaugural store in Colombia. The Colombian announcement was delivered at a press conference in Bogota, where the company's CEO explained, "Starbucks has always admired and respected Colombia's distinguished coffee tradition."

In August 2014, Starbucks opened their first store in Williamsburg, Brooklyn. This location will be one of 30 Starbucks stores that will serve beer and wine.

In September 2014, it was revealed that Starbucks would acquire the remaining 60.5 percent stake in Starbuck Coffee Japan that it does not already own, at a price of $ 913.5 million.

In August 2015, Starbucks announced that it will enter Cambodia, its 16th market in the China/Asia Pacific region. The first location will open in the capital city of Phnom Penh by the end of 2015.

8.2　Introduction

This chapter is concerned with foreign direct investment (FDI). Foreign direct investment occurs when a firm invests directly in facilities to produce and/or market a product in a foreign country. When Starbucks invested $ 10 million in Starbucks Coffee of Japan in 1996, it was engaging in its first foreign direct investment. According to the U. S. Department of Commerce, FDI occurs whenever an U. S. citizen, organization, or affiliated group takes an interest of 10 percent or more in a foreign business entity (all of Starbucks' foreign investments were for more than 10 percent of the equity of a business). Once a firm undertakes FDI, it becomes a multinational enterprise (the meaning of multinational being "more than one country").

FDI takes on two main forms. The first is a green-field investment, which involves the establishment of a wholly new operation in a foreign country. The second involves acquiring or merging with an existing firm in the foreign country. Acquisitions can be a minority (where the foreign firm takes a 10 percent to 49 percent interest in the firm's voting stock), majority (foreign interest of 50 percent to 99 percent), or full out-right stake (foreign interest of 100 percent). Here is an important distinction between FDI and foreign portfolio investment (FPI). Foreign portfolio investment is invested by individuals, firms, or public bodies (e.g., national and local governments) in foreign financial instruments (e.g., government bonds, foreign stocks). FPI does not involve taking a significant equity stake in a foreign business entity (i.e., the equity stake is less than 10 percent). FPI is determined by different factors than FDI and raises different issues.

In Chapter 2, we considered several theories that sought to explain the pattern of trade between countries. These theories focus on why countries export some products and import others. None of these theories addresses why a firm might decide to invest directly in production facilities in a foreign country, rather than exporting its domestic production to that country or licensing a foreign entity to produce its product in return for licensing fees. The theories we reviewed in Chapter 3 do not explain the pattern of foreign direct investment between countries. They do not explain, for example, why Starbucks chose to acquire Seattle Coffee in Great Britain, rather than simply license the Starbucks formula to a British firm. The theories we explore in this chapter seek to do just this.

Our central objective will be to identify the economic rationale that underlies foreign direct investment. Firms often view exports and FDI as substitutes for each other. For example, when deciding to serve the North American market, Toyota had to choose between exporting and foreign direct investment in North American production facilities. Although Toyota initially served the North American market through exports, increasingly it has turned to FDI. Toyota now has the capability to produce 600,000 cars a year in North America. This chapter attempts to understand the conditions under which firms such as Toyota prefer FDI to exporting. We will review various theories regarding these conditions.

These theories also need to explain why it is preferable for a firm to engage in FDI rather than licensing. Licensing occurs when a domestic firm, the licensor, licenses to a foreign firm, the licensee, the right to produce its product, to use its production processes, or to use its brand name or trademark. In return for giving the licensee these rights, the licensor collects royalty fees on every unit the licensee sells or on total licensee revenues. The advantage claimed for licensing over FDI is that the licensor does not have to pay for opening a foreign market; the licensee does that. Nor does the licensor have to bear the risks associated with opening a foreign market. However, despite these attractions, many firms are reluctant to engage in straight licensing arrangements, preferring to make some kind of foreign direct investment. Thus, in the opening case we saw that Starbucks originally considered a straight licensing strategy for entering the Japanese market but ultimately entered through a joint venture, which required some direct investment. Similarly, while the company did initially license its format in several Asian countries, such as Thailand and South Korea, there too it has switched to a direct investment strategy, acquiring its Thai licensee and entering into a joint venture with its South Korean licensee. What is the theoretical rationale for such a decision? The opening case hints that the need for control was a consideration. We shall develop the theoretical explanation in this chapter, and as we shall see, the need for control is an important factor in explaining the decision.

The government of a source country for FDI can also encourage or restrict FDI by domestic firms. In recent years, Japanese government has pressured many Japanese firms to undertake FDI. Japanese government sees FDI as a substitute for exporting and thus as a way of reducing Japanese politically embarrassing balance of payments surplus. In contrast, the U.S. government has, for political reasons, from time to time restricted FDI by domestic firms. For example, in response to a belief that the Iranian government actively supports terrorist organizations, the U.S. government has prohibited U.S. firms from investing in or exporting to Iran.

8.2.1 Trends in FDI

When discussing foreign direct investment, it is important to distinguish between the flow of FDI and the stock of FDI. The flow of FDI refers to the amount of FDI undertaken over a given time period (normally a year). The stock of FDI refers to the total accumulated value of foreign-owned assets at a given time. We also talk of out-flows of FDI, meaning the flow of FDI out of a country, and inflows of FDI, meaning the flow of FDI into a country.

FDI has grown more rapidly than world trade and world output for several reasons. Despite the general decline in trade barriers that we have witnessed over the past 30 years, business firms still fear protectionist pressures. Executives see FDI as a way of circumventing future trade barriers. Much of the Japanese automobile companies' investment in the United States during the 1980s and early 1990s was driven by a desire to reduce exports from Japan, thereby alleviating trade tensions between the two nations. Also, much of the recent increase in FDI is being driven by the dramatic political and economic changes that have been occurring in many of the world's developing nations. The general shift toward democratic political institutions and free market economies. Across many of Asia, Eastern Europe and Latin America, economic growth, economic deregulation, privatization programs that are open to foreign investors and the removal of many restrictions on FDI have made these countries more attractive to foreign investors. The desire of governments to facilitate FDI has also been reflected in a dramatic increase in the number of bilateral investment treaties designed to protect and promote investment between two countries.

The globalization of the world economy is also having a positive impact on the volume of FDI. Firms such as Starbucks now see the whole world as their market, and they are undertaking FDI in an attempt to make sure they have a significant presence in many regions of the world. For reasons that we shall explore later in this book, many firms now believe it is important to have production facilities based close to their major customers. This, too, is creating pressures for greater FDI.

8.2.1.1 The Direction of FDI

Historically, most FDI has been directed at the developed nations of the world as firms based in advanced countries invested in the others' markets. The United States has often been the favorite target for FDI inflows. This trend continued in the late 1990s, when the United States remained the largest recipient of foreign direct investment. In 2000, the United States was again the largest national recipient of FDI, accounting for $281 billions of the $1.3 trillion in global FDI, while Western Europe was the largest single regional recipient of FDI, with $633 billion in inflows. In 2001, the total of the United States and Western Europe dropped to $124 billion and $323 billion respectively, reflecting the drop in economic activity. Historically, the United States has been an attractive target for FDI because of its large and wealthy domestic markets, its dynamic and stable economy a favorable political environment, and the openness of the country to FDE Investors included firms based in Britain, Japan, Germany, Holland and France.

Although developed nations in general, and the United States in particular, still account for the largest share of FDI inflows, there has been some increase of FDI into the world's developing nations, From 1985 to 1990, the annual inflow of FDI into developing nations averaged $27.4 billion, or 17.4 percent of the total global flow. By 1997, the inflow into developing nations bad risen to $149billion, or 37 percent of the total. In 2001, the flow into developing nations accounted for 27 percent of the total, and it rose to $185 billion and 35 percent of the total in 2002. Most recent inflows into developing nations have been targeted at the emerging economies of South, East and Southeast Asia. Driving much of the increase has been the growing importance of China as a recipient of FDI.

Latin America emerged as the next most important region in the developing world for FDI inflows. In 2000, total inward investments into this region reached about $86 billion, and it remained at that level during 2001 before dropping to $62 billion in 2002. Much of this investment was concentrated on Mexico and Brazil and was a response to reforms in the region, including privatization, the liberalization of regulations governing FDI, and the growing importance of regional free trade areas such as MERCOSUR and NAFTA. At the other end of the scale, Africa received the smallest amount of inward investment, about $6 billion in 2002. The inability of Africa to attract greater investment is in part a reflection of the political unrest, armed conflict, and frequent changes in economic policy in the region.

Another way of looking at the importance of FDI inflows is to express them as a percentage of gross fixed capital formation. Gross fixed capital formation summarizes the total amount of capital invested in factories, stores, office buildings and the like. Other things being equal, the greater the capital investment in an economy, the more favorable its future growth prospects are likely to be. Viewed this way, FDI can be seen as an important source of capital investment and a determinant of the future growth rate of an economy. Summarizes inward flows of FDI as a percentage of gross fixed capital formation by region for 2000 (the latest year for which data are available). During 1996-2000, FDI accounted to about 11 percent of worldwide gross fixed capital formation, up from 4 percent worldwide in the early 1990s. These figures suggest that FDI is becoming an increasingly important source of investment in the world's economies.

These gross figures hide important individual country differences. For example, in 2000, inward FDI accounted for some 46 percent of gross fixed capital information in the United Kingdom,

28 percent in Brail, and 23 percent in Chile, but only 2.3 percent in India, 6.3 percent in Italy, and 0.7 percent in Japan – suggesting that FDI is an important source of investment capital, and thus economic growth, in the first three countries, but not the latter three. These differences can be explained by several factors, including the perceived ease and attractiveness of investing in a nation. To the extent that burdensome regulations limit the opportunities or foreign investment in countries such as Japan and India, these nations may be hurting themselves by limiting their access to needed capital investments.

8.2.1.2 The Form of FDI: Acquisitions Versus Green-Field Investments

FDI can take the form of a green-field investment in a new facility or an acquisition of or a merger with an existing local firm. The data suggest the majority of cross-border investment is in the form of mergers and acquisitions rather than green-field investments. UN estimates indicate that some 70 to 80 percent of all FDI inflows are in the form of mergers and acquisitions. In 2001, for example, mergers and acquisitions accounted for some 78 percent of all FDI inflows. However, there is a marked difference between FDI flows into developed and developing nations. In the case of developing nations, only about one-third of FDI is in the form of cross-border mergers and acquisitions. The lower percentage of FDI inflows that is in the form of mergers and acquisitions may simply reflect the fact that there are fewer target firms to acquire in developing nations.

When contemplating FDI, why do firms apparently prefer to acquire existing assets rather than undertake green-field investments? First, mergers and acquisitions are quicker to execute than green-field investments. This is an important consideration in the modern business world where markets evolve very rapidly. Many firms apparently believe that if they do not acquire a desirable target firm, then their global rivals will.

Second, foreign firms are acquired because those firms have valuable strategic assets, such as brand loyalty, customer relationships, trademarks or patents, distribution systems, production systems and the like. It is easier and perhaps less risky for a firm to acquire those assets than to build them from the ground up through a green-field investment.

Third, firms make acquisitions because they believe they can increase the efficiency of the acquired unit by transferring capital, technology or management skills. Thus, there are some fairly compelling arguments for favoring mergers and acquisitions over green-field investments. But many merger and acquisitions fail to realize their anticipated gains.

8.2.2 Transnational Corporations

Transnational corporations – those corporations which operate in more than one country or nation at a time – have become some of the most powerful economic and political entities in the world today.

Foreign direct investment (FDI) by transnational corporations (TNCs), and the transnational system of production and international economic transactions is now the most dominant element of the world economy, with TNCs increasingly influencing the size and nature of cross-border transactions, says an UNCTAD (United Nations Conference on Trade and Development) report.

The world's TNCs – 40,000 parent firms and 250,000 foreign affiliates – account for two-thirds of the world trade in goods and services, one-third in intra-firm transactions and the other one-third in inter-firm transactions.

This means that only one-third of world trade in goods and services is according to free-market-free-trade theories of arms-length transactions.

In releasing the report at a press conference, UNCTAD Secretary-General Rubens Ricupero said that FDI had now superseded trade as the most important mechanism for international economic integration.

The report uses this fact to argue for making "investments" part of the trade negotiation and rule-making process, through a Multilateral Investment Agreement (MIA).

At his press conference, Ricupero slightly distanced himself from the MIA of the WIR, preferring the term "multilateral framework", but did not elaborate on the distinction.

The leader of UNCTAD's investment center team responsible for the WIR, Karl Sauvant, at a Washington press conference, used the same terminology of a "multilateral framework" to argue for an agreement "creating new parameters for international business transactions". The WIR refers in this regard to the increasing number of bilateral investment agreements, several between developing countries themselves or within regional integration accords, as well as the discussions for plurilateral and multilateral agreements in the Organisation for Economic Cooperation and Development (OECD) and so on, to make the argument in favour of a multilateral agreement.

The report also advocates developing countries liberalising not only inward FDI, but also outward FDI flows, and says it would be in the interests of all countries to have a multilateral agreement to provide stable, predictable and transparent international investment relations.

Given the growing importance of FDI and international production for linking national economies and improving economic performance, and given the transnational nature of this investment, it is unavoidable that a framework will be sought that provides for stability, predictability and transparency at the multilateral level.

It refers in this connection to the built-in World Trade Organisation (WTO) agenda (of the Marrakesh agreements and the negotiations provided there for Trade-Related Investment Measures (TRIMs), Services and so on), the regional efforts (within the framework of the European Union, the North American Free Trade Agreement, Mercosur, the Asia Pacific Economic Cooperation) and the OECD negotiations for a binding Multilateral Agreement on Investment which, once it is concluded, would be open to non-OECD members to join.

UNCTAD is also helping discussions for an international framework to advance understanding on this issue, especially on the development dimensions, and to promote consensus building.

Without predicting whether these efforts would lead in the foreseeable future to a comprehensive multilateral framework, the WIR asserts that such a framework when established could well rival in importance, the international trade framework created by establishing the General Agreement on Tariffs and Trade (GATT) 50 years ago, and setting parameters within which TNCs could maintain or increase their competitiveness and countries could improve economic performance.

But whether or not there is a difference of substance between negotiations for a framework (that conceptually would imply a large leeway for individual governments to set their own rules, to suit their own conditions) and a multilateral agreement that would give rights to the TNCs to "invest" in any country for production of goods and services and "discipline" governments against interference with these rights, the European Union (the leading exponent of a WTO investment agreement) promptly welcomed the WIR, but called for a WTO working group to make progress on the idea.

8.3 Horizontal Foreign Direct Investment

Horizontal FDI is investment in the same industry abroad as a firm operates in at home. We need to understand why firms go to the trouble of acquiring or establishing operations abroad, when the alternatives of exporting and licensing are available. Other things being equal, FDI is expensive and risky compared to exporting or licensing. FDI is expensive because a firm must bear the costs of establishing production facilities in a foreign country or of acquiring a foreign enterprise. FDI is risky because of the problems associated with doing business in another culture where the "rules of the game" may be very different. Relative to firms native to a culture, there is a greater probability that a firm in a foreign culture will make costly mistakes due to ignorance. When a firm exports, it needs not bear the costs of FDI, and the risks associated with selling abroad can be reduced by using a native sales agent. Similarly, when a firm licenses its know-how, it need not bear the costs or risks of FDI. So why do so many firms apparently prefer FDI over either exporting or licensing?

The quick answer is that other things are not equal! A number of factors can alter the relative attractiveness of exporting, licensing and FDI. We will consider these factors:

①transportation costs;
②market imperfections;
③strategic behavior;
④the product life cycle;
⑤location advantages.

8.3.1 Transportation Costs

When transportation costs are added to production costs, it becomes unprofitable to ship some products a long distance. This is particularly true of products that have a low value-to-weight ratio and can be produced in almost any location (e.g., cement, soft drinks, etc.). For such products relative to either FDI or licensing, the attractiveness of exporting decreases. For products with a high value-to-weight ratio, however, transport costs are normally a very minor components of total landed cost (e.g., electronic components, personal computers, medical equipment, computer software, etc.). In such cases, transportation costs have little impact on the relative attractiveness of exporting, licensing and FDI.

8.3.2 Market Imperfections (Internalization Theory)

Market imperfections provide a major explanation of why firms may prefer FDI to either exporting or licensing. Market imperfections are factors that inhibit markets from working perfectly. The market imperfections explanation of FDI is the one favored by most economists. In the international business literature, the marketing imperfections approach to FDI is typically referred to as internalization theory.

With regard to horizontal FDI, market imperfections arise in two circumstances: when there are impediments to the free flow of products between nations, and when there are impediments to the sale of know-how (Licensing is a mechanism for selling know-how). Impediments to the free flow of products between nations decreased the profitability of exporting, relative to FDI and licensing. Impediments to the sale of know-how increase the profitability of FDI relative to licensing. Thus, the market imperfections explanation predicts that FDI will be preferred whenever there are impediments that make both exporting and the sale of know-how difficult and/or expensive.

8.3.3 Impediments to Exporting

Governments are the main source of impediments to the free flow of products between nations. By placing tariffs on imported goods, governments increase the cost of exporting relative to FDI and licensing. Similarly, by limiting imports through the imposition of quotas, governments increase the attractiveness of FDI and licensing. For example, the wave of FDI by Japanese auto companies in the United States during the 1980s was partly driven by protectionist threats from Congress and by quotas on the importation of Japanese cars. For Japanese auto companies, these factors have decreased the profitability of exporting and decreased the profitability of FDI.

8.3.4 Impediments to the Sale of Know-How

The competitive advantage many firms enjoy conies from their technological, marketing or management know-how. Technological know-how can enable a company to build a better product; for example, Nokia's technological know-how has given it a strong competitive position in the global market for wireless telephone equipment. Alternatively, technological know-how can improve a company's production process vis-a-vis competitors. For example, many claim that Toyota's competitive advantage comes from its superior production system. Marketing know-how can enable a company to better position its products in the marketplace; the competitive advantage of such companies as Kellogg, H. J. Heinz, and Procter & Gamble seems to come from superior marketing know-how. Management know-how with regard to factors such as organizational structure, human relations, control systems, planning systems, inventory management and so on can enable a company to manage its assets more efficiently than competitors. The competitive advantage of Starbucks, which was profiled in the opening case, seems to come from valuable management knowledge related to the branding and operations of retail coffee stores.

If we view know-how (expertise) as a competitive asset, it follows that the larger the market in which that asset is applied, the greater the profits that can be earned from the asset. Nokia can earn greater returns on its know-how by selling its wireless telephone equipment worldwide than by selling it only in its native Finland. However, this alone does not explain why Nokia undertakes FDI (the company has production locations around the world). For Nokia to favor FDI, two conditions must hold. First, transportation costs and/or impediments to exporting must rule out exporting as an option. Second, there must be some reason Nokia cannot sell its wireless know-how to foreign producers. Since licensing is the main mechanism by which firms sell their know-how, there must be some reason Nokia is not willing to license a foreign firm to manufacture and market its cellular telephone equipment. Other things being equal, licensing might look attractive to such a firm, since it would not have to bear the costs and risks associated with FDI yet it could still earn a good return from its know-how in the form of royalty fees.

According to economic theory, there are three reasons the market does not always work well as a mechanism for selling know-how, or why licensing is not as attractive as it initially appears.

First, licensing may result in a firm's giving away its know-how to a potential foreign competitor.

Second, licensing does not give a firm the tight control over manufacturing, marketing and strategy in a foreign country that may be required to profitably exploit its advantage in know-how. With licensing, control over production, marketing and strategy is granted to a licensee in return for a royalty fee. However, for both strategic and operational reasons, a firm may want to retain control over these functions. For example, a firm might want its foreign subsidiary to price and market very aggressively, but the licensee may be unable to do this. The opening case showed how this became an issue with Starbucks, which originally pursued a licensing strategy in Thailand, but then acquired the Thai operation because it thought the licensee was not aggressive enough in growing the market and was capital-constrained.

Or a firm may want control over the operations of a foreign entity to take advantage of differences in factor costs among countries, producing only part of its final product in a given country, while importing other parts from where they can be produced at lower cost. Again, a licensee would be unlikely to accept such an arrangement because it would limit the licensee's autonomy. When tight control over a foreign entity is desirable, horizontal FDI is preferable to licensing.

Third, a firm's know-how may not be amenable to licensing. This is particularly true of management and marketing know-how. It is one thing to license a foreign firm to manufacture a particular product, but quite another to license the way a firm does business how it manages its process and markets its products. Consider Toyota, a company whose competitive advantage in the global auto industry is acknowledged to come from its superior ability to manage the overall process of designing, engineering, manufacturing and selling automobiles; that is, from its management and organizational know-how. Toyota is credited with pioneering the development of a new production process, known as lean production, which enables it to produce higher-quality automobiles at a lower cost than its global rivals. Although Toyota has certain products that can be licensed, its real competitive advantage comes from its management and process know-how. These kinds of skills are difficult to articulate or codify; they cannot be written down in a simple licensing contract. They are organization wide and have been developed over years. They are not embodied in any one individual, but instead are widely dispersed throughout the company. Toyota's skills are embedded in its organizational culture, and culture is something that cannot be licensed. Thus, as Toyota moves away from its traditional exporting strategy, it has increasingly pursued a strategy of FDI, rather than licensing foreign enterprises to produce its cars.

All of this suggests that when one or more of the following conditions holds, markers fail as a mechanism for selling know-how and FDI is more profitable than licensing:

①when the firm has valuable know-how that cannot be adequately protected by a licensing contract;

②when the firm needs tight control over a foreign entity to maximize its market share and earnings in that country, and;

③when a firm's skills and know-how are not amenable to licensing.

8.3.5 Strategic Behavior

Another theory used to explain FDI is based on the idea that FDI flows are a reflection of strategic rivalry between firms in the global marketplace. An early variant of this argument was expounded by F T. Knickerbocker, who looked at the relationship between FDI and rivalry in oligopolistic industries. An oligopoly is an industry composed of a limited number of large firms (e. g. , an industry in which four firms control 80 percent of a domestic market would be defined as an oligopoly). A critical competitive feature of such industries is interdependence of the major players: what one firm does can have an immediate impact on the major competitors, forcing a response in kind. If one firm in an oligopoly cuts prices, this can take market share away from its competitors, forcing them to respond with similar price cuts to retain their market share. Thus, the interdependence between firms in an oligopoly leads to imitative behavior; rivals often quickly imitate what a firm does in an oligopoly.

Imitative behavior can take many forms in an oligopoly. One firm raises prices, the others follow; someone expands capacity, and the rivals imitate lest they be left at a disadvantage in the future. Knickerbocker argued that the same kind of imitative behavior characterizes FDI. Consider an oligopoly in the United States in which three firms-A, B, and C-dominate the market. Firm A establishes a subsidiary in France.

Firms B and C decide that if this investment is successful it may knock out their export business to France and give firm A a first-mover advantage. Furthermore, firm A might discover some competitive asset in France that it could repatriate to the United States to torment firms B and C on their native soil. Given these possibilities, firms B and C decide to follow firm A and establish operations in France.

Studies that looked at FDI by U. S. firms during the 1950s and 1960s show that firms based in oligopolistic industries tended to imitate each other's FDI. The same phenomenon has been observed with regard to FDI undertaken by Japanese firms during the 1980s. For example Toyota and Nissan responded its investments by Honda in the United States and Europe by undertaking their own FDI in the United States and Europe. Recently, research has shown that models of strategic behavior in a global oligopoly can explain the pattern of FDI in the global tier industry.

Knickerbocker's theory can be extended to embrace the concept of multipoint competition. Multipoint competition arises when two or more enterprises encounter each other in different regional markets, national markets or industries. Economic theory suggests that rather like chess players jockeying for advantage, firms will try to match each other's moves in different markets to try to hold each other in check. The idea is to ensure that a rival does not gain a commanding position in one market and then using the profits generated there to subsidize competitive attacks in other markets. Kodak and Fuji Photo Film Co., for example, compete against each order around the world. If Kodak enters a particular foreign market, Fuji will not be far behind. Fuji feels compelled to follow Kodak to ensure that Kodak does not gain a dominant position in the foreign market that it could then leverage to gain a competitive advantage elsewhere. The converse also holds, with Kodak following Fuji when Japanese firm is the first to enter a foreign market.

Although Knickerbocker's theory and its extensions can help to explain imitative FDI behavior by firms in oligopolistic industries, it does not explain why the first firm in an oligopoly decides to undertake FDI, rather than to export or license. In contrast, the market imperfections explanation addresses this phenomenon. The imitative theory also does not address the issue of whether FDI is more efficient than exporting or licensing for expanding abroad. Again, the market imperfections approach addresses the efficiency issue. For these reasons, many economists favor the market imperfections explanation for FDI, although most would agree that the imitative explanation tells an important part of the story.

8.3.6 The Product Life Cycle

Raymond Vernon's product life cycle theory, described in Chapter 2, also is used to explain FDI Vernon argued that often the same firms that pioneer a product in their home markets undertake FDI to produce a product for consumption in foreign markets. Thus, Xerox introduced the photocopier in the United States, and it was Xerox that set up production facilities in Japan (Fuji-Xerox) and Great Britain (Rank-Xerox) to serve those markets. Vernon's view is that firms undertake FDI at particular stages in the life cycle of a product they have pioneered. They invest in other advanced countries when local demand in those countries grows large enough to support local production (as Xerox did). They subsequently shift production to developing countries when product standardization and market saturation give rise to price competition and cost pressures. Investment in developing countries, where labor costs are lower, is seen as the best way to reduce costs.

Vernon's theory has merit. Firms do invest in a foreign country when demand in that country will support local production, and they do invest in low-cost locations (e. g. , developing countries) when cost pressures become intense. However, Vethen's theory fails to explain why it is profitable for a firm to undertake FDI at such times, rather than continuing to export from its home base and rather than licensing a foreign firm to produce its product. Just because demand in a foreign country is large enough to support local production, it does not necessarily follow that local production is the most profitable option. It may still be more profitable to produce at home and export to that country (to realize the scale economies that arise from serving the global market from one location). Alternatively, it may be more profitable for the firm to license a foreign company to produce its product for sale in that country. The product life-cycle theory ignores these options and, instead, simply argues that once a foreign market is large enough to support local production, FDI will occur. This limits its explanatory power and its usefulness to business in that it fails to identify when it is profitable to invest abroad.

8.3.7 Location-Specific Advantages

The British economist John Dunning has argued that in addition to the various factors discussed above, location-specific advantages can explain the nature and direction of FDI. By location and specific advantages, Dunning means the advantages that arise from using resource endowments or assets that are tied to a particular foreign location and that a firm finds valuable in combine with its own unique assets (such as the firm's technological, marketing, or management know-how). Dunning accepts the internalization argument that market failures make it difficult for a firm to license its own unique assets (know-how). Therefore, he argues that combining location-specific assets or resource endowments and the firm's own unique assets often requires FDI. It requires the firm to establish production facilities where those foreign assets or resource endowments are located (Dunning refers to this argument as the eclectic paradigm.).

An obvious example of Dunning's arguments is natural resources, such as oil and other minerals, which are specific to certain locations. Dunning suggests that a firm must undertake FDI to exploit such foreign resources. This explain the FDI under taken by many of the world's oil companies, which have to invest where oil is located to combine their technological and managerial knowledge with this valuable location specific resource. Another example is valuable human resources, such as low-cost, highly skilled labor. The cost and skill of labor varied from country to country. Because labor is not internationally mobile, according to Dunning it makes sense for a firm to locate production facilities where the cost and skills of local labor are most suited to its particular production processes.

However, the implications of Dunning's theory go beyond basic resources such as minerals and labor. Consider Silicon Valley, which is the world center for the computer and semiconductor industry. Many of the world's major computer and semiconductor companies, such as Apple Computer, Silicon Graphics and Intel are located close to each other in the Silicon Valley region of California. As a result, much of the cutting-edge research and product development in computers and semiconductors occur here. According to Dunning's arguments, knowledge being generated in Silicon Valley with regard to the design and manufacture of computers and semiconductors is available nowhere else in the world. As it is commercialized, that knowledge diffuses throughout the world, but the leading edge of knowledge generation in the computer and semiconductor industries is to be found in Silicon Valley. In Dunning's language, this means Silicon Valley has a location-specific advantage in the generation of knowledge related to the computer and semiconductor industries. In part, this advantage comes from the sheer concentration of intellectual talent in this area, and in part it arises from a network of informal contacts that allows firms to benefit from each other's knowledge generation. Economists refer to such knowledge "spillovers" as externalities, and one well-established theory suggests that firms can benefit from such externalities by locating close to their source.

In so far as this is the case, it makes sense for foreign computer and semiconductor firms to invest in research and (perhaps) production facilities so they too can learn about and utilize valuable new knowledge before those based elsewhere, thereby giving them a competitive advantage in the global marketplace. Evidence suggests that European, Japanese, South Korean and Chinese Taiwan province computer and semiconductor firms are investing in the Silicon Valley region, precisely because they wish to benefit from the externalities that arise there. Others have argued that direct investment by foreign firms in the U.S. biotechnology industry has been motivated by desires to gain access to the unique location-specific technological knowledge of U.S. biotechnology firms. Dunning's theory, therefore, seems to be a useful addition to those outlined above, for it helps explain how location factors affect the direction of FDI.

8.4　Vertical Foreign Direct Investment

Vertical FDI takes two forms. There is backward vertical FDI into an industry abroad that provides inputs for a firm's domestic production processes. Historically, most backward vertical FDI has been in extractive industries (e.g., oil extraction bauxite mining, tin mining, copper mining). The objective has been to provide inputs into a firm's downstream operations (e.g., oil refining, aluminum smelting and fabrication, tin smelting and fabrication). Firms such as Royal Dutch/Shell, British Petroleum (BP), RTZ, Consolidated Gold Fiel and ALcoa are among the classic examples of such vertically integrated multinationals.

A second form of vertical FDI is forward vertical FDI in which an industry abroad sells the outputs of a firm's domestic production processes, and forward vertical FDI is less common than backward vertical FDI. For example, when Volkswagen entered the U.S. market, it acquired a large number of dealers rather than distributed its cars through independent U.S. dealers.

With both horizontal and vertical FDI, the question that must be answered is why would a firm go to all the trouble and expense of setting up operations in a foreign country? Why, for example, did petroleum companies such as BP and Royal Dutch/ Shell vertically integrate backward into oil production abroad? The location-specific advantages argument helps explain the direction of such FDI vertically integrated multinationals in extractive industries invest where the raw materials are. However, this argument does not clarify why they did not simply import raw materials extracted by local producers. And why do companies such as Volkswagen feel it is necessary to acquire their own dealers in foreign markets, when in theory it might seem less costly to rely on foreign dealers. There are two basic answers of these kinds of questions. The first is a strategic behavior argument, and the second draws on the market imperfections approach.

8.4.1 Strategic Behavior

According to economic theory, by vertically integrating backward to gain control over the source of raw material, a firm can raise entry barriers and shut new competitors out of an industry. Such strategic behavior involves vertical FDI if the raw material is found abroad. A famous example occurred in the 1930s when North American firms such as Alcoa pioneered commercial smelting of aluminum. Aluminum is derived by smelting bauxite. Although bauxite is a common mineral, the percentage of aluminum in bauxite is typically so low that it is not economical to mine and smelt. During the 1930s, only one large-scale deposit of bauxite with an economical percentage of aluminum had been discovered, and it was on the Caribbean island of Trinidad. Alcoa and Alcan vertically integrated backward and acquired ownership of the deposit. This action created a barrier to entry into the aluminum industry. Potential competitors were deterred because they could not get access to high-grade bauxite – it was all owned by Alcoa and Alcan. Those that did enter the industry bad to use lower-grade barite than Alcan and Alcoa and found themselves at a cost disadvantage. This situation persisted until the 1950s and 1960s, when new high-grade deposits were discovered in Australia and Indonesia.

However, despite the bauxite example, the opportunities for barring entry through vertical FDI seem tar too limited to explain the incidence of vertical FDI among the world's multinationals, In most extractive industries, mineral deposits are not as concentrated as in the case of bauxite in the 1930s; new deposits are constantly being discovered. Consequently, any attempt to monopolize all viable raw material deposits is bound to prove very expensive if not impossible.

Another strand of the strategic behavior explanation of vertical FDI sees such investment not as an attempt to build entry barriers, but as an attempt to circumvent the barriers established by firms already doing business in a country. This may explain Volkswagen's decision to establish its own dealer network when it entered the North American auto market. GM, Ford and Chrysler then dominated the market.

Each firm had its own network of dealers. Volkswagen believed that the only way to get quick access to the United States was to promote its cars through company owned dealerships.

8.4.2 Market Imperfections

As in the case of horizontal FDI, a more general explanation of vertical FDI can be found in the market imperfections approach. The market imperfections approach offers two explanations for vertical FDI. As with horizontal FDI, the first explanation revolves around the idea that there are impediments to the sale of know-how through the market mechanism. The second explanation is based on the idea that investments in specialized assets expose the investing firm to hazards that can be reduced only through vertical FDI.

8.4.3 Impediments to the Sale of Know-How

Consider the case of oil refining companies such as British Petroleum and Royal Dutch/Shell. Historically, these firms pursued backward vertical FDI to supply their British and Dutch oil refining facilities with crude oil when this occurred in the early decades of the 20th century; neither Great Britain nor the Netherlands had domestic oil supplies. However, why did these firms not just import oil from firms in oil-rich countries such as Saudi Arabia and Kuwait?

Originally, there were no Saudi Arabian or Kuwaiti firms with the technological expertise for finding and extracting oil. BP and Royal Dutch/Shell had to develop this know-how to get access to oil. This alone does not explain FDI, however, for once BP and Shell had developed the necessary know-how; they could have licensed it to Saudi Arabian or Kuwaiti firms. However, as we saw in the case of horizontal FDI, licensing can be self-defeating as a mechanism firm the sale of know-how, If the oil refining firms had licensed their prospecting and extraction know-how to Saudi Arabian or Kuwaiti firms, they would have risked giving away their technological know-how to those firms, creating future competitors in the process. Once they had the know-how, the Saudi and Kuwaiti firms might have gone prospecting for oil in other parts of the world, competing directly against BP and Royal Dutch/Shell. Thus, it made more sense for these firms to undertake backward vertical FDI and extract the oil themselves instead of licensing their hard-earned technological expertise to local firms.

Generalizing from this example, the prediction is that backward vertical FDI will occur when a firm has the knowledge and the ability to extract raw materials in another country and there is no efficient producer in that country that can supply raw materials to the firm.

8.4.4 Investment in Specialized Assets

Another strand of the market imperfections argument predicts that vertical FDI will occur when a firm must invest in specialized assets whose value depends on inputs provided by a foreign supplier. In this context, a specialized asset is an asset designed to perform a specific task and whose value is significantly reduced in its next-best use, consider the case of an aluminum refinery, which is designed to refine bauxite ore and produce aluminum. Bauxite ores vary in content and chemical composition from deposit to deposit. Each type of ore requires a different type of refinery. Running one type of bauxite through a refinery designed for another type increases production costs by 20 to

100 percent. Thus, the value of an investment in an aluminum refinery depends on the availability of the desired kind of bauxite ore.

Imagine that a U.S. aluminum company must decide whether to invest in an aluminum refinery designed to refine a certain type of ore. Assume further that this ore is available only through an Australian mining firm at a single bauxite mine. Using a different type of ore in the refinery would raise production costs by at least 20 percent.

Therefore, the value of the U.S. company's investment depends on the price it must pay the Australian firm for this bauxite. Recognizing this, once the U.S. company has invested in a new refinery, what is to stop the Australian firm from raising bauxite prices? Absolutely nothing; and once it has made the investment, the U.S. firm is locked into its relationship with the Australian supplier. The Australian firm can increase bauxite prices, secure in the knowledge that as long as the increase in the total production costs is less than 20 percent, the U.S. firm will continue to buy from it. (It would become economical for the U.S. firm to buy from another supplier only if total production costs increased by more than 20 percent.)

The U.S. firm can reduce the risk of the Australian firm opportinistically raising prices in this manner by buying out the Australian firm. If the U.S. firm can buy the Australian firm, or its bauxite mine, it need no longer fear that bauxite prices will be increased after it has invested in the refinery. In other words, it would make economic sense for the U.S. firm to engage in vertical FDI. In practice, these kinds of considerations have driven aluminum firms to pursue vertical FDI to such a degree that a large percentage of the total volume of bauxite is transferred within vertically integrated firms.

8.5 Entry Strategies

Once a firm decides to enter a foreign market, the question arises as to the best mode of entry. Firms can use six different modes to enter foreign markets: exporting, turnkey projects, licensing, franchising, establishing joint ventures with a host-country firm or setting up a new wholly owned subsidiary in the host country. Each entry mode has advantages and disadvantages. Managers need to consider these carefully when deciding which to use.

8.5.1 Export

Many manufacturing firms begin their expansion as exporters and only later switch to anther mode for serving a foreign market. We take a close look at the mechanics of exporting in the next chapter. Here we focus on the advantages of exporting as an entry mode.

8.5.1.1 Advantages

Exporting has two distinct advantages. First, it avoids the often substantial costs of establishing manufacturing operations in the host country. Second, exporting may help a firm achieve experience curve and location economies. By manufacturing the product in a centralized location and exporting it to other national markets, the firm way may realize substantial scale economies from its global sales volume.

8.5.1.2 Disadvantages

Exporting has a number of drawbacks. First, exporting from the firm's home base may not be appropriate if lower cost locations for manufacturing the product can be found abroad (i. e. , if the firm can realize location economies by moving production elsewhere). Thus, particularly for firms pursuing global standardization or transnational strategies, it may be preferable to manufacture where the mix of factor conditions is most favorable from a value-creation perspective and to export to the rest of the world from that exporting form the firm's home country. Many U. S. electronics firms have moved some of their manufacturing to the Far East because of the availability of low-cost, highly skilled labor there. They then export from that location to the rest of the word, including the United States.

A second drawback to exporting is that high transportation costs can make exporting uneconomical, particularly for bulk products. One way of getting around this is to manufacture bulk products regionally. This strategy enables the firm to realize some economies from large-scale production and at the same time to limit its transportation costs.

Another drawback is that tariff barriers can make exporting uneconomical. Similarly, the threat of tariff barriers by the host-country government can make it very risky. A fourth drawback to exporting arises when a firm delegates its marketing, sales and service in each country where it does business to another company. This is a common approach for manufacturing firms that are just beginning expand internationally. The other company may be a local agent, or it may be another multinational with extensive international distribution operations. Local agents often carry the products of competing firms and so have divided loyalties. In such cases, the local agent may not do as good a job as the firm would if it managed its marketing itself. Similar problems can occur when another multinational take on distribution.

The way around such problems is to set up wholly subsidiaries in foreign nations to handle local marketing, sales and service. By doing this, the firm can excise tight control over marketing and sales in the country while reaping the cost advantages of manufacturing the product in a single location or a few choice locations.

8.5.2 Turnkey Projects

Firms that specialize in the design, construction and start-up of turnkey plants are common in some industries. In a turnkey project, the contractor agrees to handle every detail of the project for a foreign client, including the training of operating personnel. At completion of the contract, the foreign client is handled the "key" to a plant that is ready for full operation-hence, the term turnkey. This is a means of exporting process technology to other countries. Turnkey projects are most common in the chemical, pharmaceutical, petroleum refining and metal refining industries, all of which use complex, expensive production technologies.

8.5.2.1 Advantages

The know-how required to assemble and run a technologically complex process, such as refining petroleum or steel, is a valuable asset. Turnkey projects are a way of earning great economic returns from that asset. The strategy is particularly useful where foreign direct investment (FDI) is limited by host-government regulations. For example, the governments of many oil-rich countries have set out to build their own petroleum refining industries, so they restrict FDI in their oil and refining sectors. But because many of these countries lack petroleum-refining technology, they gain it by entering into turnkey projects with foreign firms that have the technology. Such deals are often attractive to the selling firm because without them, they would have no way to earn a return on their valuable know-how in that country. A turnkey strategy can also be less risky than conventional FDI. In a country with unstable political and economic environments, a longer-term investment might expose the firm to unacceptable political or economic risks (e.g., the risk of nationalization or of economic collapse).

8.5.2.2 Disadvantages

Three main drawbacks are associated with a turnkey strategy. First, the firm that enters into a turnkey deal will have no long-term interest in the foreign country. This can be a disadvantage if that country subsequently proves to be a major market for the output of the process that has been exported. One way around this is to take a minority equity interest in the operation. Second, the firm that enters into a turnkey project with a foreign enterprise may inadvertently create a competitor. Third, if the firm's process technology is a source of competitive advantage, then selling this technology through a turnkey project is also selling competitive advantage to potential or actual competitors.

8.5.3 Licensing

Licensing is a contractual arrangement whereby one company (the licensor) makes a legally protected asset available to another company (the licensee) in exchange for royalties, license fees or some other form of compensation. The licensed asset may be a brand name, company name, patent, trade secret or product formulation. Licensing is widely used in the fashion industry. For example, the namesake companies associated with Bill Blass, Hugo Boss, and other global design icons typically generate more revenue from licensing deals for jeans, fragrances and watches than from their high-priced couture lines. Organizations as diverse as Disney, Caterpillar inc., the National Basketball Association and Coca-cola also make extensive use of licensing. None is an apparel manufacturer; however, licensing agreements allow them to leverage their brand names and generate substantial revenue streams. As these examples suggest, licensing is a global market entry and expansion strategy with considerable appeal. It can offer an attractive return on investment for the life of the agreement, provided that the necessary performance clauses are included in the contract. The only cost is signing the agreement and policing its implementation.

Two key advantages are associated with licensing as a market entry mode. First, because the licensee is typically a local business that will produce and market the goods on a local or regional basis, licensing enables companies to circumvent tariffs, quotas or similar export barriers. Disney's success with licensing illustrates a second key advantage of this entry mode. When appropriate, licensees are considerable autonomy and are free to adapt the licensed goods to local tastes. Disney licenses trademarked cartoon characters, names and logos to producers of clothing, toys, and watches for sale throughout the world. Licensing allows Disney to create synergies based on its core theme park, motion picture and television businesses. Its licensees are allowed considerable leeway to adapt colors, materials or other design elements to local tastes. This helps explain why, in the Asia-Pacific region alone, sales of, Disney products doubled between 1988 and 1990 and doubled again by 1994. In China, licensed goods were practically unknown until a few years ago. Similarly, yearly worldwide sales of licensed Caterpillar merchandise are running at $900 million as consumers make a fashion statement with boots, jeans and handbags bearing the distinctive black-and-yellow Cat label.

Stephen Palmer is the head of London-based Overland Ltd., which holds the world-wide license for Cat apparel. He notes, "Even if people here don't know the brand, they have a feeling that they know it. They have seen Caterpillar tractors from an early age. It's subliminal, and that's why it's working."

Sanofi-Aventis, a French pharmaceutical company, has pursued a licensing strategy with great success. Drug research is extremely expensive; even so, Sanofi has dozens of under development, with each program costing as much as $400 million. Sanofi's chief executive turns to rivals such as Bristol-Myers Squibb to help find the research; licensees are then permitted to market the new drugs in return for royalties of up to 15 percent of total sales. Licensing was also the cornerstone of Pilkington's market expansion strategy. In the 1950s, after 7 years of research and an investment of $21 million, the British company developed a process innovation that dramatically lowered the cost of producing high-quality plate glass for the automotive and building industries. In addition to exporting its new "float glass" to dozens of countries, Pilkington licensed its technology to competition and created a worldwide industry standard. As Richard D'Aveni has noted, this strategy "generated substantial income for Pilkington, helping to assure its continued technological leadership in the industry for decades."

Licensing is associated with several disadvantages and opportunity costs. First, licensing agreement offer limited market control. Because the licensor typically does not become involved in the licensee's marketing program, potential returns from marketing may be lost. The second disadvantage is that the agreement may have a short life if the licensee develops its own know-how and begins to innovate in the licensed product or technology area. In a worst-case scenario (from the licensor's point of view), licenses, especially those working with process technologies, can develop into strong competitors in the local market and, eventually, into industry leaders. This is because licensing, by its very nature, enables a company to "borrow" – that is, leverage and exploit – another company's resource. A case in point is Pilkington, which has seen its leadership position in the glass industry erode as Glaverbel, Saint-Gobain, PPG, and other competitors have achieved higher levels of production efficiency and lower costs. The ice cream industry in Japan provides another example. Meiji Milk produced and marketed Lady Borden premium ice cream under a licensing agreement with Borden Inc. Meiji learned important skills in dairy product processing; as the expiration dates of the licensing contracts drew near, Meiji rolled out its own premium ice cream brands. When Borden tried to market ice cream without Meiji's help, it had problems developing new sales channels.

Perhaps the most famous example of the opportunity costs associated with licensing dates back to the mid-1950s, when Sony cofounder Masaru Ibuka obtained a licensing agreement for the transistor from AT&T's Bell Laboratories. Ibuka dreamed of using transistors to small, battery-powered radios. However, the Bell engineers with whom he spoke insisted that it was impossible to manufacturer transistors that could handle the high frequencies required for a radio; they advised him to try making hearing aids. Undeterred, Ibuka presented the challenge to his Japanese engineers who spent many months improving high-frequency output. Sony was not the first company to unveil a transistor radio; a U.S.-built product, the Regency, featured transistors from Texas Instruments and a colorful plastic case. However, it was Sony's high quality, distinctive approach to styling, and marketing savvy that ultimately translated into worldwide success.

Conversely, the failure to seize an opportunity to license can also lead to dire consequences. In the mid-1980s, Apple computer chairman John Sculley decided against a broad licensing program for Apple's famed operating system (OS). Such a move would have allowed other computer manufacturers to produce Mac-compatible units. Meanwhile, Microsoft's growing world dominance in both OS and applications got a boost in 1985 from Windows, which featured a Mac-like graphic interface. Apple sued Microsoft for infringing on its intellectual property; however, attorneys for the software giant successfully argued in court that Apple had in fact shared crucial aspects of its OS without limiting Microsoft's right to adapt and improve it. Belatedly, in the mid-1990s, Apple began licensing its operating system to other manufactures. However, the global market share for machines running the Mac OS continues to hover in the low single digits. The return of Steven Jobs and Apple's introduction of the new iMac in 1998 marked the start of a new era for Apple. Recently, the popularity of the company's iPod music players and iTunes Music Store have boosted its fortunes. However, Apple's failure to license its technology in the pre-Windows era arguably cost the company tens of billions of dollars.

As the Borden and transistor stories make clear, companies may find that the up-front easy money obtained from licensing turns out to be an expensive source of revenue. To prevent a licensor-competitor from gaining unilateral benefit, licensing agreements should provide for a cross-technology exchange between all parties. At the absolute minimum, any companies that plans to remain in business must ensure that its license agreements include a provision for full cross-licensing (i. e,. that the license shares its developments with the licensor). Overall the licensing strategy must ensure ongoing competitive advantage. For example, license arrangement can create export market opportunities and open the door to low-risk manufacturing relationships. They can also speed diffusion of new products or technologies.

8.5.3.1 Special Licensing Arrangements

Contract manufacturing requires a global company – Nike, for example – to provide technical specification to a subcontractor or local manufacturer. The subcontractor then oversees production. Such arrangements offer several advantages. The licensing firm can specialize in product design and marketing, while transferring responsibility for ownership of manufacturer facilities to contractors and subcontractors. Other advantages include limited commitment of financial and managerial resources and quick entry into target countries, especially when the target market is too small to justify significant investment. One disadvantage, as already noted, is that companies may open themselves to public scrutiny and criticism if workers in contract factories are poorly paid or labor in inhumane circumstance.

Franchising is another variation of licensing strategy. A franchise is a contract between a parent company-franchisor and a franchisee that allows the franchisee to operate a business developed by the franchisor in return for a fee and adherence to franchise-wide policies and practices. Franchising has great appeal to local entrepreneurs anxious to learn and apply Western-style marketing techniques. William Le Sante, a franchising consultant in Miami, suggests that would-be franchisors ask the following questions before expanding overseas:

(1) Will local consumers buy your product?

(2) How touch is the local competition?

(3) Does the government respect trademark and franchisor rights?

(4) Can your profits be easily repatriated?

(5) Can you buy all the supplies you need locally?

(6) Is commercial space available and are rents affordable?

(7) Are your local partners financially sound and do they understand the basics of franchising?

The specialty retailing industry favors franchising as a market entry mode. For example, there are nearly 2000 The Body Shop stores around the world; 70 percent of the stores are operated by franchisees. Franchising is also a cornerstone of global growth in the fast-food industry; McDonald's reliance on franchising to expand globally is a case in point. The fast-food giant has a well-known country markets. Crucially, McDonald's headquarters has learned the wisdom of leveraging local market knowledge by granting franchisees considerable leeway to tailor restaurant interior designs and menu offerings to suit country-specific preference and tastes. Generally speaking, however, franchising is a market entry strategy that is typically executed with less localization than licensing.

When companies do decide to license, they should sign agreements that anticipate more extensive market participation in the future. Insofar as is possible, a company should keep options and paths open for other forms of market participation. Many of these forms require investment and give the investing company more control than possibility with licensing.

A licensing agreement is an arrangement whereby a licensor grants the rights to intangible property to another entity (the license) for a specified period, and in return, the licensor receives a royalty fee from the licensee. Intangible property includes patents, inventions, formulas, processes, designs, copyrights and trademarks.

8.5.3.2 Advantages

In the typical international licensing deal, the licensee puts up most of the capital necessary to get the overseas operation going. Thus, a primary advantage of licensing is that the firm does have to bear the development costs and risks associated with opening a foreign market. Licensing is attractive for firms lacking the capital to develop operations overseas. In addition, licensing can be attractive when a firm is unwilling to commit substantial financial resources to an unfamiliar or politically volatile foreign market. A firm may use licensing when it wishes to participate in a foreign market but is prohibited from doing so by barriers to investment.

Finally, licensing is frequently used when a firm possesses some intangible property that might have business applications, but it does not want to develop those applications itself. For example, Bell Laboratories at AT&T originally invented the transistor circuit in the 1950s, but AT&T decided it did not want to produce transistors, so it licensed the technology to a number of other companies, such as Texas Instruments. Similarly, Coca-Cole has licensed its famous trademark to clothing manufacturers, which have incorporated the design into clothing.

8.5.3.3 Disadvantages

Licensing has three serious drawbacks. First, it does not give a firm the tight control over manufacturing, marketing, and strategy that is required for realizing experience curve and location economics. Licensing typically involves each licensee setting up his own production operations. This severely limits the firm's ability to realize experience curve and location economies by producing its product in a centralized location. When these economies are important, licensing may not be the best way to expand overseas.

Second, competing in a global market may require a firm to coordinate strategic moves across countries by using profits earned in one country to support competitive attacks in another. By its very nature, licensing limits a firm's ability to utilize a coordinated strategy. A licensee is unlikely to allow a multinational firm to use its profits (beyond those due in the form of royalty payments) to support a different licensee operating in another country.

The third problem with licensing is when we reviewed the economic theory of FDI. This is the risk associated with licensing technological know-how to foreign companies. Technological know-how constitutes the basis of many multinational firms' competitive advantage. Most firms wish to maintain control over how their know-how is used, and a firm can quickly lose control over its technology by licensing it. Many firms have made the mistake of thinking they could maintain control over their know-how within the framework of a licensing agreement. The Japanese firms quickly assimilated the technology, improved on it, and used it to enter the U. S. market, taking substantial market share away from RCA.

There are ways of reducing this risk. One way is to enter into a cross-licensing agreement with a foreign firm. Under a cross-licensing agreement, a firm might license some valuable intangible property to a foreign partner, but in addition to a royalty payment, the firm might also request that the foreign partner license some of its valuable know-how to the firm. Such agreements may reduce the risks associated with licensing technological know-how because the licensee realizes that if it violates the licensing contract (by using the knowledge obtained to complete directly with the licensor), the licensor can do the same to it. Cross – licensing agreements enable firms to hold each other hostage, which reduces the probability that they will behave opportunistically toward each other. Such cross-licensing agreements are increasingly common in high-technology industries.

Another way of reducing the risk associated with licensing is to follow the Fuji-Xerox model and link an agreement to license know-how with the formation of a joint venture in which the licensor and licensee take important equity stakes. Such an approach aligns the interests of licensor and licensee, because both have a stake in ensuring that the venture is successful. Thus, the risk that Fuji Photo might appropriate Xerox's technological know-how, and then complete directly against Xerox in the global photocopier marker, was reduced by the establishment of a joint venture in which both Xerox and Fuji Photo had an important stake.

8.5.4 Franchising

Franchising is similar to licensing, although franchising tends to involve longer-term commitments than licensing. Franchising is basically a specialized form of licensing in which the franchiser not only sells intangible property (normally a trademark) to the franchisee but also insists that the franchisee agrees to abide by strict rules as to how it does business. The franchiser will also often assist the franchisee to run the business on an ongoing basis. As with licensing, the franchiser typically receives a royalty payment, which amounts to some percentage of the franchisee's revenues. Whereas licensing is pursued primarily by manufacturing firms, franchising is employed primarily by service firms. McDonald's is a good example of a firm that has grown by using a franchising strategy. McDonald's strict rules as to how franchisees should operate a restaurant extend to control over the menu, cooking methods, staffing policies and design and location. McDonald's also organizes the supply chain for its franchisees and provides management training and financial assistance.

8.5.4.1 Advantages

The advantages of franchising as an entry mode are similar to those of licensing. The firm is relieved of many of cost and risks of opening a foreign market on its own. Instead, the franchisee typically assumes those costs and risks. This creates a good incentive for the franchising strategy, a service firm can build a global presence quickly and at a relatively low cost and risk, as McDonald's has.

8.5.4.2 Disadvantages

The disadvantages of franchising can be less pronounced than in the case of licensing. Many service companies, such as hotels, use franchising; in such instances, the firm has no reason to consider the need for coordination of manufacturing to achieve experience curve and location economies. But franchising may inhibit the firm's ability to take profits out of one country to support competitive attacks in another. A more significant disadvantage of franchising is quality control. The foundation of franchising arrangements is that the firm's brand name conveys a message to consumers about the quality of the firm's product. Thus, a business traveler checking in at a Four Seasons hotel in Chinese Hong Kong can reasonably expect the same quality of room, food and service that she would receive in China New York. The Four Seasons name is supposed to guarantee consistent product quality. This presents a problem in that foreign franchisees may not be as concerned about quality as they are supposed to be, and the result of poor quality can extend beyond lost sales in a particular foreign market to a decline in the firm's worldwide reputation. The geographical distance of the firm from its foreign franchisees can make poor quality difficult to detect. In addition, the sheer numbers of franchisees – in the case of McDonald's, tens of thousands – can make quality control difficult. Due to these factors, quality problems may persist.

One way around this disadvantage is to set up a subsidiary in each country in which the firm expands. The subsidiary might be wholly owned by the company or a joint venture with a foreign company. The subsidiary assumes the rights and obligations to establish franchises throughout the particular country or region. McDonald's, for example, establishes a master franchisee in many countries. Typically, this master franchisee is a joint venture between McDonald's and a local firm. The proximity and the smaller number of franchises to oversee reduce the quality control challenge. In addition, because the firm at least partially owns the subsidiary (or master franchisee), it can place its own managers there to help ensure that it is doing a good job of monitoring the franchises. This organizational arrangement has proven very satisfactory for McDonald's, KFC and others.

8.5.5 Joint Ventures

A joint venture entails establishing a firm that is jointly owned by two or more otherwise independent firms. Fuji-Xerox, for example, was set up as a joint venture between Xerox and Fuji Photo. Establishing a joint venture with a foreign firm has long been a popular mode for entering a new market. The most typical joint venture is a 50/50 venture, in which there are two parties, each of which holds a 50 percent ownership stake and contributes a steam of managers to share operating control (this was the case with the Fuji-Xerox joint venture until 2001; it is now a 25/75 venture, with Xerox holding 25 percent). Some firms, however, have sought joint ventures in which they have a majority share and thus tighter control.

8.5.5.1 Advantages

Joint ventures have a number of advantages. First, a firm benefits from a local partner's knowledge of the host country's competitive conditions, culture, language, political systems and business systems. Thus, for many U. S. firms, joint ventures have involved the U. S. company providing technological know-how and products and the local partner providing the marketing expertise and the local knowledge necessary for competing in that country. Second, when the development costs or risks of opening a foreign market are high, a firm might gain by sharing these costs and or risks with a local partner. Third, in many countries, political considerations make joint ventures the only feasible entry mode. Research suggests joint ventured with local partners face a low risk of being subject to nationalization or other forms of adverse government interference. This appears to be because local equity partners, who may have influence on host-government policy, have a vested interest in speaking out against nationalization or government interference.

8.5.5.2 Disadvantages

Despite these advantages, joint ventures have major disadvantages. First, as with licensing, a firm that enters into a joint venture risks giving control of its technology to its partner. Thus, a proposed joint venture in 2002 between Boeing and Mitsubishi Heavy Industries to build a new widebody jet raised fears that Boeing might unwittingly give away its commercial airline technology to the Japanese. However, joint-venture agreements can be constructed to minimize this risk. One option is to hold majority ownership in the venture. This allows the dominant partner to excise greater control over its technology. But it can be difficult to find a foreign partner who is willing to settle for minority ownership. Another option is to "wall off" from a partner technology that is central to the core competence of the firm, while sharing other technology.

The second disadvantage is that a joint venture does not give a firm the tight control over subsidiaries that that it might need to realize experience curve or location economies, nor does it give a firm the tight control over a foreign subsidiary that it might need for engaging in coordinated global attacks against its rivals.

The third disadvantage with joint venture is that the shared ownership arrangement can lead to conflicts and battles for control between the investing firms if their goals and objectives change or if they take different views as to what the strategy should be. This was apparently not a problem with the Fuji-Xerox joint venture. According to Yotaro Yobayasdi, currently the chairman of Fuji-Xerox, a primary reason is that both Xerox and Fuji Photo adopted an arm's-length relationship with Fuji-Xerox, giving the venture's management considerable freedom to determine its strategy. However, a great deal of researches indicated that conflicts of interest over strategy and goals often arise in joint ventures. These conflicts tend to be greater when the venture is between firms of different nationalities, and they often end in the dissolution of the venture. Such conflicts tend to be triggered by shifts in the relative bargaining power of venture. A foreign partner's knowledge about local market conditions increases, it depends less on the expertise of a local partner. This increases the bargaining power of the foreign partner and ultimately leads to conflicts over control of the venture's strategy and goals. Some firms have sought to limit such problems by entering into joint ventures in which one partner has a controlling interest.

8.5.6 Wholly Owned Subsidiaries

In a wholly owned subsidiary, the firm owns 100 percent of the stock. Establishing a wholly owned subsidiary in a foreign market can be done in two ways. The firm either can set up a new operation in that country, often referred to as a Greenfield venture, or it can acquire an established firm in that host nation and use that firm to promote its products. For example, as we saw in the Management Focus, ING's strategy for entering the U. S. market was to acquire established enterprises rather than try to build an operation from the ground floor.

8.5.6.1 Advantages

Wholly owned subsidiaries have several clear advantages. First, when a firm's competitive advantage is based on technological competence, a wholly owned subsidiary will often be the preferred entry mode because it reduces the risk of losing control over that competence. (See Chapter 7 for more details.) Many high-tech firms prefer this entry mode for overseas expansion (e. g., firms in the semiconductor, electronics, and pharmaceutical industries). As discussed in the chapter's opening case, for example, JCB was unwilling to transfer key technology to its Indian joint venture with Escorts and only did so once it had purchased its venture partner.

Second, a wholly owned subsidiary gives a firm tight control over operations in different countries. This control is necessary for engaging in global strategic coordination (i. e., using profits from one country to support competitive attacks in anther).

Third, a wholly owned subsidiary may be required if a firm is trying to realize location and experience curve economies (as firms pursuing global and transnational strategies try to do). When cost pressures are intense, it may pay a firm to configure its value chain in such a way that the value added at each stage is maximized. Thus, a national subsidiary may specialize in manufacturing only part of the product line or certain components of the end product, exchanging parts and products with other subsidiaries in the firm's global system. Establishing such a global production system requires a high degree of control over the operations of each affiliate. The various operations must be prepared to accept centrally determined decisions as to how they will produce, how much they will produce, and how their output will be priced for transfer to the next operation. Because licensees or joint-venture partners are unlikely to accept such a subservient role, establishing wholly owned subsidiaries may be necessary. Finally, establishing a wholly owed subsidiary gives the firm a 100 percent share in the profits generated in a foreign market.

8.5.6.2 Disadvantages

Establishing a wholly owned subsidiary is generally the most expensive method of serving a foreign market from a capital investment standpoint. Firms doing this must bear the full capital costs and risks of setting up overseas operations. The risks associated with learning to do business in a new culture are less if the firm acquires an established host-country enterprise. However, acquisitions raise additional problems, including those associated with trying to marry divergent corporate cultures. These problems may more than offset any benefits derived by acquiring an establishing operation. Because the choice between Greenfield ventures and acquisitions is such an important one, we shall discuss it in more detail later in the chapter. Table 8.1 shows us top 100 global brands.

Table 8.1 Top 100 Global Brands

2014 Rank	Brand	Region/Country	Sector	Brand Value	Change in Brand Value
01	Apple	United States	Technology	118,863 $ m	+21%
02	Google	United States	Technology	107,439 $ m	+15%
03	Coca-Cola	United States	Beverages	81,563 $ m	+3%
04	IBM	United States	Business Services	72,244 $ m	-8%
05	Microsoft	United States	Technology	61,154 $ m	+3%
06	GE	United States	Diversified	45,480 $ m	-3%
07	Samsung	South Korea	Technology	45,462 $ m	+15%
08	Toyota	Japan	Automotive	42,392 $ m	+20%
09	McDonald's	United States	Restaurants	42,254 $ m	+1%
10	Mercedes-Benz	Germany	Automotive	34,338 $ m	+8%
11	BMW	Germany	Automotive	34,214 $ m	+7%
12	Intel	United States	Technology	34,153 $ m	-8%
13	Disney	United States	Media	32,223 $ m	+14%
14	Cisco	United States	Technology	30,936 $ m	+6%
15	Amazon	United States	Retail	29,478 $ m	+25%
16	Oracle	United States	Technology	25,980 $ m	+8%
17	HP	United States	Technology	23,758 $ m	-8%
18	Gillette	United States	FMCG	22,845 $ m	-9%
19	Louis Vuitton	France	Luxury	22,552 $ m	-9%
20	Honda	Japan	Automotive	21,673 $ m	+17%
21	H&M	Sweden	Apparel	21,083 $ m	+16%
22	Nike	United States	Sporting Goods	19,875 $ m	+16%
23	American Express	United States	Financial Services	19,510 $ m	+11%
24	Pepsi	United States	Beverages	19,119 $ m	+7%
25	SAP	Germany	Technology	17,340 $ m	+4%

Continued

2014 Rank	Brand	Region/Country	Sector	Brand Value	Change in Brand Value
26	IKEA	Sweden	Retail	15,885 $ m	+15%
27	UPS	United States	Transportation	14,470 $ m	+5%
28	eBay	United States	Retail	14,358 $ m	+9%
29	Facebook	United States	Technology	14,349 $ m	+86%
30	Pampers	United States	FMCG	14,078 $ m	+8%
31	Volkswagen	Germany	Automotive	13,716 $ m	+23%
32	Kellogg's	United States	FMCG	13,442 $ m	+4%
33	HSBC	United Kingdom	Financial Services	13,142 $ m	+8%
34	Budweiser	United States	Alcohol	13,024 $ m	+3%
35	J.P. Morgan	United States	Financial Services	12,456 $ m	+9%
36	Zara	Spain	Apparel	12,126 $ m	+12%
37	Canon	Japan	Electronics	11,702 $ m	+6%
38	Nescafé	Switzerland	Beverages	11,406 $ m	+7%
39	Ford	United States	Automotive	10,876 $ m	+18%
40	Hyundai	South Korea	Automotive	10,409 $ m	+16%
41	Gucci	Italy	Luxury	10,385 $ m	+2%
42	Philips	Netherlands	Electronics	10,264 $ m	+5%
43	L'Oréal	France	FMCG	10,162 $ m	+3%
44	Accenture	United States	Business Services	9,882 $ m	+4%
45	Audi	Germany	Automotive	9,831 $ m	+27%
46	Hermès	France	Luxury	8,977 $ m	+18%
47	Goldman Sachs	United States	Financial Services	8,758 $ m	+3%
48	Citi	United States	Financial Services	8,737 $ m	+10%
49	Siemens	Germany	Diversified	8,672 $ m	+2%
50	Colgate	United States	FMCG	8,215 $ m	+5%
51	Danone	France	FMCG	8,205 $ m	+3%
52	Sony	Japan	Electronics	8,133 $ m	-3%
53	AXA	France	Financial Services	8,120 $ m	+14%
54	Nestlé	Switzerland	FMCG	8,000 $ m	+6%
55	Allianz	Germany	Financial Services	7,702 $ m	+15%
56	Nissan	Japan	Automotive	7,623 $ m	+23%
57	Thomson Reuters	Canada	Media	7,472 $ m	-8%

Continued

2014 Rank	Brand	Region/Country	Sector	Brand Value	Change in Brand Value
58	Cartier	France	Luxury	7,449 $m	+8%
59	Adidas	Germany	Sporting Goods	7,378 $m	-2%
60	Porsche	Germany	Automotive	7,171 $m	+11%
61	Caterpillar	United States	Diversified	6,812 $m	-4%
62	Xerox	United States	Business Services	6,641 $m	-2%
63	Morgan Stanley	United States	Financial Services	6,334 $m	+11%
64	Panasonic	Japan	Electronics	6,303 $m	+8%
65	Shell	Netherlands	Energy	6,288 $m	+14%
66	3M	United States	Diversified	6,177 $m	+14%
67	Discovery	United States	Media	6,143 $m	+7%
68	KFC	United States	Restaurants	6,059 $m	-2%
69	Visa	United States	Financial Services	5,998 $m	+10%
70	Prada	Italy	Luxury	5,977 $m	+7%
71	Tiffany & Co.	United States	Luxury	5,936 $m	+9%
72	Sprite	United States	Beverages	5,646 $m	-3%
73	Burberry	United Kingdom	Luxury	5,594 $m	+8%
74	Kia	South Korea	Automotive	5,396 $m	+15%
75	Santander	Spain	Financial Services	5,382 $m	+16%
76	Starbucks	United States	Restaurants	5,382 $m	+22%
77	Adobe	United States	Technology	5,333 $m	+9%
78	Johnson & Johnson	United States	FMCG	5,194 $m	+9%
79	John Deere	United States	Diversified	5,124 $m	+5%
80	MTV	United States	Media	5,102 $m	+2%
81	DHL	United States	Transportation	5,084 $m	NEW
82	Chevrolet	United States	Automotive	5,036 $m	+10%
83	Ralph Lauren	United States	Apparel	4,979 $m	+9%
84	Duracell	United States	FMCG	4,935 $m	+6%
85	Jack Daniel's	United States	Alcohol	4,884 $m	+5%
86	Johnnie Walker	United Kingdom	Alcohol	4,842 $m	+2%
87	Harley-Davidson	United States	Automotive	4,772 $m	+13%
88	MasterCard	United States	Financial Services	4,758 $m	+13%
89	Kleenex	United States	FMCG	4,643 $m	+5%

Continued

2014 Rank	Brand	Region/Country	Sector	Brand Value	Change in Brand Value
90	Smirnoff	United Kingdom	Alcohol	4,609 $ m	+8%
91	Land Rover	United Kingdom	Automotive	4,473 $ m	NEW
92	FedEx	United States	Transportation	4,414 $ m	NEW
93	Corona	Mexico	Alcohol	4,387 $ m	+3%
94	Huawei	China	Technology	4,313 $ m	NEW
95	Heineken	Netherlands	Alcohol	4,221 $ m	-3%
96	Pizza Hut	United States	Restaurants	4,196 $ m	-2%
97	Hugo Boss	Germany	Apparel	4,143 $ m	NEW
98	Nokia	Finland	Technology	4,138 $ m	-44%
99	Gap	United States	Apparel	4,122 $ m	+5%
100	Nintendo	Japan	Electronics	4,103 $ m	-33%

Exercises

1. Define the key terms listed below:
FDI (Foreign Direct Investment);
Transnational Corporations;
Monopolistic Advantage Theory;
The Product Life Cycle.

2. "Most FDI is made to gain access to low-wage labor." Do you agree or disagree? Why?

3. "Industrialized countries are the source of most FDI because they have large amounts of financial capital that they must invest somewhere." Do you agree or disagree? Why?

4. "Multinational enterprises often establish affiliates using little of their own financial capital because they want to reduce their exposure to risks." Do you agree or disagree? Why?

5. Why does much FDI occur in such industries as pharmaceuticals and electronic products while little FDI occurs in such industries as clothing and paper products?

6. A country currently prohibits any FDI into the country. Its government is considering liberalizing this policy. You have been hired as a consultant to a group of foreign firms that wants to see the policy loosened. They ask you to prepare a report on the major arguments for why the country should liberalize this policy. What will you report?

Chapter 9 Chinese Foreign Trade

Peace, development and cooperation are the trends in today's world. Since the adoption of the reform and opening up policy more than 30 years ago, China has conformed to the trend of economic globalization by opening wider to the outside world and promoting economic and trade cooperation with other countries on the basis of equality and mutual benefit. Through years of development, foreign trade has become one of China's most dynamic and fastest-growing sectors, placing China among the world's largest trade countries. China's foreign trade development has strengthened the nation's ties with the rest of the world, effectively pushing forward the country's modernization, and promoted world prosperity and progress.

China entered the World Trade Organization (WTO) in 2001. During the past decade, China has quickened its integration into the global economy while its foreign trade has been further invigorated. On the 10th anniversary of China's accession to the WTO, the Chinese government issues this White Paper to give a comprehensive introduction to Chinese foreign trade development.

9.1 Historic Progress in Chinese Foreign Trade

After the founding of the People's Republic of China (PRC) in 1949, China adhered to the principle of independence and self-reliance, and gradually carried out economic and trade exchanges with foreign countries. However, hindered by the international political environment at that time and the country's planned economic system, Chinese foreign trade development was relatively slow.

In 1978 China entered the new period of reform and opening up. Devoting major efforts to the development of foreign trade became an important approach to accelerate modernization, shake off backwardness, promote the growth of economy, and improve comprehensive national strength. Over the past more 30 years or so, has been seizing the opportunity of the world economy's long-term prosperity and the deepening economic globalization, China has opened wider to the outside world, attracted and utilized foreign investment, introduced advanced technology, transformed and upgraded domestic industries, and achieved rapid development in foreign trade through all-round participation in the international division of labor and competition.

Chinese total trade volume in goods ranks high globally. In 1978 the total value of Chinese import and export was only 20.6 billion U.S. dollars, ranking 32nd in world trade and accounting for less than 1 percent of the world's total. In 2010 the total value of China's import and export reached 2.974 trillion U.S. dollars, 144 times as much as that in 1978, averaging an annual growth of 16.8 percent. In 2010 the total value of China's export was 1.5778 trillion U.S. dollars, showing a 17.2 percent annual growth on average, and the total value of its import was 1.3962 trillion U.S. dollars, showing a 16.4 percent annual growth on average. In 2010, the total volumes of China's export and import accounted for 10.4 percent and 9.1 percent of the world's total respectively. By the end of 2010 China had been the world's largest exporter and second-largest importer for two consecutive years.

The structure of China's trade in goods has fundamentally changed. Chinese export commodity structure shifted from the primary products dominated to manufactured goods dominated in the 1980s, and from mainly light industrial and textile products to mainly mechanical and electronic products in the 1990s. In the new century, Chinese export of high-tech products, led by electronics and information technology commodities, has been increasingly expanded. In addition to state-owned enterprises, foreign-invested enterprises and private enterprises also engage in foreign trade, and their total value of import and export has each exceeded that of the state-owned enterprises. From the 1980s to the early 21st century, Chinese processing trade flourished, accounting for half of the country's foreign trade volume. Throughout Chinese foreign trade development, foreign-invested enterprises and processing trade have played very significant roles.

China has formed an all-round and diversified import and export market. Since the adoption of the reform and opening up policy, China has been promoting foreign trade on all fronts, and established trade relations with the vast majority of the world's countries and regions. Chinese trade partners have increased from a small number of countries and regions in 1978 to 231 countries and regions now. The European Union (EU), the United States, the Association of Southeast Asian Nations (ASEAN), Japan and the other BRIC countries have become Chinese major trade partners. In this new century Chinese trade with newly emerging markets and developing countries has maintained sustained and relatively rapid growth. In Chinese total trade in goods from 2005 to 2010 the proportion of trade with ASEAN increased from 9.2 percent to 9.8 percent, with other BRIC countries from 4.9 percent to 6.9 percent, with Latin America from 3.5 percent to 6.2 percent and with Africa from 2.8 percent to 4.3 percent.

Chinese international competitiveness in services trade has been enhanced. With its WTO entry, Chinese trade in services entered a new stage of development. With its scale rapidly enlarged and its pattern gradually optimized, Chinese trade in services now ranks among the top in the world. Chinese trade in tourism, transport and other fields has maintained a steady growth momentum. Chinese cross-border services in construction, communications, insurance, finance, computers and information, royalties and license fees, consultation and related fields, as well as service outsourcing, have been growing rapidly. From 2001 to 2010 Chinese total services trade value (excluding government services) witnessed a more-than-five-fold growth from 71.9 billion U.S. dollars to 362.4 billion U.S. dollars. Chinese proportion in world services trade exports rose from 2.4 percent to 4.6

percent, worth 170.2 billion U.S. dollars in 2010, and jumped from the 12th place in the world to the 4th; Chinese proportion in world services trade imports increased from 2.6 percent to 5.5 percent, worth 192.2 billion U.S. dollars in 2010, moving from the 10th place in the world to the 3rd.

Chinese foreign trade development has greatly pushed forward the country's modernization drive. China has grown into an open economy. Participation in the international division of labor and competition, introduction of advanced technology, equipment and management methods and utilization of foreign direct investment have greatly promoted Chinese technological progress and industrial upgrading, and also improved the management and market competitiveness of its enterprises. The rapid growth of processing trade has brought into play Chinese comparative advantages of an abundant labor force, and accelerated the country's industrialization and urbanization. Foreign trade has directly contributed to the employment of over 80 million Chinese, more than 60 percent of whom are from rural areas, and employees' income and living standards have been remarkably improved. Foreign trade, domestic investment and domestic consumption have become the three major engines propelling Chinese economic growth.

The historic progress in Chinese foreign trade has been closely connected with the changes in the international and domestic situations. Starting in the 1980s, peace and development became the theme of the times. With the acceleration of economic globalization, the flow and allocation of capital, technology, products, markets, resources, labor force and similar elements became more dynamic around the world. Scientific and technological progress, led by information and communications technology, has greatly improved production efficiency; international industrial transfer has continuously deepened and developed. Economic globalization, scientific and technological progress, international industrial transfer and strengthened cooperation between countries have provided historic opportunities for Chinese integration into the world economy. The Chinese government, conforming to the trend of the times and taking economic construction as the central task, has implemented the reform and opening up policy, developed economic and technological cooperation with other countries, vigorously and rationally utilized foreign investment, brought its comparative advantages into full play, promoted the deepening of the division of labor in the international industrial chain, and provided favorable conditions for its own foreign trade development. During this process foreign enterprises and multinational corporations in particular, have obtained abundant opportunities to invest in China, added value to their capital, technology, management experience, marketing channels and other elements, and shared the fruits of Chinese rapid economic growth. Chinese foreign trade development benefited greatly from its reform and opening up, from economic globalization, and from taking the path of cooperation and mutual benefit. Chinese cannot develop itself in isolation from the rest of the world, and global prosperity and stability cannot be maintained without Chinese participation.

China remains a developing country. Compared with other world trade powers, Chinese export industry remains at the low end of the global industrial chain. Chinese resource and energy inputs and environmental cost are relatively high, while the international competitiveness of enterprises and the risk-resistance of some industries are relatively weak. Chinese transformation from a large trading country to a strong trading power will be a comparatively long-term process requiring arduous efforts.

9.2　Reform of and Improvements to Chinese Foreign Trade System

Before China adopted the reform and opening up policy in 1978, its foreign trade was governed by mandatory planning, and the state absorbed both the profits and the losses of enterprises. Since the reform and opening up policy was initiated, Chinese foreign trade system has completed the transformation from mandatory planning to giving full play to the fundamental role of the market - from state monopoly to full openness, and from indiscriminate egalitarianism to giving enterprises discretionary management power and making them responsible for their own profits and losses. During the negotiations over the restoration of its GATT (General Agreement on Tariffs and Trade) membership and entry into the WTO, and after it became a WTO member, China gradually adopted international trade practices, and established a unified, open foreign trade system compatible with multilateral trade rules.

During the initial period of reform and opening up, Chinese foreign trade system reform focused on the transformation of its unitary planning, transfer of management and operation power in foreign trade to lower levels, implementation of the system of allowing enterprises to retain a certain portion of foreign exchange earnings, and establishment of a foreign exchange coordination market. China absorbed foreign direct investment to introduce foreign-invested enterprises as new business entities in its foreign trade sector, breaking the monopoly of state-owned foreign trade enterprises. After that, China introduced a responsibility system in doing foreign trade, gradually replacing mandatory planning with guided planning. The state also set up an export tax rebates system in line with the general practice of international trade. In October 1992, China clearly put forward the goal of reform toward a socialist market economy. A comprehensive reform of the systems of finance, taxation, banking, foreign trade and foreign exchange was carried out accordingly. In January 1994, the Chinese government discontinued all export subsidies, making all import and export enterprises fully responsible for their own profits and losses. The official and market-regulated exchange rates of Chinese currency, the Renminbi (RMB), coexisted in a unitary and managed floating exchange rate system based on market demand and supply. Foreign trade enterprises were incorporated, and pilot programs for the import and export agency system were carried out. In the same year, the Foreign Trade Law of the People's Republic of China was promulgated, establishing principles such as safeguarding a foreign trade order of equity and freedom, and a basic legal system for foreign trade. In December 1996, China realized current account convertibility for the RMB. Meanwhile, China voluntarily made significant tariff cuts, and reduced non-tariff measures such as quotas and licenses. These reform measures helped China initially establish a foreign trade administration and regulation system based on the market economy, giving full play to such economic levers as the exchange rate, taxation, tariffs and finance.

On December 11th, 2001, China became the 143rd member country of the World Trade Organization after 16 years of negotiations. To honor its commitments upon entry into the WTO, China expanded its opening-up in the fields of industry, agriculture and the services trade, and accelerated trade and investment facilitation and liberalization. Meanwhile, the state deepened the reform of its foreign trade system, improved its foreign trade legal system, reduced trade barriers and administrative intervention, rationalized government responsibilities in foreign trade administration, made government behavior more open, more impartial and more transparent, and promoted the development of an open economy to a new stage.

After its entry into the WTO, China reviewed over 2 300 laws and regulations, and departmental rules. Those that did not accord with WTO rules and Chinese commitments upon entry into the WTO were abolished or revised. Administrative licensing procedures are reduced and regulated in the revised laws and regulations, and a legal system of trade promotion and remedy has been established and improved. In accordance with the Agreement on Trade-related Aspects of Intellectual Property Rights (TRIPS) administered by the WTO, China revised its laws and regulations and judicial interpretations related to intellectual property rights, and thereby constructed a complete legal system that conforms to Chinese actual conditions and international practices.

Taking further measures to lower tariffs and reduce non-tariff measures. During the transitional period following China's entry into the WTO, the general level of Chinese import tariffs was lowered from 15.3 percent in 2001 to 9.9 percent in 2005. By January 2005, the majority of Chinese tariff reduction commitments had been fulfilled; China had removed non-tariff barriers, including quota, licensing and designated bidding, measures concerning 424 tariff lines, and only retained licensing administration over imports that are controlled for the sake of public safety and the environment in line with international conventions and WTO rules. By 2010 Chinese overall tariff level had dropped from 9.8 percent to 15.2 percent in the case of agricultural products and 8.9 percent in the case of industrial products. Since 2005, China has completely maintained its bound tariff rate.

9.2.1 Fully Liberalizing Access to Foreign Trade Operations

According to the Foreign Trade Law of the People's Republic of China that was revised in 2004, starting from July 2004, foreign trade dealers only need to register with the authority responsible, and no longer have to ask for approval from the Chinese government. This change has facilitated the diversification of Chinese foreign trade entities, consisting of state-owned, foreign-invested and private enterprises. The imports and exports of state-owned and foreign-invested enterprises have maintained sustained growth, while private enterprises have seen their foreign trade developed rapidly and their share of Chinese import and export market keep expanding, becoming key players in Chinese foreign trade. In 2010 the import and export volume of state-owned enterprises, foreign-invested enterprises and private enterprises in the country's total was 20.9 percent, 53.8 percent and

25.3 percent respectively.

Further opening the services market, China has earnestly fulfilled its commitments upon entry into the WTO by offering market access to international service providers in a wide range of fields, including finance, telecommunications, construction, distribution, logistics, tourism and education. China has opened up 100 of the WTO's 160 sub-sectors of services trade, approaching the average level of developed countries. In 2010 a total of 13905 foreign-invested enterprises in the services sector had been set up in China, with 48.7 billion U.S. dollars of foreign investment actually used, accounting for 50.7 percent of the total number of newly founded foreign-invested enterprises in Chinese non-financial sectors and 46.1 percent of the total amount of foreign investment actually utilized that year respectively.

9.2.2 Creating a Level Playing Field

China has striven to provide a flexible, fair and stable market for domestic and international enterprises by establishing and improving the legal system and the law-enforcement and supervisory mechanism for fair trade, and curbing and cracking down on unfair practices in foreign trade operations, such as infringement of rights, dumping, smuggling and disruption of the market order. Following domestic laws and international trade rules, China has strengthened its efforts in monitoring and early warning, and adopted measures such as trade remedy and antitrust investigation to correct the unfair practices of its trade partners, and to safeguard the legitimate rights and interests of domestic industries and enterprises. Facing the international financial crisis, China worked hand in hand with the international community to firmly oppose all forms of trade protectionism, strictly adhered to relevant WTO rules, and treated domestic and foreign products equally while carrying out the stimulus plan, promoting fair competition between domestic and foreign enterprises.

By 2010, all of Chinese commitments made upon entry into the WTO had been fulfilled. Chinese earnest efforts are commended by the majority of the WTO members. The Chinese government received three trade policy reviews from the WTO in 2006, 2008 and 2010 respectively. The WTO's basic principles, such as non-discrimination, transparency and fair competition, have been included in Chinese laws, regulations and related systems. A deeper understanding of concepts such as market orientation, opening up, fair competition, and the rule of law and intellectual property rights has been achieved among the Chinese people, promoting the further opening up of the national economy and more improvements to the market economy.

9.3 The Development of Chinese Foreign Trade Contributes to the World Economy

The development of Chinese foreign trade has accelerated the modernization of the national economy, enhanced the country's comprehensive strength, and improved the standard of living of more than 1.3 billion Chinese. It has also helped integrate the Chinese economy into the world economy, and make economic globalization conducive to the common prosperity of all countries and regions.

Chinese reform and opening up and its active participation in economic globalization have made the country one of the world's fastest-growing economies. Over the past more than 10 years, China, along with other emerging economies, has become an increasingly important force propelling world economic growth. According to the World Bank, from 2001 to 2010, Chinese GDP increased by 4.6 trillion U.S. dollars, representing 14.7 percent of the increase in the world aggregate, and the share of Chinese GDP in the world rose to 9.3 percent over the same period. Data from the WTO shows that from 2000 to 2009, the average annual growth rates of Chinese exports and imports were 17 percent and 15 percent, respectively, much higher than the 3 percent annual growth rate of world trade.

During the international financial crisis, Chinese foreign trade was among the first to stabilize, promoting the recovery of the world economy. After the crisis broke out in 2008, the Chinese government adopted in time a series of policies and measures to stimulate the economy expand domestic demand and stabilize imports and exports. In 2009, global goods imports decreased by 12.8 percent, while Chinese goods imports increased by 2.9 percent, making it the only country to maintain growth among the world's largest economies. The Chinese factors sustained the exports of many countries affected by the financial crisis, stimulated demand in the global commodities market, and boosted confidence, giving a new momentum to the world's economic recovery and growth. During its third review of Chinese trade policy, the WTO pointed out that China had played a constructive role in stimulating global demand during the international financial crisis, and had thus made significant contributions to the stability of the world economy.

The development of Chinese foreign trade has helped enhance the national welfare of China and its trading partners. As it accelerated its integration into the global division of labor, China has gradually developed into a major producer and exporter of industrial products relying on its labor cost advantages, relatively strong industrial supporting, processing and manufacturing capabilities, and increasing labor productivity. It provides inexpensive and quality commodities to meet the diverse demands of the international market. Chinese advantages due to economies of scale and low processing costs in the global manufacturing industry partially offsets the rising prices of upstream factors of production, playing an important role in curbing global inflation and raising the real purchasing power of consumers of its trading partners.

The development of Chinese foreign trade has provided a broad market for its trading partners. Since 2001, Chinese import of goods has increased by approximately five times, representing an annual growth rate of around 20 percent. Chinese rapidly expanding imports have become a major driving force for global economic growth, creating an enormous market for its trading partners to augment their exports. At present, China is the largest export market for Japan, South Korea, Australia, ASEAN, Brazil and South Africa, the second largest for the EU, and the third largest for the U.S. and India. As Chinese industrialization and urbanization are moving forward rapidly, and its domestic demand keeps growing, the country's continuously expanding and opening market will offer increasing opportunities to its trading partners.

Meanwhile, China is one of the developing countries granting the biggest market access to the least-developed countries (LDCs). By July 2010, China had granted zero-tariff treatment to over 4700 commodities from 36 LDCs which had established diplomatic ties with China. The zero-tariff commodities accounted for 60 percent of the total imports from those countries. China has promised to continue expanding its preferential treatment to the LDCs having diplomatic ties with China until the zero-tariff commodities reach 97 percent of the total imports from those countries. The zero-tariff measure has helped increase the exports of LDCs to China. Since 2008, China has been the largest export market for LDCs. In 2010, Chinese import of goods from LDCs accounted for approximately one quarter of those countries' total exports, an increase of 58 percent over the previous year.

China has participated in and helped push forward the reform of the global economic governance mechanism. The Chinese government actively advocates a "balanced, inclusive and mutually beneficial" multilateral trade system, and strives to establish a fair and equitable new international economic and trade order. As a large developing country with a rapidly growing economy, China plays an active role in the G20 and BRICs summits, Doha Round talks, and other international dialogue and cooperation mechanisms. China does its best to assume international responsibilities that suit its development level and strength. China continuously consolidates its cooperation with emerging countries in the fields of economy, finance, trade and investment, and works toward an equitable and rational international economic order that benefits all countries.

In addition, China strictly fulfills its international obligations regarding export controls. It consistently advocates the complete prohibition and thorough dismantling of all weapons of mass destruction, and firmly opposes the proliferation of such weapons and their carriers. Chinese relevant laws clearly prescribe that the state may take necessary measures to restrict the import and export of goods and technologies relating to fissionable materials or the materials, from which they are derived, as well as the import and export relating to arms, ammunition or other military supplies. China earnestly abides by international conventions regarding export controls, and fulfills its non-proliferation commitments, actively contributing to world peace and regional stability. Over the past few years, Chinese government has adopted a wide range of internationally recognized norms and practices, and formed a complete export control system covering nuclear, biological, chemical, missile and other sensitive items and technologies, providing legal grounds and institutional guarantees for the better realization of the goal of non-proliferation.

9.4 Promoting Basically Balanced Growth of Foreign Trade

The primary factors determining whether a country's foreign trade is in surplus or deficit are its economic structure and the international competitiveness of its products or services. China does not pursue a foreign trade surplus intentionally. There has been a certain amount of deficit in Chinese services trade for a long time, and the trade in goods was in deficit for most of the years prior to 1990. After 1990, with large-scale industrial outsourcing and relocation, China enhanced its competitiveness in manufactured goods. Growth in exports overtook that of imports, turning the overall deficit to a surplus in trade in goods. In 2005 Chinese surplus in trade in goods reached 100 billion U. S. dollars for the first time, which was followed by vigorous growth for four consecutive years. In 2008 the surplus hit 298.1 billion U. S. dollars, the highest point in history, before slowing down gradually. The surpluses in trade in goods for 2009 and 2010 were 195.7 billion U. S. dollars and 181.6 billion U. S. dollars, down 34.4 percent and 7.2 percent year-on-year respectively. In 2010 Chinese surplus in trade in goods accounted for 6.1 percent of the total import and export volume and 3.1 percent of the GDP. Of the nine nations with the largest trade balances (favorable or unfavorable), China was not high up in the league table in terms of the two ratios.

The fact that China is enjoying a surplus in trade in goods reflects its position in the international division of labor at the current stage. China has now relatively big advantages in the processing and assembling of industrial products, and is the largest producer and exporter of industrial products. The United States, European Union and some other countries and regions are the major end consumer markets. With the transfer of large numbers of labor-intensive processing and assembling sectors to China from Japan, South Korea, Singapore and other nations and regions, their surpluses with the United States and Europe were also transferred to China. The result is that while China is currently enjoying a surplus in trade in goods primarily with the United States and Europe, it also has long-term trade deficits with Japan, South Korea, ASEAN and other major intermediate producers. In 2010 Chinese surpluses in trade in goods with the United States and the European Union were 181.3 billion U. S. dollars and 142.8 billion U. S. dollars respectively, and its total deficit in trade in goods with Japan, South Korea and ASEAN was 141.6 billion U. S. dollars. To produce and export industrial products, China needs to import large quantities of primary goods, thus creating a deficit in trade in goods with certain exporters of primary goods. It is the country's different level and status of participation in the international division of labor in manufacturing and the services industry that leads to Chinese big surplus in trade in goods but a long-term deficit in services trade.

Chinese surplus in trade in goods mainly comes from foreign-invested enterprises and processing trade. With the spread of economic globalization as well as the refinement of the division of labor and the development of economies of scale, an increasing amount of international trade – intra-industry trade or processing trade based on value-chain specialization – is predominated by multinationals. Since the adoption of the reform and opening up policy in 1978, China has experienced rapid growth in attraction of foreign direct investment. For a fairly long period of time the import and export business of foreign-invested enterprises and processing trade mainly operated by foreign-invested enterprises accounted for about 50 percent of Chinese trade volume in goods, and were also the major source of the country's surplus in trade in goods. In 2009 and 2010 the surplus in trade in goods created by foreign-invested enterprises reached 127 billion U. S. dollars and 124. 3 billion U. S. dollars respectively, accounting for 64. 8 percent and 68. 4 percent of the total surplus of Chinese trade in goods in the two years. Processing trade surplus of foreign-invested enterprises in the same period hit 264. 6 billion U. S. dollars and 322. 9 billion U. S. dollars, significantly higher than the country's total trade surplus for 2009 and 2010. While foreign-invested enterprises and processing trade enjoyed a big favorable trade balance, the import and export of Chinese state-owned enterprises, general trade and other forms of trade were in deficit.

The limits on certain high-tech trade set by developed countries also affect the trade balance between China and some of its trading partners. As China is currently accelerating its pace of industrialization, it needs to import advanced equipment and technologies from developed countries. Unfortunately, some developed countries, sticking to their old way of thinking, impose various restrictions on the export of high-end equipment and advanced technologies to China, resulting in slow growth in the export of these sectors. To a certain extent such limits hinder Chinese imports from these countries, posing an unfavorable impact on bilateral trade balance.

As China turned its trade deficit into a surplus, the country improved its international balance of payments and enhanced its resistance to external risks. However, the sharp increase in surplus also created trouble for the Chinese economy. The large volume of RMB input in export settlement complicates macroeconomic control, and the rapid expansion of Chinese surplus in trade in goods also results in more trade frictions between China and its trading partners, as well as persistent pressure on the RMB to appreciate.

The Chinese government attaches great importance to the imbalance in the development of foreign trade, and has adopted a series of policies and measures to curb overheated surplus growth.

First, it proactively adjusts the economic structure, strives to expand domestic demand, and especially increases investment in projects to improve the people's livelihood and stimulate household consumption.

Second, it enacts a series of policies to expand imports, simplify the procedures of import administration and import payment, lower the temporary tax rates on certain imported commodities, improve the import promotion system and facilitate import businesses.

Third, it has adjusted the export tax rebates policy, lowered or cancelled export tax rebates for some products that consume too much energy and cause serious pollution and certain resource-based products.

Fourth, it has amended the prohibited and restricted categories of processing trade, expanding the scope of the prohibited category and promoting this sector's restructuring and upgrading.

Fifth, it has changed the situation of the pegged exchange rate of the yuan against the U. S. dollar since the Asian financial crisis, and adopted the administered floating exchange rate system based on market demand, and adjusted it with reference to a basket of currencies from July 21, 2005. During the period from the exchange rate reform in July 2005 to the end of August 2011, the nominal exchange rate of the yuan against the dollar appreciated by about 30 percent.

Chinese measures to promote balanced foreign trade growth have achieved obvious effects. The nation's surplus in trade in goods has been on a steady decline since 2009, and the proportion of surplus in the total import and export trade volume and the GDP also started to drop in 2008, moving toward a balance in foreign trade. Chinese efforts not only serve the development of its own economy, but are also practical moves to promote the structural adjustment and the rebalancing of the global economy.

9.5 Constructing All-Round Economic and Trade Partnerships with Mutually Beneficial Cooperation

China stresses all-round development in its foreign trade. China adheres to the developing economic and trade partnerships based on practical cooperation and mutual benefit with all countries, no matter they are big or small, rich or poor.

China enjoys steady growth in its trade with developed countries, and realizes complementary advantages as well as reciprocity and mutual benefit. Chinese trade with the European Union has been developing steadily in recent years. The European Union mainly exports manufactured products to China, including advanced mechanical and electronic products, transport vehicles, complete plants, core parts and components, precision components and other High-tech products which are highly competitive in the Chinese market. Foreign trade between China and the United States has a solid development base. China exports a large variety of consumer goods to meet the demands of American consumers, while satisfying its own need for development by constantly expanding imports of electronic, aerospace, biological, medical, agricultural and services trade items from the United States. China and Japan are geographically proximate to each other and this is an advantage in bilateral trade. Chinese-Japanese trade promotes continuous cooperation and progress in industry while spurring the development of regional economic comparative advantages and cooperation in East Asia. Chinese trade and investment cooperation with developed countries such as Canada, Australia, Switzerland and New Zealand also maintain a good momentum of development.

Chinese trade with emerging economies and developing countries is experiencing robust growth, with huge development potential. With the comprehensive implementation of the China-ASEAN Free Trade Agreement in 2010, tariffs have been cancelled for 90 percent of the commodities traded between them, vigorously promoting the rapid growth of bilateral trade between China and ASEAN. The free entry of specialties and competitive products into each other's market suits the various needs of the two sides. Foreign trade between China and Democratic People's Republic of Korea keeps growing constantly and steadily. Bilateral investment and economic cooperation also present broad prospects. Chinese trade with the other BRIC countries has been enjoying rapid growth in recent years, which promotes the development of the member countries' respective advantageous industries and shows the broad development prospects of emerging markets. In recent years, China has seen relatively fast growth in its trade with other developing countries, further development of trade with its historical trading partners in the Arab world, broadening areas of economic and trade cooperation with Latin American countries, and bilateral trade with African countries, which gives full play to the complementary advantages of the two sides' resources and economic structures.

China attaches great importance to the institutional set-up of bilateral and regional economic and trade cooperation. Currently over 150 countries and regions have signed agreements on bilateral trade or economic cooperation with China, which has established and maintains high-level economic dialogue mechanisms with the United States, Europe, Japan, Great Britain, Russia and other major economies. China proactively participates in the Asia-Pacific Economic Cooperation, ASEAN (10 + 3) meetings, which also include Japan and Democratic people's republic of Korea, the East Asia Summit, Forum on China-Africa Cooperation, Greater Mekong Sub-regional Economic Cooperation Committee, Central Asia Regional Economic Cooperation Committee, Greater Tumen Initiative and other regional and sub-regional economic cooperation mechanisms. China adheres to the principle of "good neighborly friendship and partnership" in establishing and developing various forms of border economic and trade cooperation.

China takes proactive initiatives to participate in and promote regional economic integration. By the end of 2010 China had held 15 rounds of negotiations on free trade or closer economic partnership arrangements with 28 countries and regions on five continents, and signed and implemented 10 free trade agreements or closer economic partnership arrangements. Currently five free trade agreement talks are under way. China advocates the establishment of an East Asia free trade zone. In 2010 the total volume of bilateral trade in goods between China and its trade partners in its ten free trade agreements or closer economic partnership arrangements (ASEAN, Pakistan, Chile, Singapore, New Zealand, Peru, Costa Rica, Chinese Hong Kong SAR, Chinese Macau SAR and Chinese Taiwan) reached U.S. \$782.6 billion, accounting for over a quarter of the country's total import and export volume.

China has actively participated in and promoted the World Trade Organization's Doha Round talks, and strives to safeguard the authority of the multilateral trading system. China stresses that the negotiations should be conducive to the implementation of the principle of fairness and justice of the multilateral trading system, and reflects the goal of the Doha Round as a development round. China takes part in the Doha Round's talks on agriculture, non-agricultural goods, services, rules and other issues, submitting over 40 negotiating texts on its own and over 100 texts with other members. To promote the Doha Round talks, China repeatedly expressed its wish to make constructive contributions suited to its level of development.

In settling disputes with its trading partners, China gives consideration to the interests of all parties, and seeks common ground while shelving differences. Since Chinese entry into the WTO and with the continuous growth of its imports and exports, the number of trade disputes and frictions between China and its trading partners has increased. These cases mainly involved textile products, shoes, tires, car parts and components, steel and chemical products, and mainly covered the issues of IPR, trade balance, fair trade, food safety, environmental protection and other areas of concern. China has always preferred dialogue to confrontation, and cooperation to pressure, and chooses to settle disputes between trading partners through consultation and negotiation. China adheres to giving consideration to and balancing the interests of all parties and settling disputes through dialogue, consultation and negotiation by utilizing bilateral and multilateral channels and following the rules and under the framework of the WTO. In recent years China has adopted various measures to further open up its market, protect IPR, promote trade balance, reform the exchange rate formation mechanism of the RMB and standardize the operational order of imports and exports, among other areas, fully taking into account the concerns of its trading partners. When consultations fail to settle a dispute, China appropriately handles the issue with its trading partners through the WTO dispute settlement mechanism, in order to maintain the stability of the multilateral trading system.

9.6 Realizing Sustainable Development of Foreign Trade

At present, unbalanced, inconsistent and unsustainable development factors persist in Chinese foreign trade. They are manifested in the following ways: Export growth mainly relies on the input and consumption of resources, energy, land, manpower, environment, etc., while the input of science and technology, management, innovation and other factors are insufficient, resulting in an ever more conspicuous contradiction between foreign trade development and the constraint on resource supply and environmental carrying capacity; enterprises are not competitive enough in R&D, design, marketing and services and products with their own intellectual property rights and with their own brands account for only a small proportion of the exports; the contribution of foreign trade to Chinese primary, secondary and tertiary industries is unbalanced; central and western China falls behind other regions in the scale and level of foreign trade; and foreign trade needs improvement in terms of the quality of its products and profits. The Chinese government is clearly aware of these problems and has taken active measures to accelerate the change of the development pattern of foreign trade, and achieve sustainable development.

Foster comprehensive competitive edge of foreign trade development. In recent years, with the rising labor cost and spiraling prices of resources, energy and other production factors, the low-cost advantage of export-oriented industries has been greatly weakened. In the face of these new conditions, the Chinese government has set the strategic goal of turning the mode of foreign trade from extensive to intensive development. During the 11th Five-year Plan period (2006-2010) the Chinese government adjusted import and export taxation policies and implemented the strategies of fostering foreign trade by science and technology, market diversification and putting quality first. It launched pilot projects for transforming and upgrading processing trade, improved financial and insurance services for import and export enterprises, and encouraged enterprises to accelerate technical progress and optimize product structure. With these measures, China enhanced the comprehensive competitiveness of its foreign trade. Most of import and export enterprises withstood challenges of the international financial crisis, and Chinese foreign trade recovered soon after the crisis. During the 12th Five-year Plan period (2011-2015) China will make efforts to maintain its current competitive edge in exports, foster new advantages centering on technology, branding, quality and services at a faster pace, promote industrial transformation and upgrading, extend the value-added chain of processing trade, and the competitiveness and added value of enterprises and products. It will vigorously develop trade in services to promote balanced development between it and trade in goods. It will open the services trade wider to the outside world, promote service outsourcing, and try to expand the export of new services. It will improve and implement state policies in the fields of finance and taxation, banking and insurance, foreign currency management, customs clearance, inspection and quarantine and logistics and transportation, in a bid to speed up trade and investment facilitation for the stable and healthy development of foreign trade.

Promote energy conservation and emission reduction in foreign trade development. As early as in 1994, the Chinese government published Chinese Agenda 21 – White Paper on Chinese Population, Environment and Development in the 21st Century, setting goals on energy conservation and emission reduction for national economic and social development. In both the 11th and 12th five-year plans, the government made the reduction of energy consumption and CO_2 emission intensity two obligatory targets. Since 2004, the Chinese government has lowered and even abolished export tax rebates for some energy-intensive, heavily-polluting and resource-based products, banned or limited the processing trade in some such products, and encouraged import and export enterprises to keep up with the world's advanced environmental standards. As a result, in recent years such products have seen their proportion in exports decreasing, while the export of new-energy, energy-conserving and environmental-friendly products has grown by a big margin. Most of import and export enterprises above a designated scale have obtained ISO 14000 certification or other environmental standard certifications. China will try to readjust its economic and industrial structure, accelerate the application of advanced energy-conserving and environmental technologies, and promote more balanced development between foreign trade and resource conservation and environmental protection.

Strengthen trade-related intellectual property protection. Strengthening intellectual property protection is necessary for China to comply with its international obligations. It is also an essential move if China seeks to transform its economic growth mode and build an innovative country. The Chinese government has made tremendous efforts in this regard, and made significant progress in legislation, law enforcement, publicity, training and enhancing the social awareness of IPR protection. In 2008 China promulgated the Outline of the National Intellectual Property Strategy, making IPR protection a national strategy. From 2006 to 2011, China published the Action Plan on Intellectual Property Protection for six consecutive years, putting in place over 1000 concrete measures covering the fields of legislation, law enforcement, education and training, cultural communication and exchanges with the outside world. In 2010, China filed 12295 applications for international patents in accordance with the Patent Cooperation Treaty, registering a growth rate of 55.6 percent over 2009, which was the fastest increase in the world. China also rose from the fifth to the fourth place in terms of patent application in the world. At present, it is a common challenge facing all countries to strengthen foreign trade-related intellectual property protection, and a world trend to strengthen dialogue and cooperation in this area. Under related international conventions and within its own legislative framework, the Chinese government will strengthen exchanges and cooperation with other countries and regions for the healthy development of intellectual property.

Enhance the quality and safety requirements of export products. Generally speaking, the quality of Chinese export products is constantly improving, and they are becoming more and more popular among consumers around the world. In 2009 and 2010, 11.032 million batches and 13.054 million batches respectively, of Chinese export products were examined by inspection and quarantine authorities, with only 0.15 percent and 0.14 percent being substandard; the export values totaled 429.27 billion U.S. dollars and 552.18 billion U.S. dollars respectively, with 0.12 percent and 0.13 percent respectively, found substandard. In 2010 China exported 127 000 batches of food to the United States, with 99.53 percent up to standard, and 138 000 batches to the European Union, with 99.78 percent up to standard. According to a report from the Ministry of Health, Labor and Welfare of Japan on imported food, in 2010 tests on 20 percent of food imported from China found that 99.74 percent was up to standard, higher than that of food imported from the United States and European Union in the same period. However, a small number of Chinese enterprises still ignore product quality and safety to bring down cost, while some foreign importers turn a blind eye to quality and credibility, and try every means to bring down the price or even authorize Chinese producers to use substandard materials. All this harms the image of "made in China" products. To tackle these problems, in recent years, the chinese government has improved laws and regulations on product quality and safety, strengthened supervision at every link, and strictly investigated and punished the few enterprises that had violated laws and regulations and caused quality problems. In March 2011, China launched the Year of Improving the Quality of Foreign Trade Products, through which it aimed to improve the mechanism of approval, certification and supervision of the quality and safety of foreign trade products, thereby enhancing the quality and safety of export products.

Raise import and export enterprises' sense of social responsibility. As China opens wider to the outside world, more and more enterprises have come to realize that along with development and expansion they should shoulder their corresponding social responsibilities. This can not only help promote social harmony and progress, but also enhance enterprises' competitiveness and capacity for sustainable development. Advocating the Scientific Outlook on Development and the idea of a harmonious society, Chinese governments at all levels encourage enterprises to enhance their sense of social responsibility, respect labor rights, safeguard consumers' rights and protect the ecological environment. In the meantime, the Chinese government encourages enterprises to accept relevant social responsibilities in the field of foreign trade and try to get necessary certifications. Since the new Law on Labor Contracts and its implementation regulations took effect in 2008, import and export enterprises have established the system of "five insurances" (old-age insurance, medical insurance, unemployment insurance, work injury insurance and maternity insurance), as well as a housing fund. The Chinese government regards it as an important task in the course of promoting foreign trade transformation and upgrading to enhance enterprises' sense of social responsibility. It is therefore determined to strengthen publicity and training in this regard, establish and improve a management system marked by integrity for import and export enterprises, improve public supervision on enterprises to make sure they fulfill their social responsibilities, carry out international cooperation in fostering and managing enterprises' sense of social responsibility, and call on import and export enterprises to constantly enhance their performance in this regard.

Promote international cooperation in emerging industries of strategic importance. To develop new strategic industries is of great significance for China to realize foreign trade transformation and upgrading, and sustainable development. After over 30 years of reform and opening up, China has seen its overall strength grown remarkably, its science and technology advancing and its industrial system improving markedly, laying a solid foundation for the development of emerging industries of strategic importance. However, compared to developed countries, these industries in China are still in their infancy. In the wake of the 2008 international financial crisis, all the world major economies have been developing emerging industries at a faster pace, and China has taken the development of these industries as an important task in the course of its industrial rejuvenation. To promote the priority areas, while giving play to the basic role of the market in allocating resources, the Chinese government has strengthened its policy guidance, regulated market order, improved its investment environment and encouraged enterprises to enhance their technological innovation capabilities. This basic policy of supporting emerging industries of strategic importance conforms to international trade rules. China is willing to strengthen communication with other countries in scientific research, technological development and capacity building, and work with them to create a new situation for international cooperation and development in emerging industries.

At present, the underlying impact of the international financial crisis, the protracted, arduous and complicated nature of the world economic recovery is manifesting itself, and the global economic structure and trade layout face in-depth readjustment. China will make new adjustments to its foreign trade, in an effort to turn foreign trade from scale expansion to quality and profit improvement, and from mainly relying on its low-cost advantage to enhancing its comprehensive competitive edge, thereby turning China from a big trading country to a strong trading power.

Chinese foreign trade is still hampered by many uncertainties and is bound to meet new difficulties and challenges. During the 12th Five-year Plan period China will open itself wider to the outside world as a driver for further reform, development and innovation, make full use of its advantages, strengthen international cooperation in all respects, and integrate itself into the world economy on a wider scale and at a higher level. China is willing to work with its trading partners to cope with the various challenges facing the world economy and trade, and promote its foreign trade to realize a more balanced, coordinated and sustainable development, and share prosperity and mutually-beneficial results with its trading partners.

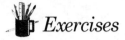
Exercises

1. Which four areas in the field of foreign trade does China have not met?
2. Briefly talk about the historic progress in Chinese foreign trade?
3. How does the development of Chinese Foreign Trade contribute to the World Economy?
4. After learning from this chapter, can you predict the trend of Chinese foreign trade?

References

[1] 托马斯 A 普格尔,彼得 H 林德特.国际经济学[M].北京:经济科学出版社,2001.
[2] 弗里德里希·李斯特.政治经济学的国民体系[M].北京:商务印书馆,1961.
[3] 陈同仇,薛荣久.国际贸易[M].北京:对外贸易教育出版社,1997.
[4] 卢进勇.入世与中国利用外资和海外投资[M].北京:对外经济贸易大学出版社,2001.
[5] PAUL R KRUGMAN, MAURICE OBSTFELD. International Economics Theory and Policy Fifth Edition. 国际经济学理论与政策[M]. 5 版.北京:清华大学出版社,2001.
[6] 多米尼克·萨尔瓦多.国际经济学[M].北京:清华大学出版社,2004.
[7] ROBERT J CARBAUGH. International Economics[M]. 北京:高等教育出版社,2005.
[8] 罗塞·罗伯茨.抉择——关于自由贸易与贸易保护主义的寓言[M].北京:中国人民大学出版社,2002.
[9] 保罗·克鲁格曼.地理和贸易[M].北京:中国人民大学出版社,2000.
[10] 保罗·克鲁格曼.战略性贸易政策与国际经济学[M].北京:中国人民大学出版社,2000.
[11] 保罗·克鲁格曼.克鲁格曼国际贸易新理论[M].北京:中国社会科学出版社,2001.
[12] 黄卫平,彭刚.国际经济学教程[M].北京:中国人民大学出版社,2004.
[13] 李坤望.国际经济学[M].北京:高等教育出版社,2005.
[14] 赵春明.非关税壁垒的应对及运用[M].北京:人民出版社,2001.
[15] 亚蒂什 M 巴格瓦蒂,等.高级国际贸易学[M].上海:上海财经大学出版社,2004.
[16] 姜波克.国际金融新编[M].北京:复旦大学出版社,2005.
[17] 田青.国际经济一体化理论与实证研究[M].北京:中国经济出版社,2005.
[18] 海闻,P 林德特,王新奎.国际贸易[M].上海:上海人民出版社,2003.
[19] G 甘道尔夫,等.国际贸易理论与政策[M].上海:上海财经大学出版社,2005.
[20] 格林纳韦.国际贸易前沿问题[M].北京:中国税务出版社,2000.
[21] Robson P.国际一体化经济学[M].上海:上海译文出版社,2001.
[22] 亚当·斯密.国民财富的性质和原因的研究[M].北京:商务印书馆,1979.
[23] 劳伦斯 S 科普兰.汇率与国际金融[M]. 3 版.北京:中国金融出版社,2002.
[24] 金仁淑.投资大国的兴衰——日本对外直接投资模式及效用研究[M].长春:吉林人民出版社,2002.
[25] 杨帆.人民币汇率研究——兼谈国际金融危机与涉外经济[M].北京:首都经济贸易大学出版社,2000.

[26] HALLWOOD C PAUL, RONALD MACDONALD. International money and finance[M]. 3rd Edition. Blackwell, 2000.

[27] 原毅军. 国际经济学[M]. 北京:高等教育出版社,2005.

[28] PAUL R KRUGMAN, MAURICE OBSTFELD. International economics theory and policy Fifth edition[M]. 5 版. 北京:清华大学出版社,2001.

[29] MADURA J. International financial management[M]. 7th Edition. 北京:Peking University Press/Thomson Learning, 2003.

[30] ARNDT S HENRYK KIERZKOWSKI. Fragmentation: new production and Trade Patterns in the World Economy[M]. Oxford University Press, 2001.

[31] BETH V YARBROUGH, ROBERT M YARBROUGH. The world economy[M]. 4th Edition. The Dryden Press, 2000.

[32] KRUGMAN PAUL MAURICE OBSTFELD. International economic theory and policy[M]. 5th Edition. Addison-Wesley, 2000.

[33] PETER B KENEN. The International economy[M]. 4th Edition. Cambridge University Press, 2000.

[34] THOMAS PUGEL. International economics[M]. MacGraw Hill, 2001.